Best of Friends 3

The yearbook of Creative Monochrome

Editor

Roger Maile

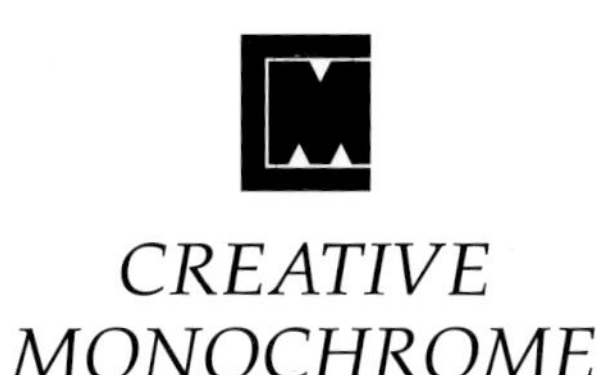

CREATIVE MONOCHROME

BEST OF FRIENDS 3

The yearbook of Creative Monochrome

Editor: ROGER MAILE

Published in the UK by Creative Monochrome Ltd
20 St Peters Road, Croydon, Surrey, CR0 1HD.

British Library Cataloguing-in-Publication Data:
A catalogue record for this book is available from the British Library

ISBN 1 873319 25 8
First edition, 1996

ISSN 1359-446X

Printed in England by Penshurst Press,
Buckingham House, Longfield Road,
Tunbridge Wells, Kent, TN2 3EY.

Introduction

Roger Maile

Selecting the images for *Best of Friends* is very much a labour of love. I am a self-confessed photographic junkie: viewing stimulating images simply increases my urge to see more. The best entries get me itching to dust off my own cameras and try to achieve more satisfying results, and I hope the selection in the book will have the same effect on many readers of all levels of photographic experience.

The entry for this year's book established new records: 420 photographers submitted a total of 3638 prints. What such statistics do not reveal is my impression that the overall standard of entry was the strongest yet. Because I believe that staying power is an essential quality for images in a book, the prints are reviewed over three 'rounds': 1381 photographs survived to the second round and 711 were still vying for selection at the final stage, where they were joined by 76 prints which were retained from the previous year's entry. At the end of the process, 143 images claimed their space in the book.

It would be wrong to claim that these were the best prints submitted, or even my opinion of what were the best. This disclaimer is not borne out of false modesty – not a trait I am often accused of! – but from the fact that a book such as *Best of Friends* needs to have some sense of balance, both of subject matter and style, and the images have to flow not only across page spreads but from the beginning to end of the book.

Such factors mean inevitably that some excellent work gets omitted for reasons which are totally beyond the control of individual entrants. The best I can do in such situations is to retain the prints for consideration in the following year. I was pleased to be able to find a place this year for quite a number of the prints which were pipped at the post last time.

The most obvious question I am asked, and yet the most difficult to answer, is what it is about an image that determines whether it gets selected or not. The search for the photographic elixir is as understandable as it is pointless: if there were a magic formula, its discovery would destroy the magic. That is not intended to dodge the question, but to indicate that the answer lies in emotional response rather than in the intellect. At its simplest, I choose photographs because I like them and want others to share my pleasure (or sometimes anguish or discomfort) in seeing them.

Responding in this way probably poses more questions than it answers. Although the reaction to an image is primarily emotional, it is also possible to rationalise some of the factors which contribute to the decision-making process. I have, for example, already mentioned 'staying power' as a criterion – the ability of a print to hold the interest. Some people will jump to the conclusion that this means that the subject matter itself is the most important influence on selection. Whilst the intrinsic appeal of the subject is often a factor, it is the photographic interpretation of the subject which makes the difference – witness the fact that so many people return from their holidays in beautiful locations with images guaranteed to put any audience to sleep within five minutes. And yet a talented photographer can take a subject as mundane as a couple of pears and produce a work of art that you would want to hang on your wall.

There are several elements at work in the distinctive photographic image, from the original selection of subject matter to composition, arrangement of the elements within the picture space, the angle of view, lighting and the technical ability to produce on paper the pre-visualised finished print. And each of these elements is a matter of personal preference. Even when a photographer gets all of these elements 'right' – ie he or she produces a print which captures what was in their mind's eye at the time of exposure – they may well find that others do not share the same emotional response to the image. The best analogy I can recall is with radio wavelengths: some people's images 'transmit' across a broad band and have wide appeal, while others have a much narrower focus and some are on a different channel altogether.

I see it as part of my job as the selector to 'tune in' to as wide a range of styles and subject matter as possible. It will never be wide enough for some people and it will, just as surely, be too wide for others. So long as the cries of "too pretty" are roughly balanced by the shouts of "too arty-farty", I think the balance must be about right. I treasure a notion that the first group may be encouraged to appreciate the quality of more 'romantic' or 'pictorial' images, while the second may begin to understand what the more 'contemporary' image-makers are trying to achieve. Creative Monochrome has always encouraged a 'broad church' philosophy in which a gospel of tolerance is preached, but I guess that also means tolerating the 'narrow band' outlook of some Friends.

One area where I do retain an old fashioned and dogmatic view is that of technical quality. I am aware that there are some photographers who believe they have 'got beyond that', but this strikes me as the sort of trendy nonsense which taught a generation of school children that spelling and grammar could be neglected in the cause of self expression. Just as technical writing skills are aids to self expression and effective communication, so technical quality assists the photographer in making his thoughts and moods accessible to others. In my opinion, too many photographers are trying to pass off as 'contemporary' work which is really just sloppy self-indulgence – the intellectual equivalent of the holiday snap.

Technical quality is rather more subjective in its interpretation than the rules of spelling and grammar. I feel that the important consideration is that the technical quality should be appropriate to the 'feel' of the image. It is not always the case, for example, that there needs to be detail in the shadow and highlight areas, just as prints with a very narrow tonal range can convey a sympathetic mood for certain subject treatments. It is a question of context: one person's 'minor key' is another's 'flat print', while the max-black in one image is the blocked shadow area in another.

The other element in the selection process of which I am conscious is the distinctiveness or originality of the image. We are all bombarded by a plethora of images and, whether consciously or not, these are bound to influence the way we see or interpret different subjects. Equally, it is surprising how often photographers produce what they genuinely believe to be a totally original image only to find that someone separated by time and geography has, quite independently, produced a virtually identical photograph. It becomes tempting to feel that there is no such thing as an original image, so perhaps this is as subjective a criterion as the others I have mentioned.

Whilst I have tried to rationalise my approach to the selection after the event, the fact remains that, of its essence, it is not an intellectual exercise. When I was first faced with the task of judging a competitive salon along with two 'old hands', one advised me not to think about it, but to go with my initial gut feeling; that was pragmatic advice in the context of having only a few seconds to decide on the relative merits of each image, but I feel it is also sound advice in a much broader context. Some images just jump out and speak to you – one doesn't have to think, just react. Sometimes they will not succeed in holding the attention, or maybe their attraction is not related to their photographic merits, and this is where the protracted selection process for the book helps.

And so the images presented in this book are very much a personal selection. They are the ones that grabbed and held my attention; the images which created and sustained a positive response. I can only hope that readers will experience the same feelings as they peruse what I believe to be another remarkable collection of photographs.

Voting for the BoF awards

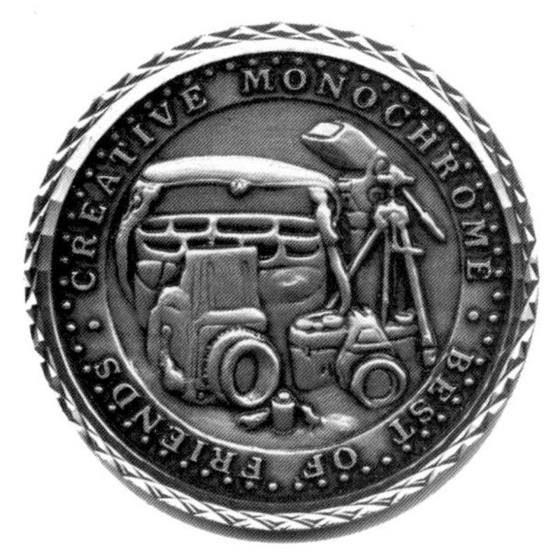

Six medals – one gold, two silver, and three bronze – are awarded each year

The images in *Best of Friends 3* are the equivalent of an exhibition of Friends' work. As is customary in such exhibitions, there are awards for a small number of prints which especially capture the judges' attention. All Friends of Creative Monochrome are invited to be the judges and to cast votes to determine the award winners.

Here's what to do. Each Friend has a maximum of 10 votes to award. Within that limit, you may allocate the votes as you see fit. For example, you can choose 10 prints to give one vote each; or you could give all 10 votes to one image; or somewhere in between. Votes can only be used in whole numbers. Friends may not vote for their own work.

To vote, for each image selected, write down the image number (*not* the page number), photographer and number of votes awarded. Please also include your own name and address (or membership number). Send your vote to: Creative Monochrome Ltd, 20 St Peters Road, Croydon, Surrey, CR0 1HD, England, **to arrive by 31 March 1997**, or vote by fax on 0181-681 0662.

To join the Friends of Creative Monochrome, or for further information, write to the above address or telephone 0181-686 3282.

The prints on this page are the six medal winners in the second BoF Awards (and, of course, are not eligible this time).

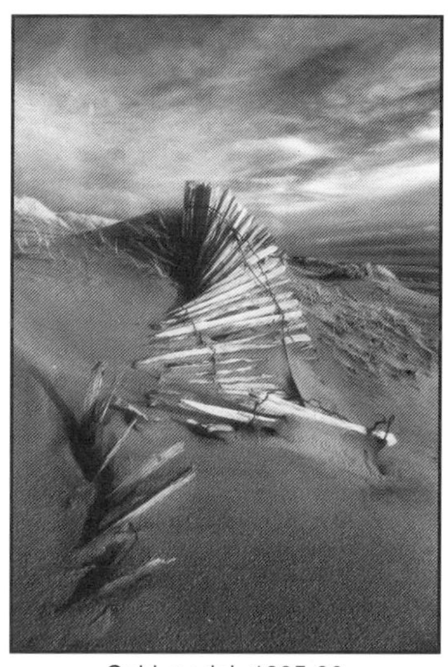

Gold medal, 1995-96
Storm damage, Camber Sands
David Dixon

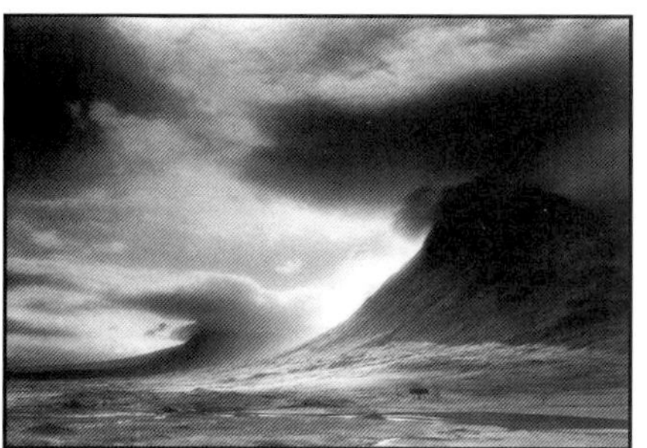

Silver medal, 1995-96
Glencoe
John Nasey

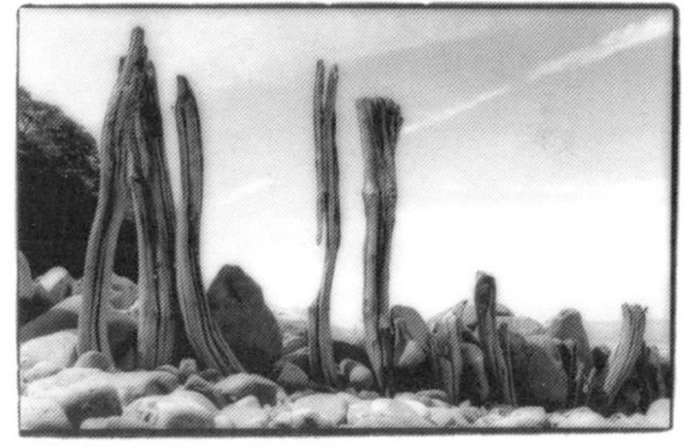

Silver medal, 1995-96
Weathered groyne
Michael Milton

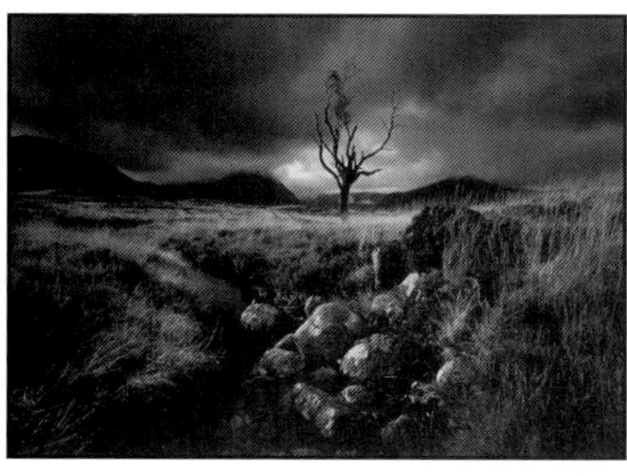

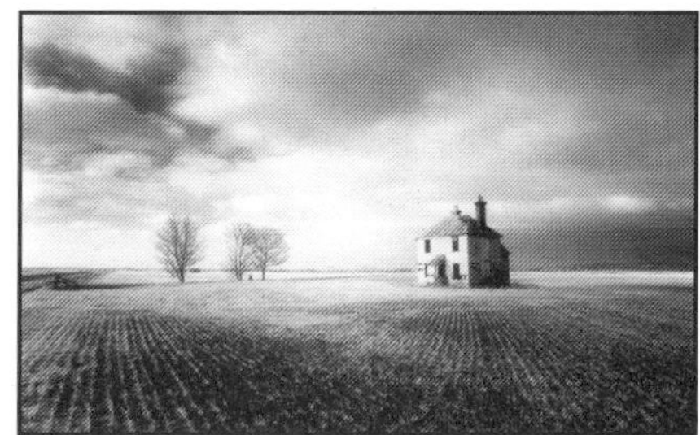

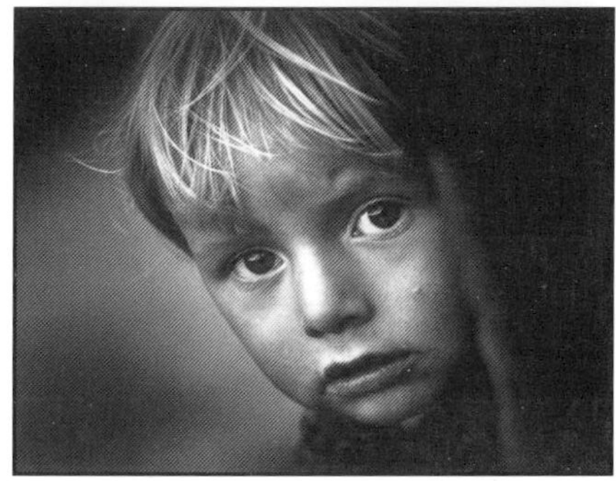

Bronze medals, 1995-96

above: Rannoch Moor
Peter Clark

opposite above: The house on Walland Marsh
David Dixon

opposite below: Yorkshire lad
Bill Carden

Index of contributors

(The index references are to image numbers, rather than page numbers. Brief profiles of all the contributors are included towards the back of the book.)

Portfolio

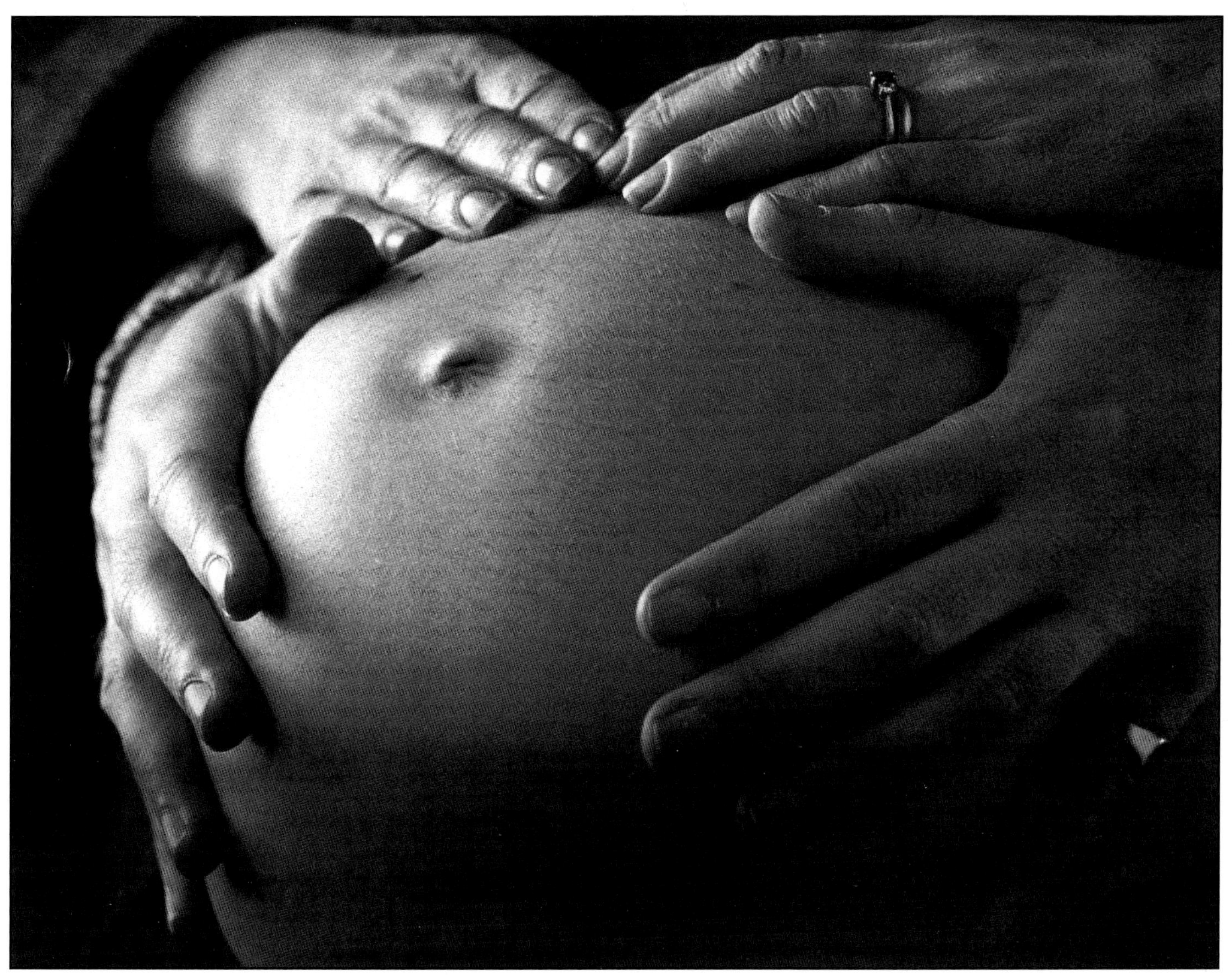

1
Expectation
Rosemary Cooper

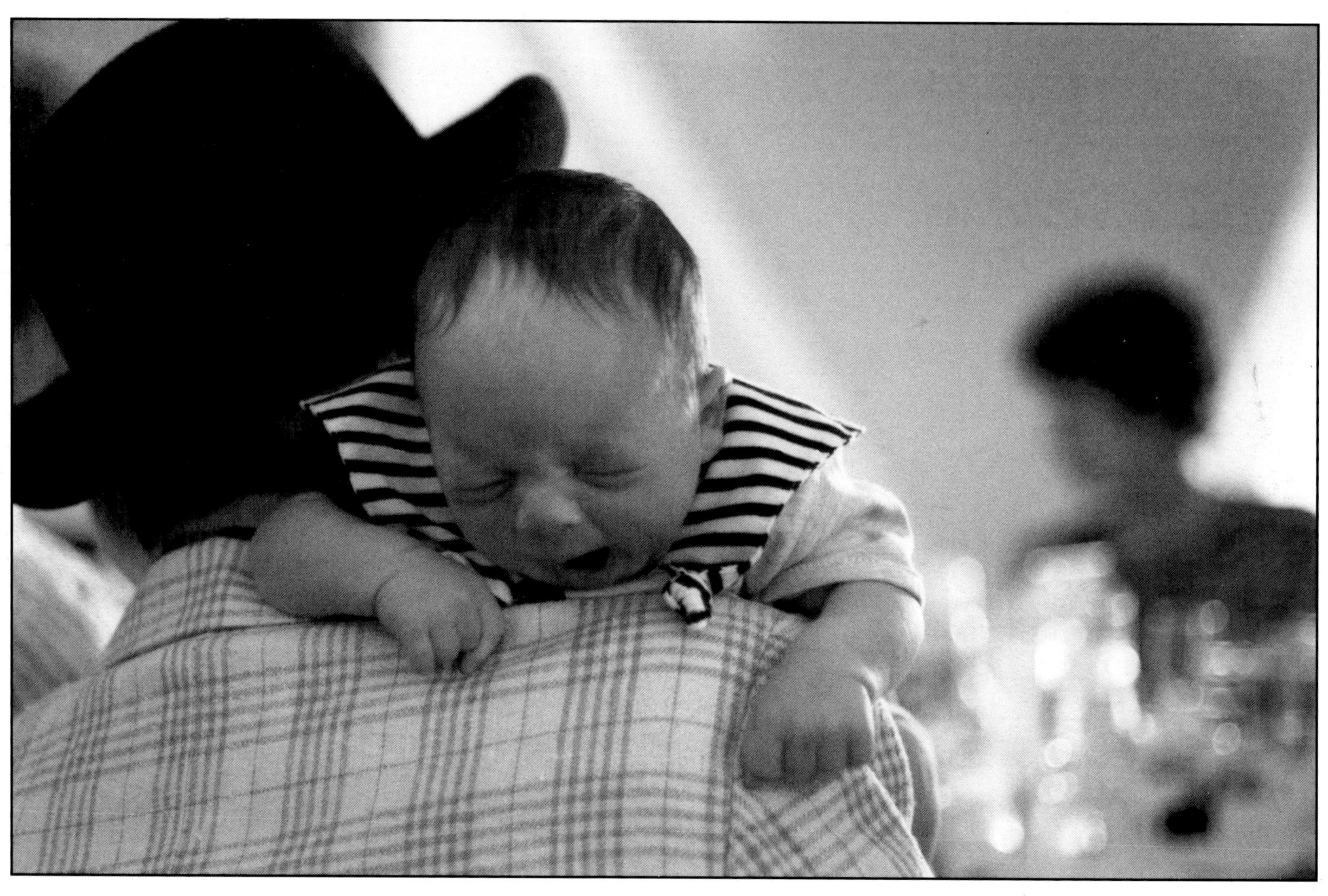

2
Baby William
Peter Bryenton

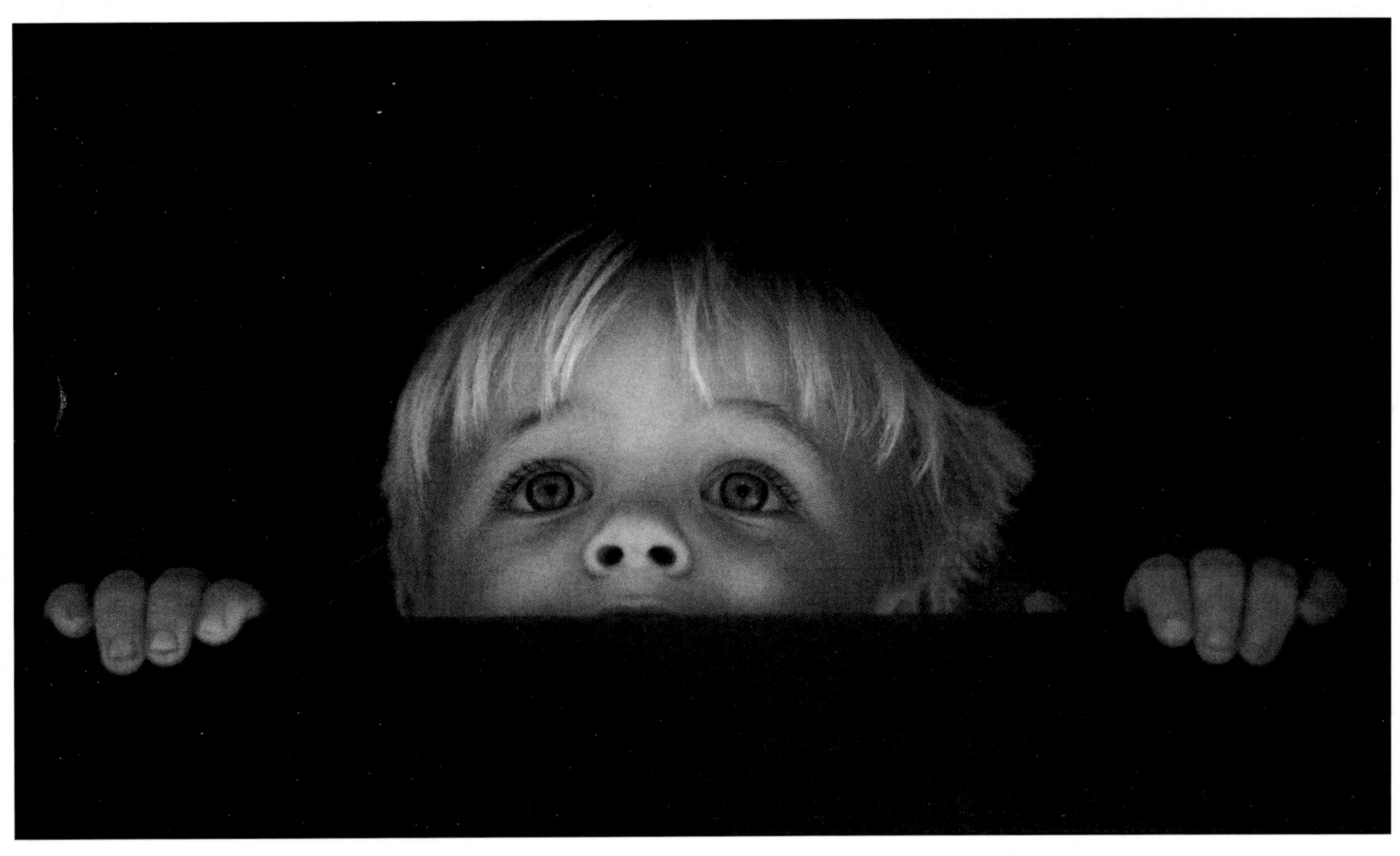

3
Archie
Robert Visick

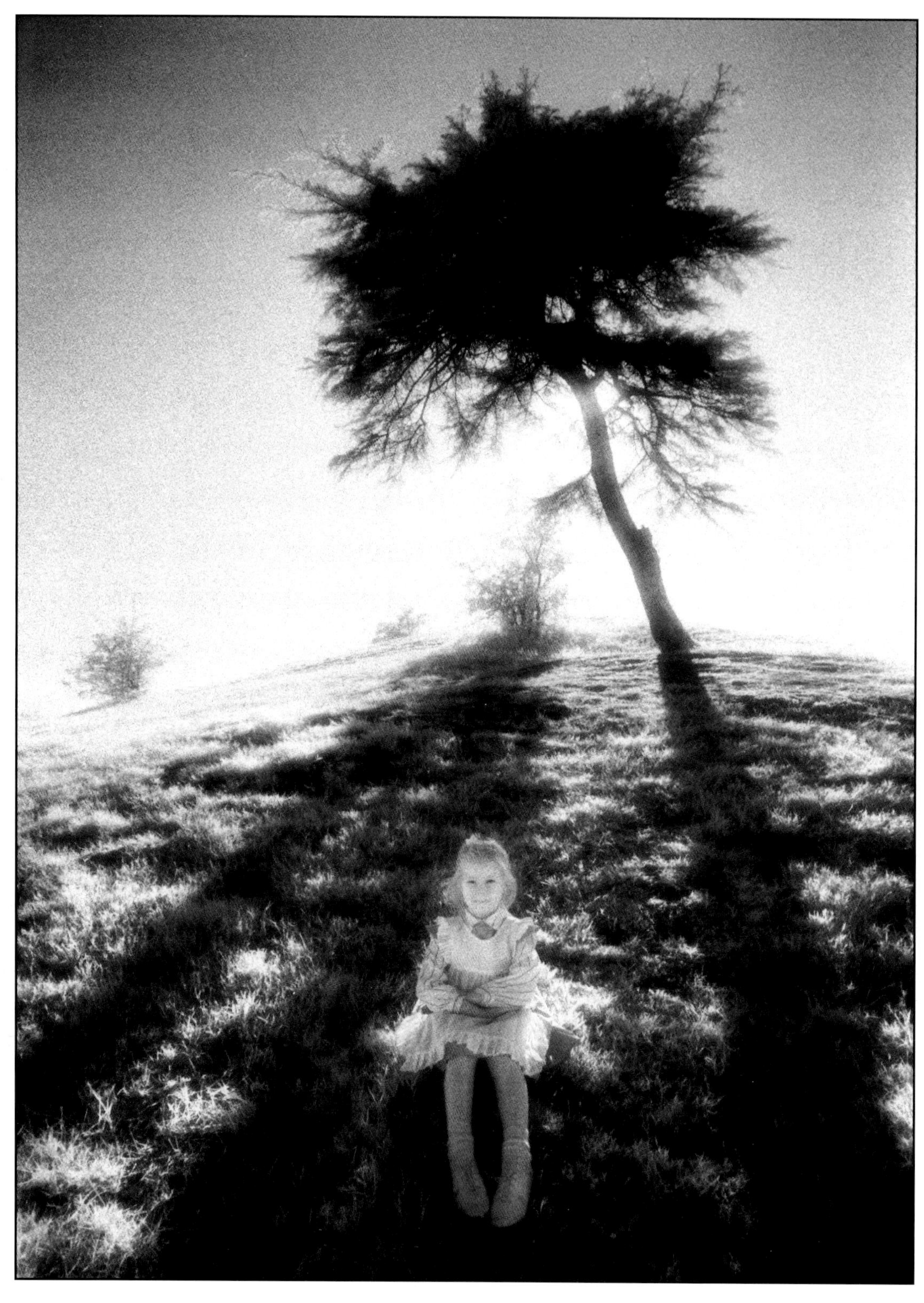

4
Victoria
Trevor Crone

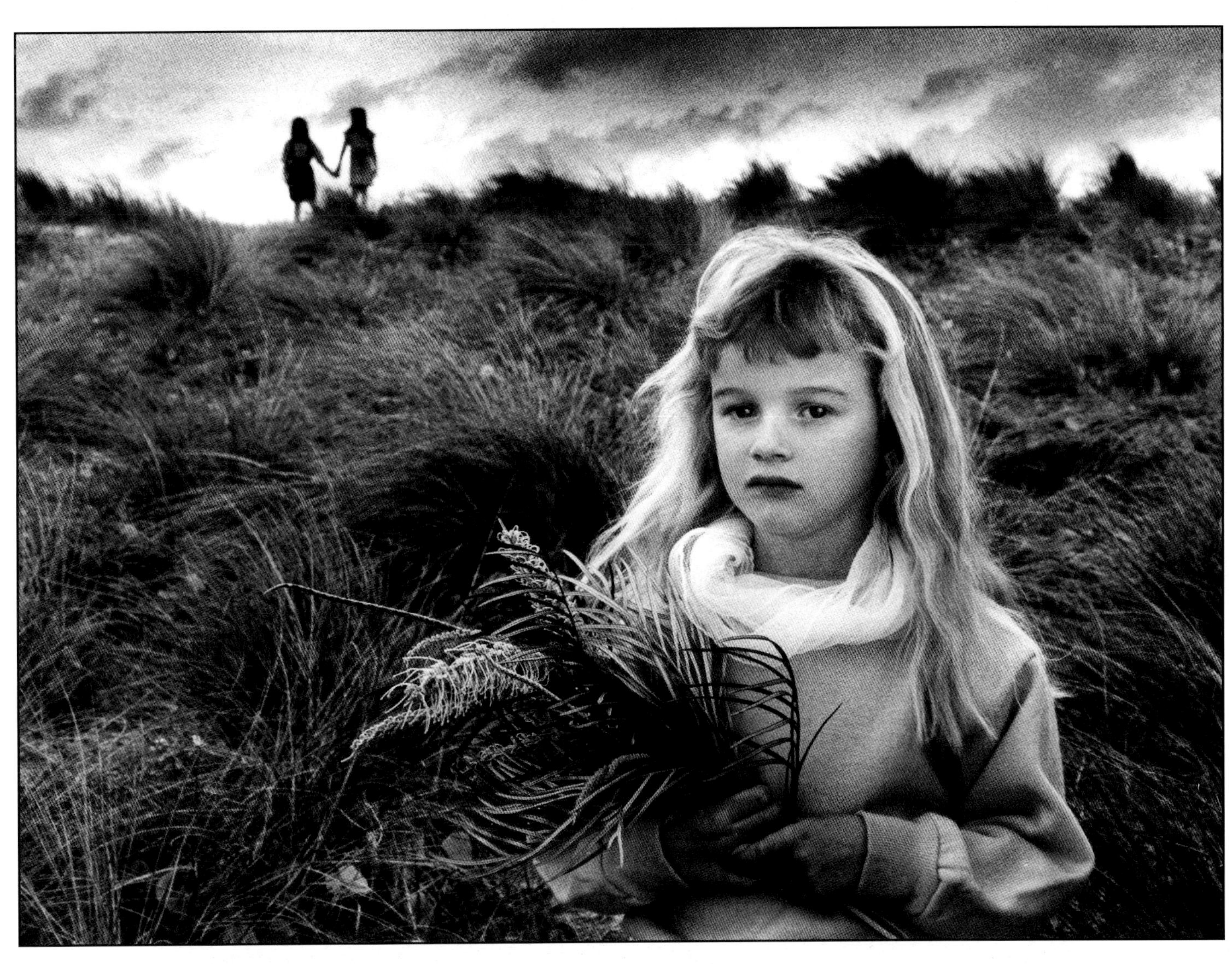

5
Little sister
David Mahony

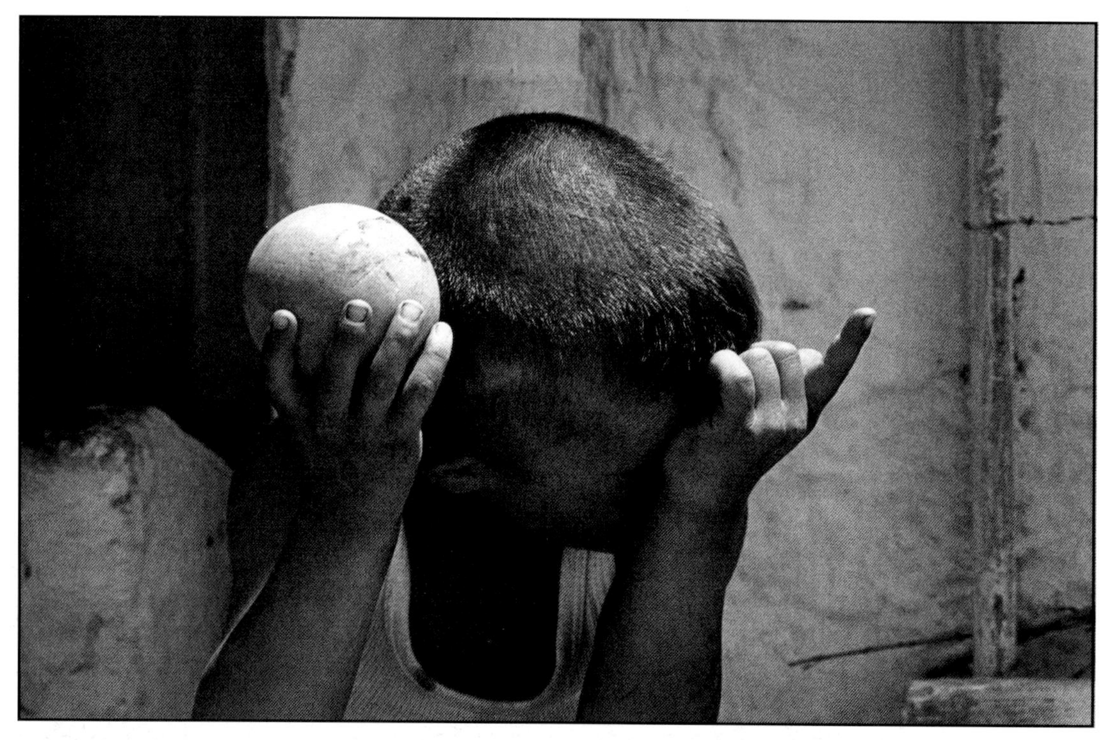

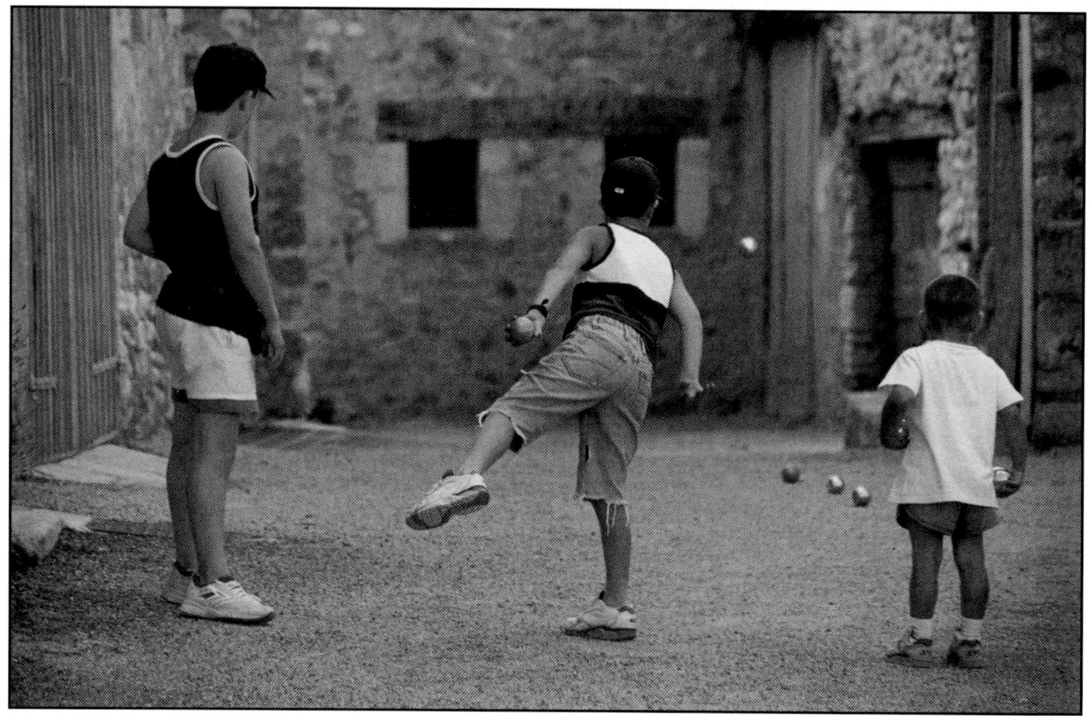

(top) 6 **His world**, *Bill Wisden*

(below) 7 **The boule players**, *John Devenport*

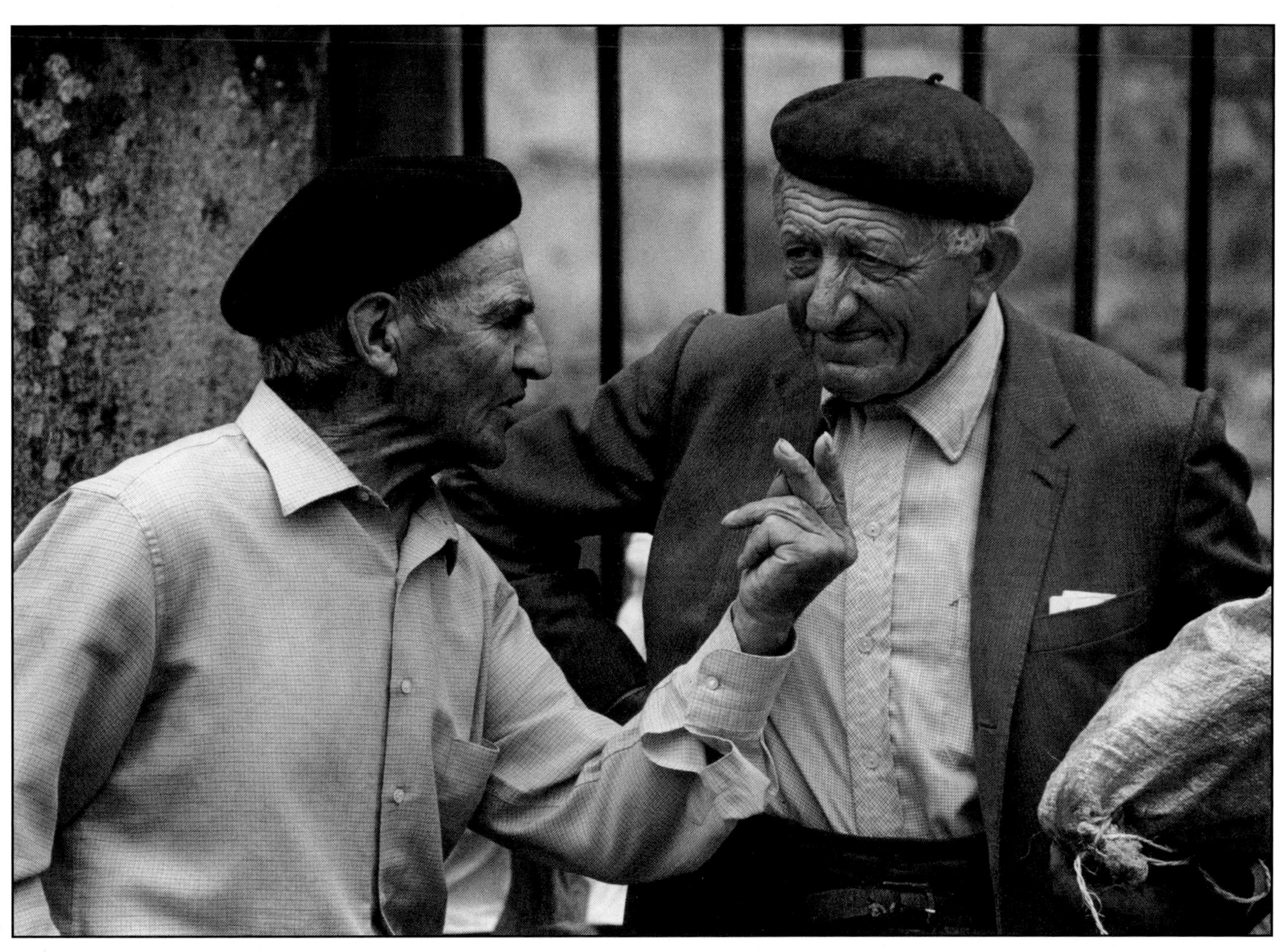

8
Spanish conversation
John Devenport

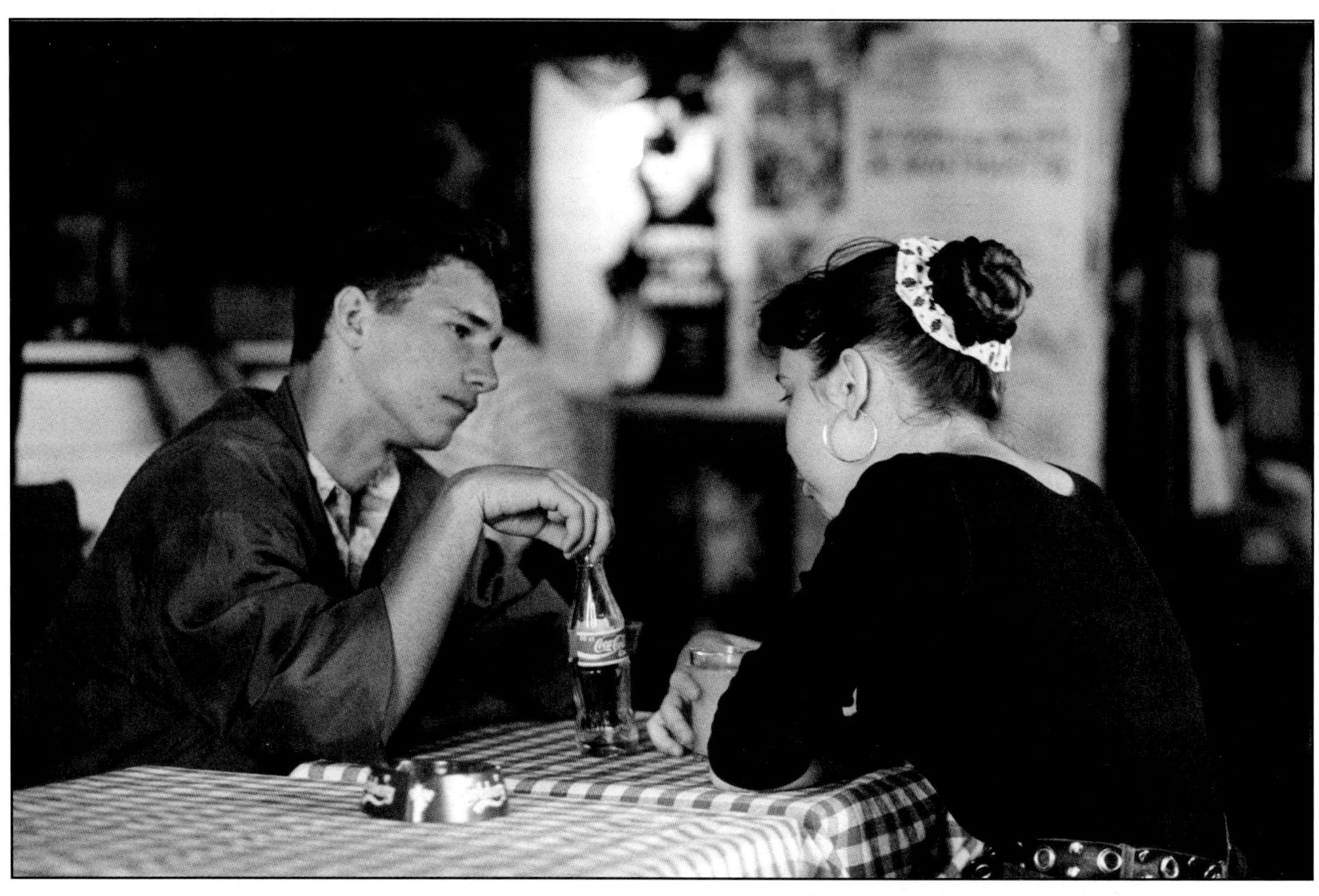

9
Monmartre
Gerry Walden

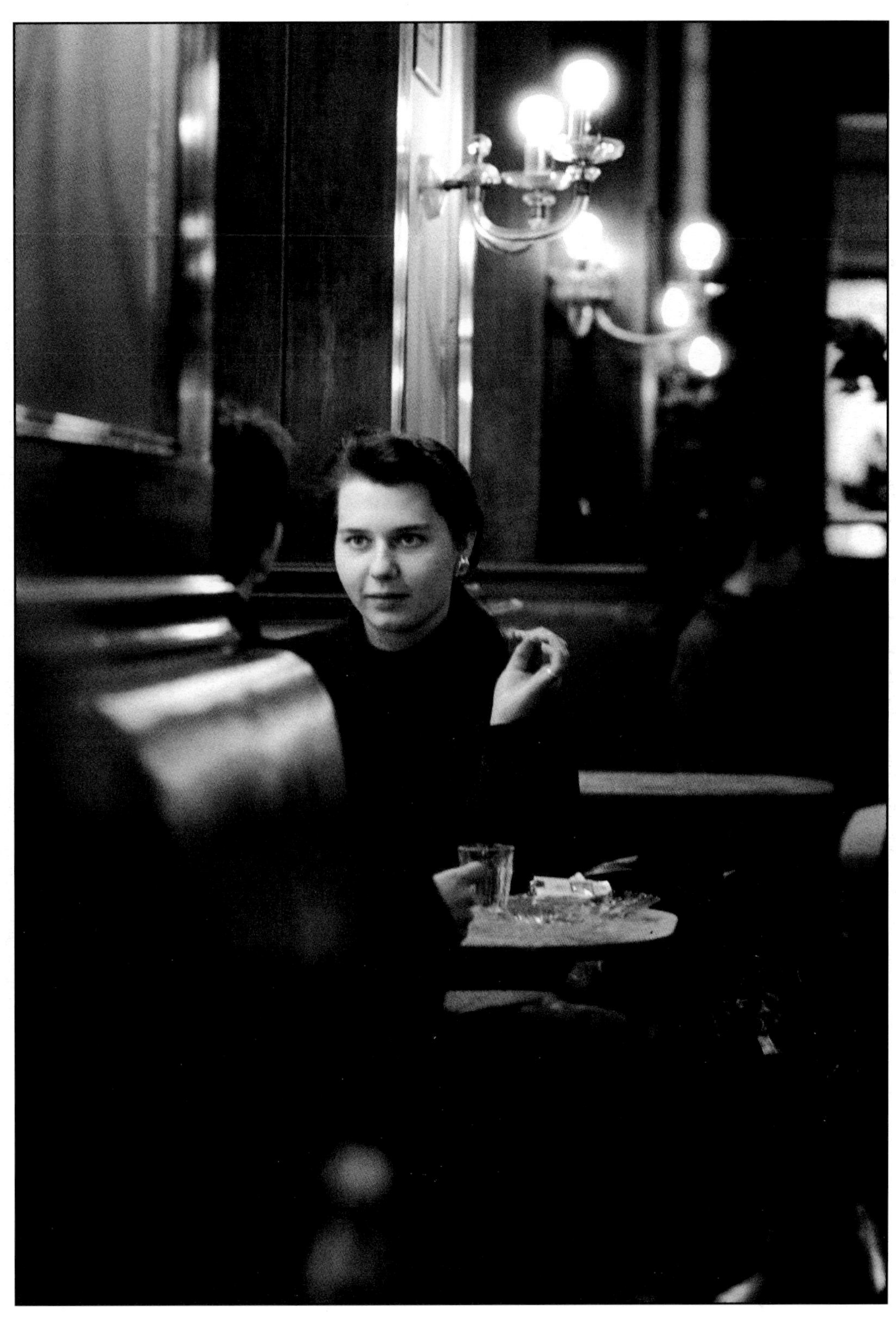

10
Vienna
Gerry Walden

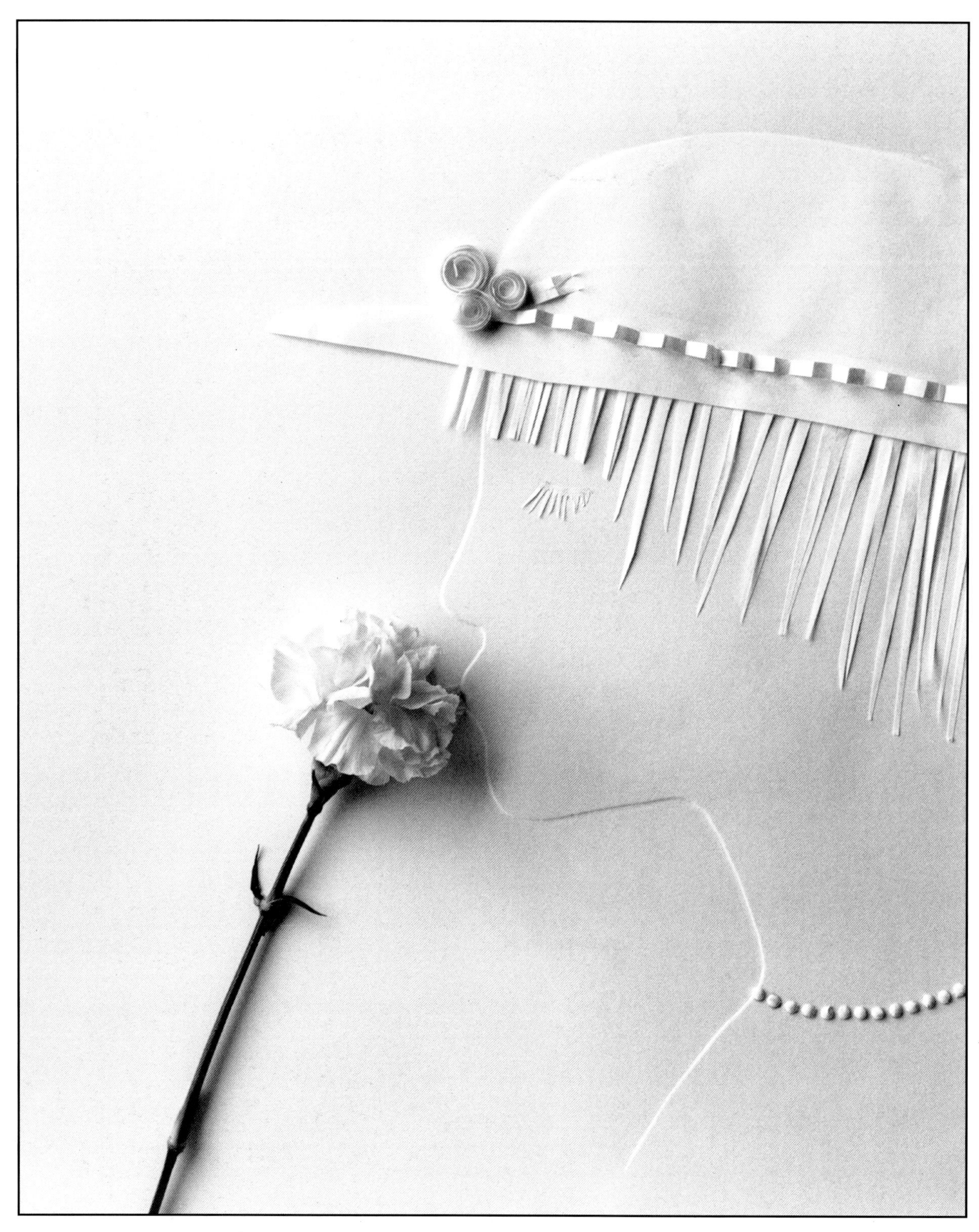

11
Girl with carnation
Christine Chambers

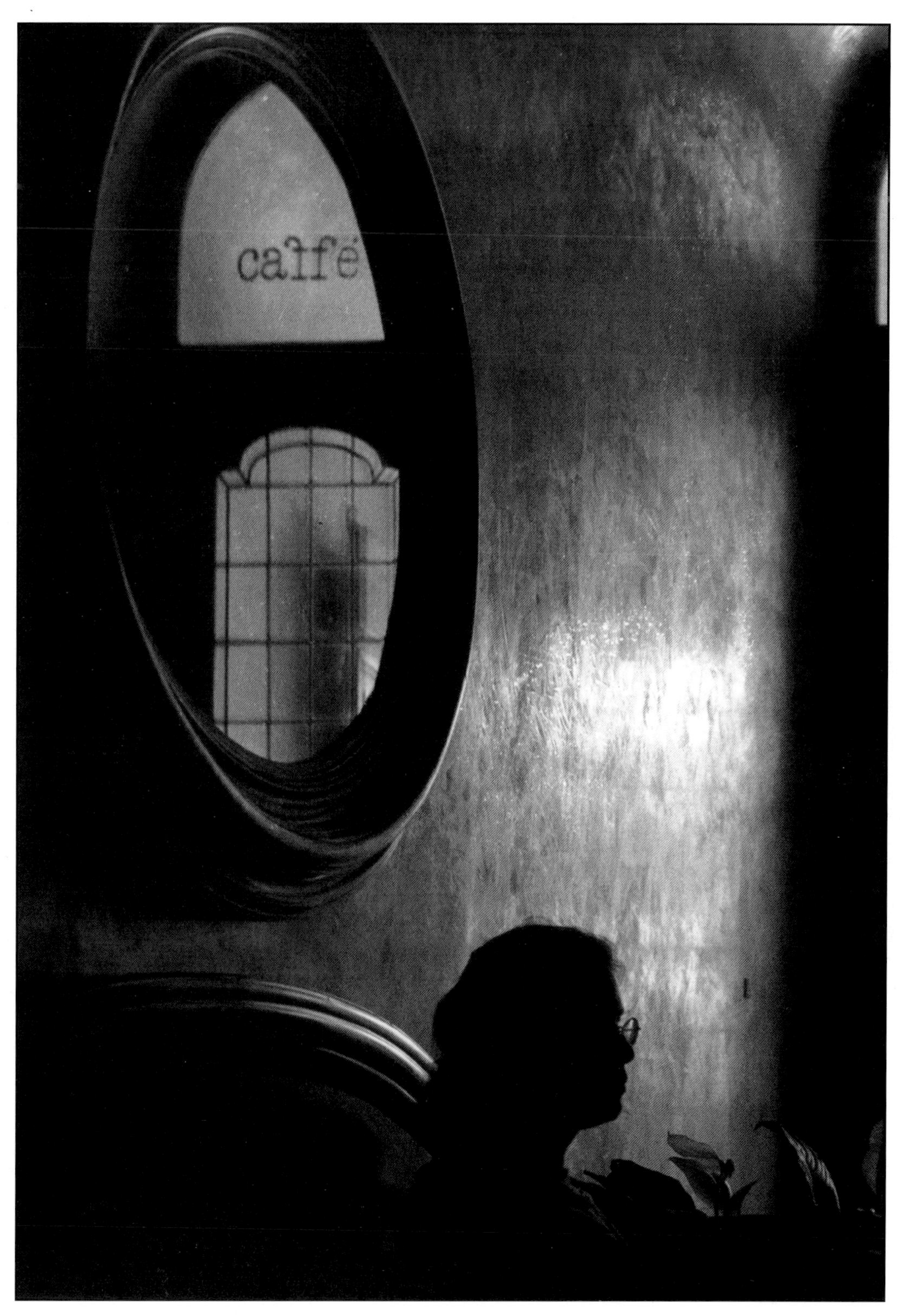

12
The assignation
Rosemary Cooper

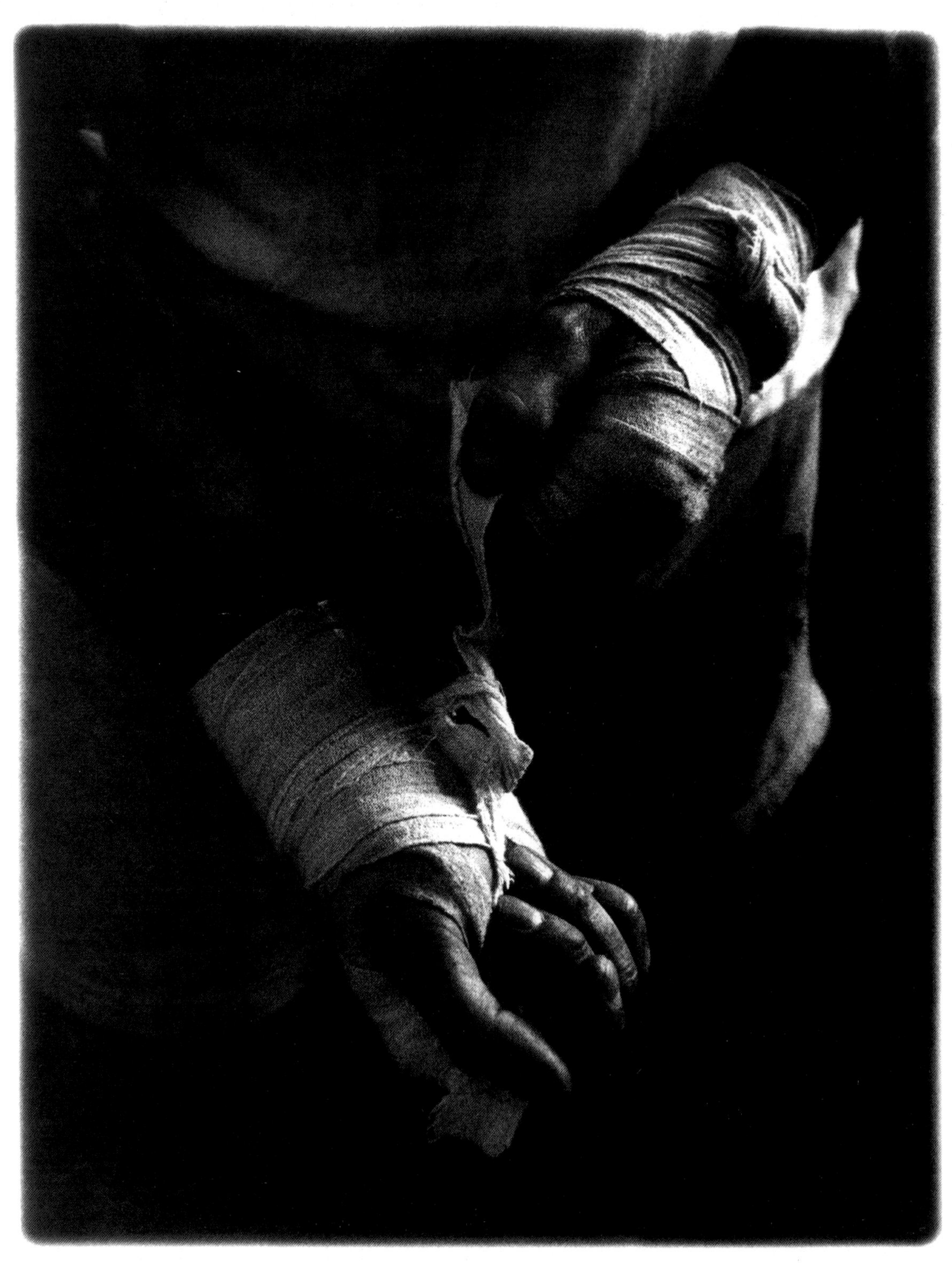

13
Knotty hands
Peter Doughty

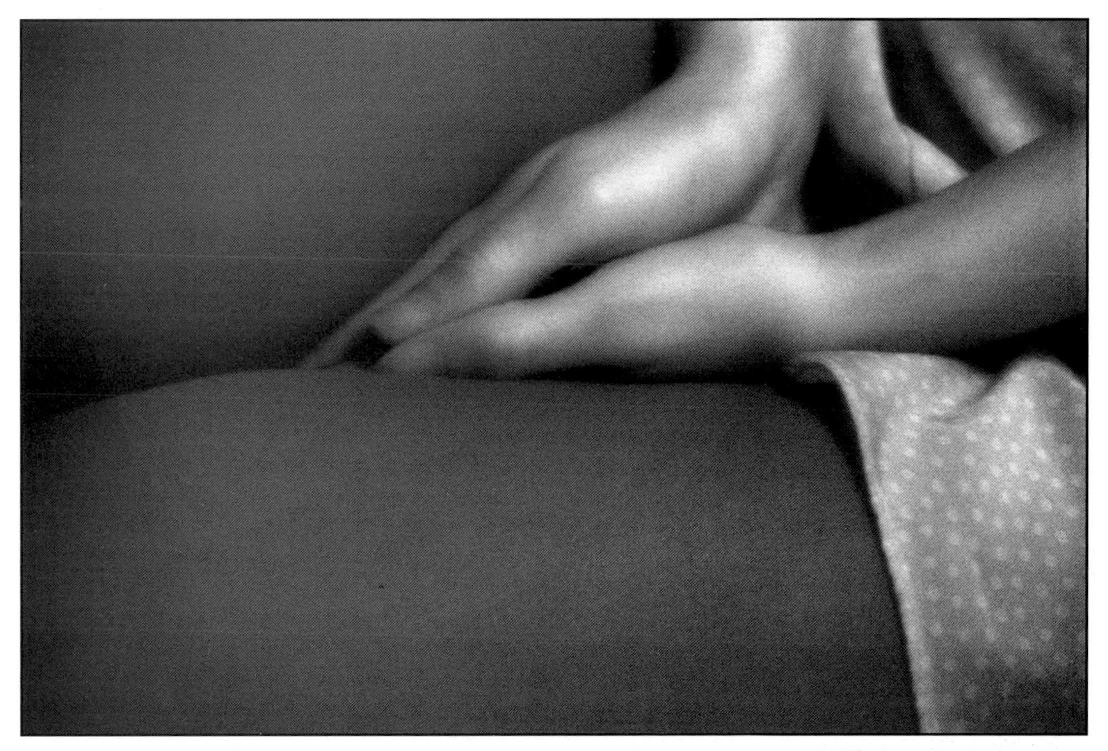

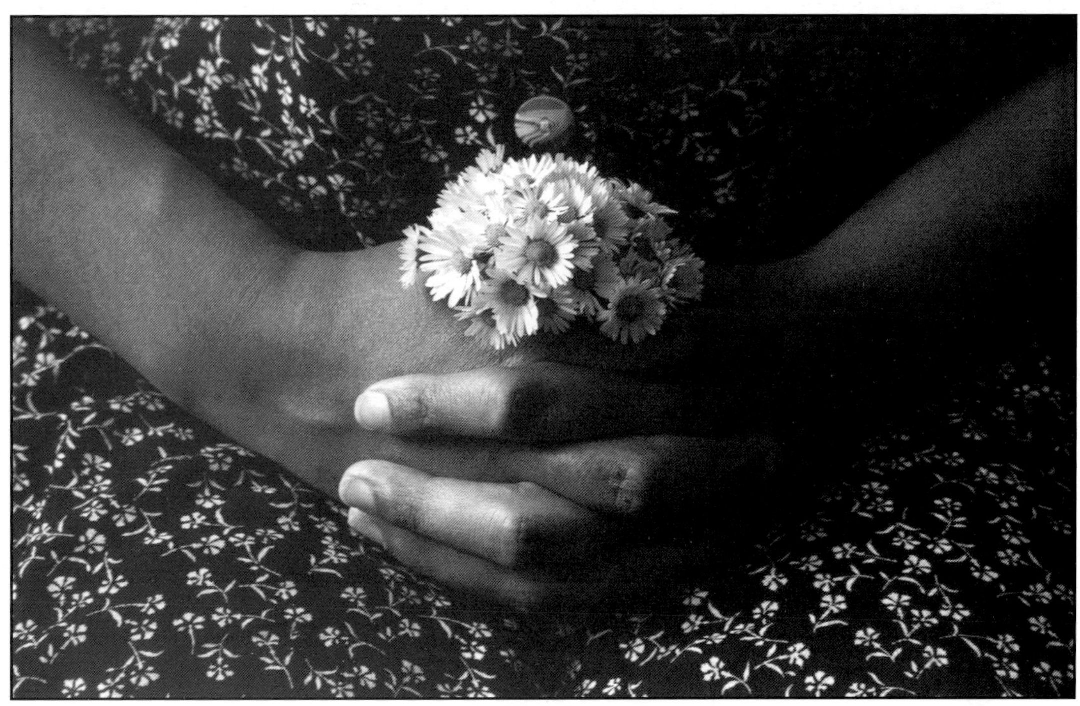

(top) 14, **Mains jointes**, *Denis Bourg*

(below) 15, **Daisies**, *Ken Bates*

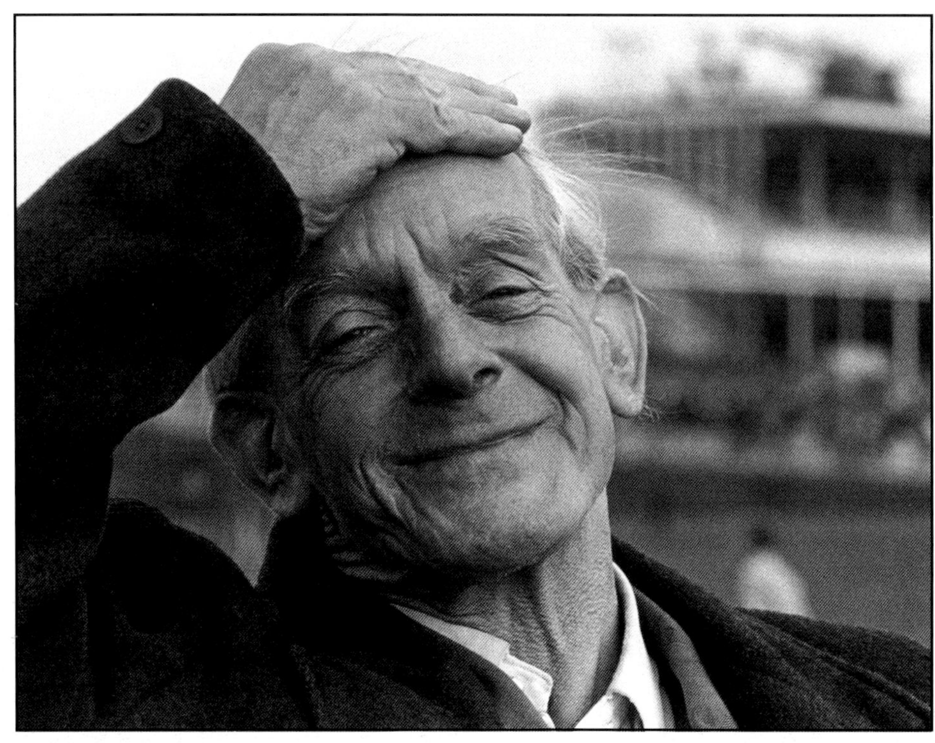

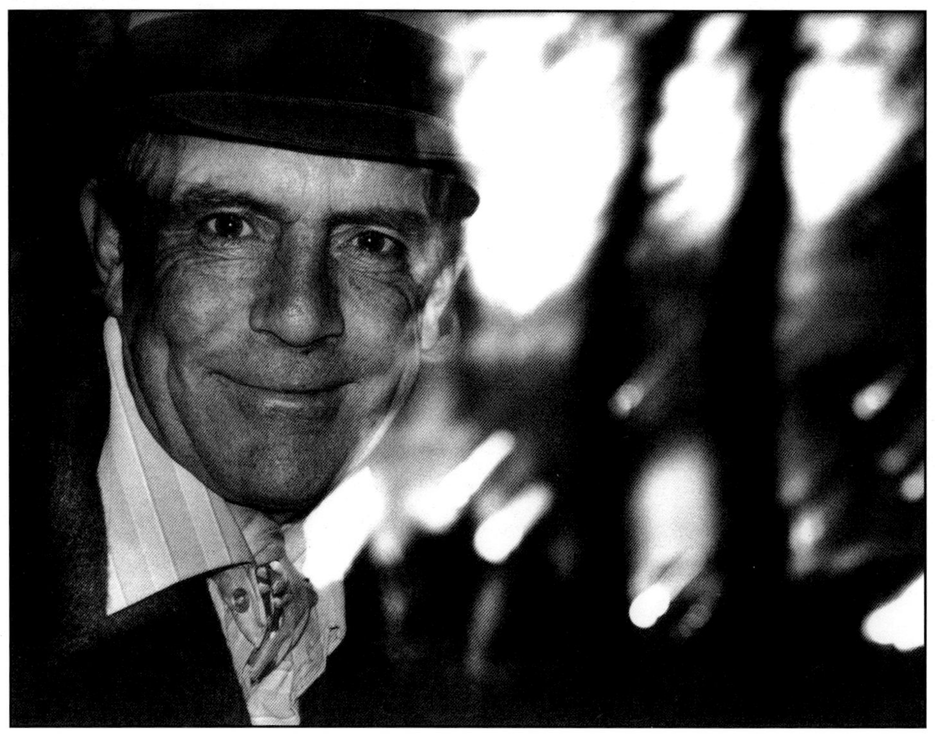

(top) 16, **Frank at the races**; *(below)* 17, **Jockey**,

Moyra Peralta

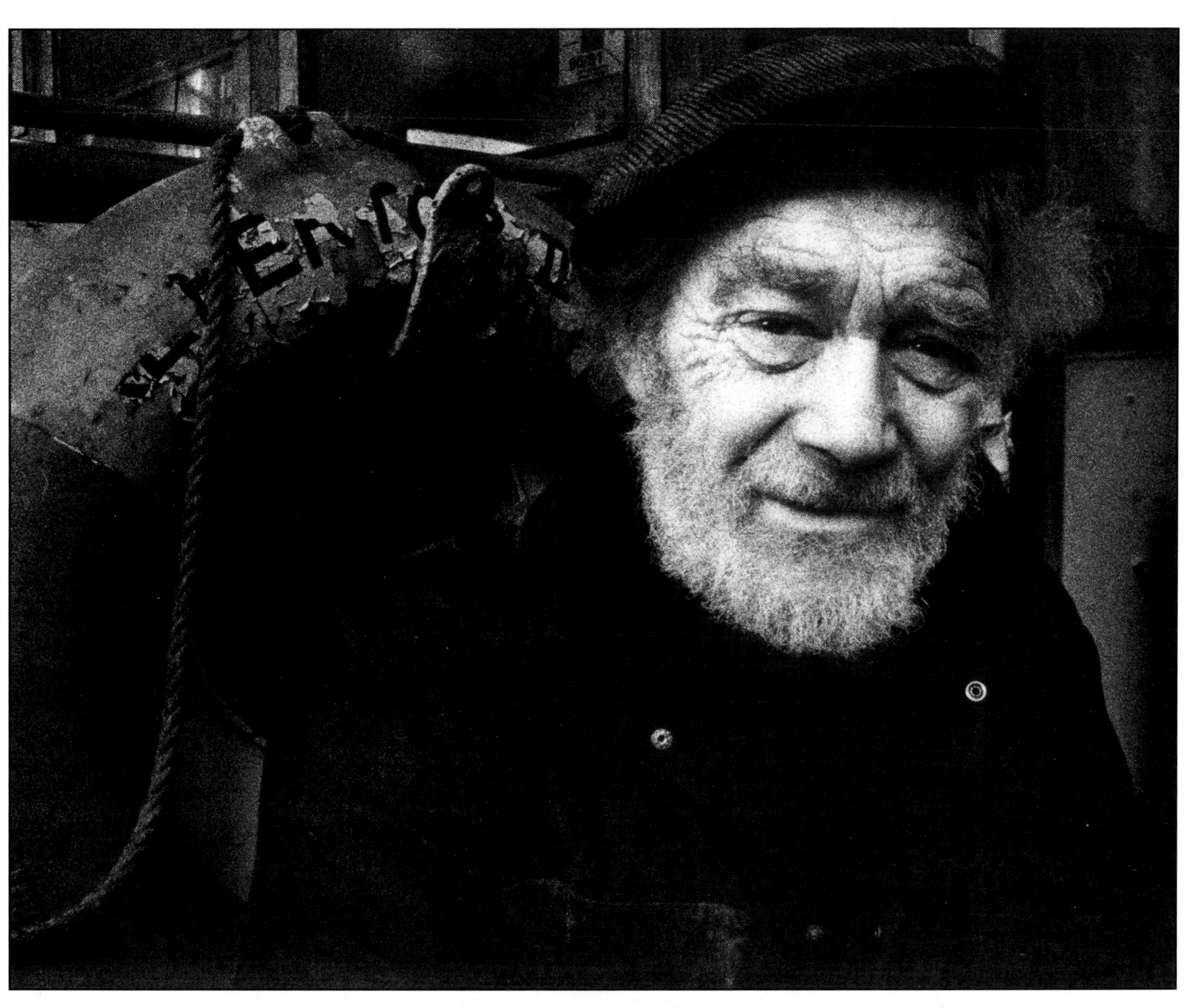

18
Man of the sea
Steve Zalokoski

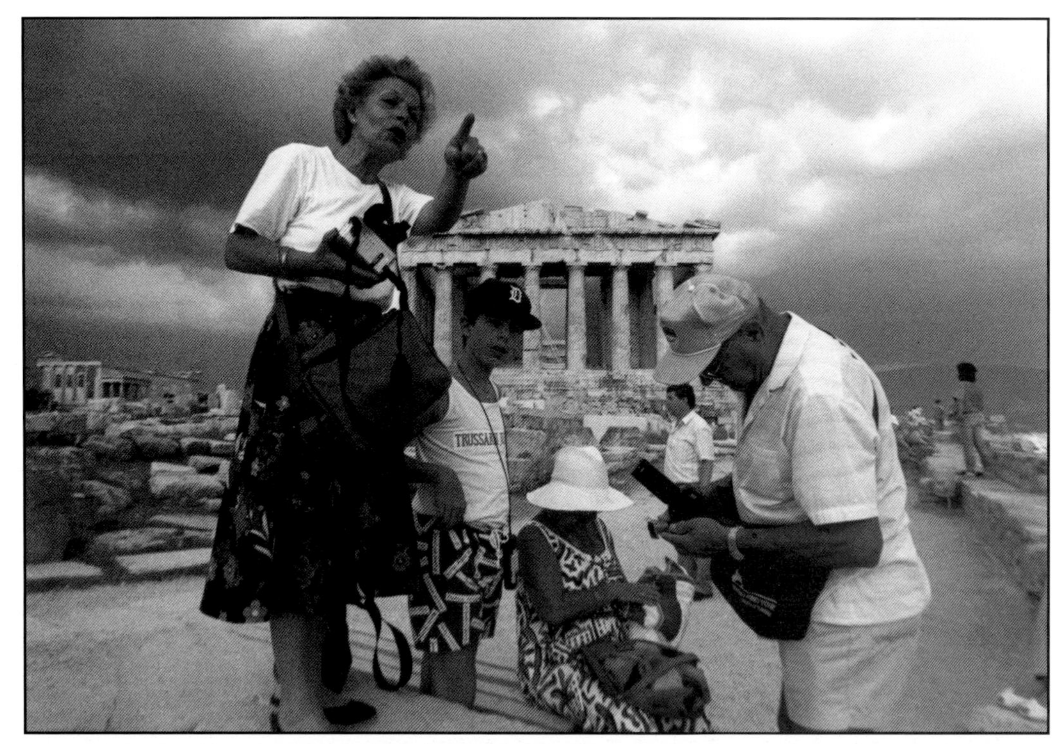

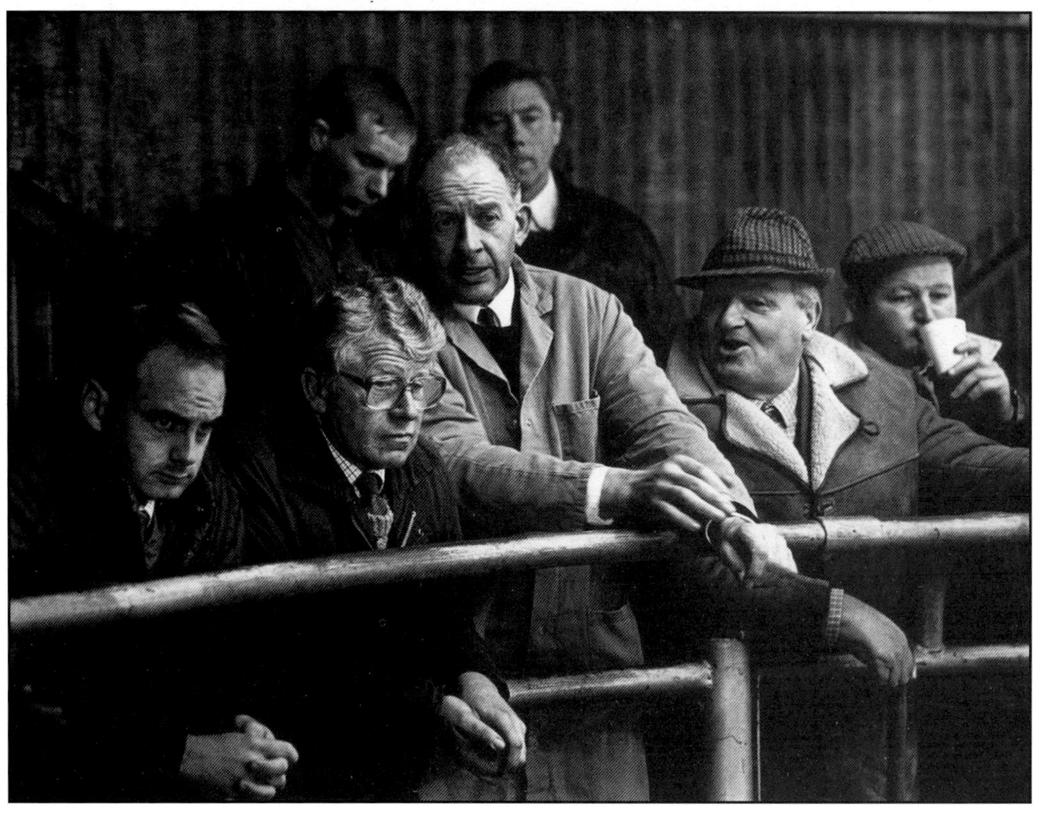

(top) 19, **Tourists, Athens**, *Mike Coles (London)*

(below) 20, **There's a bargain!**, *Trevor Fry*

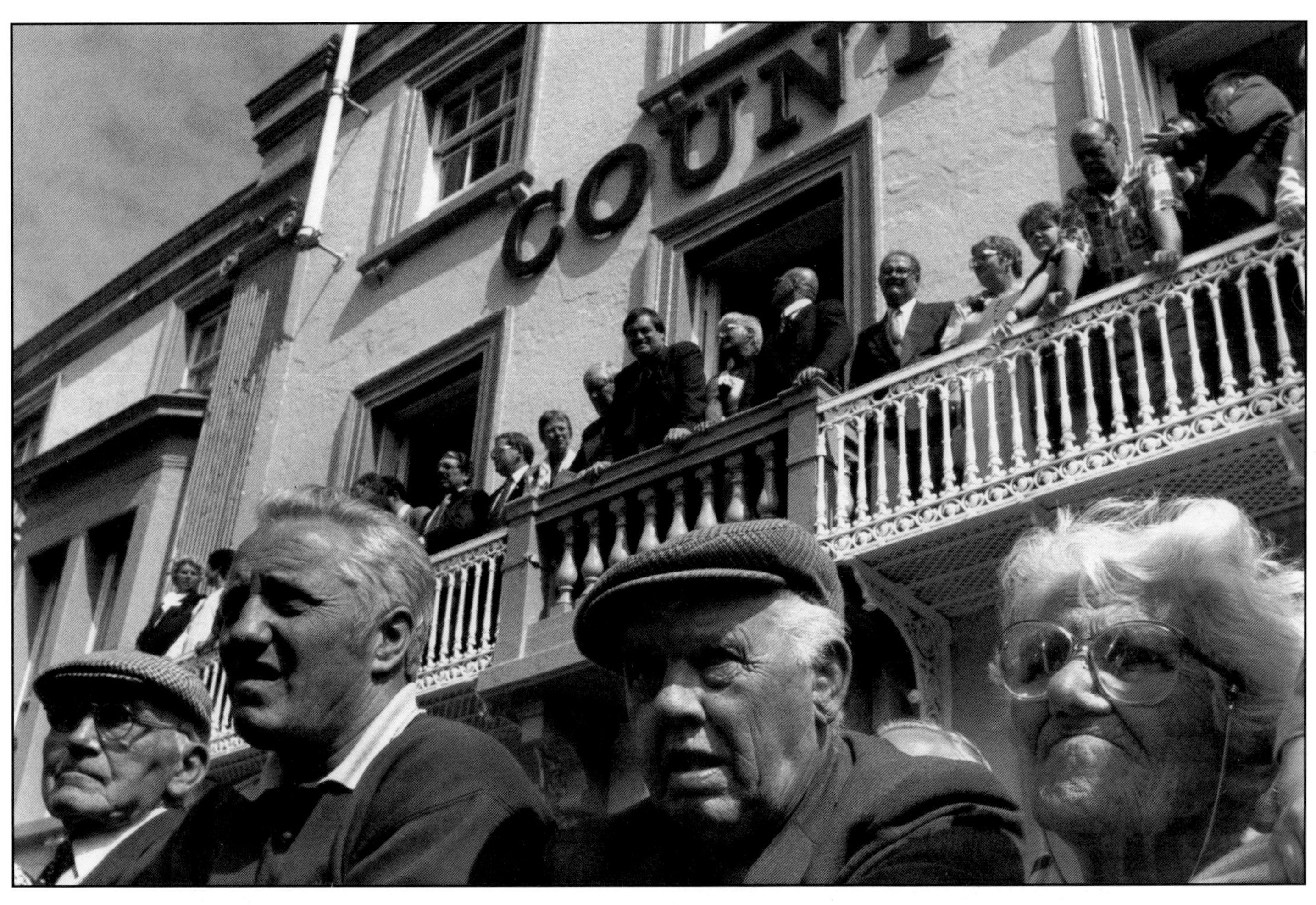

21
New Labour
Alan Brown

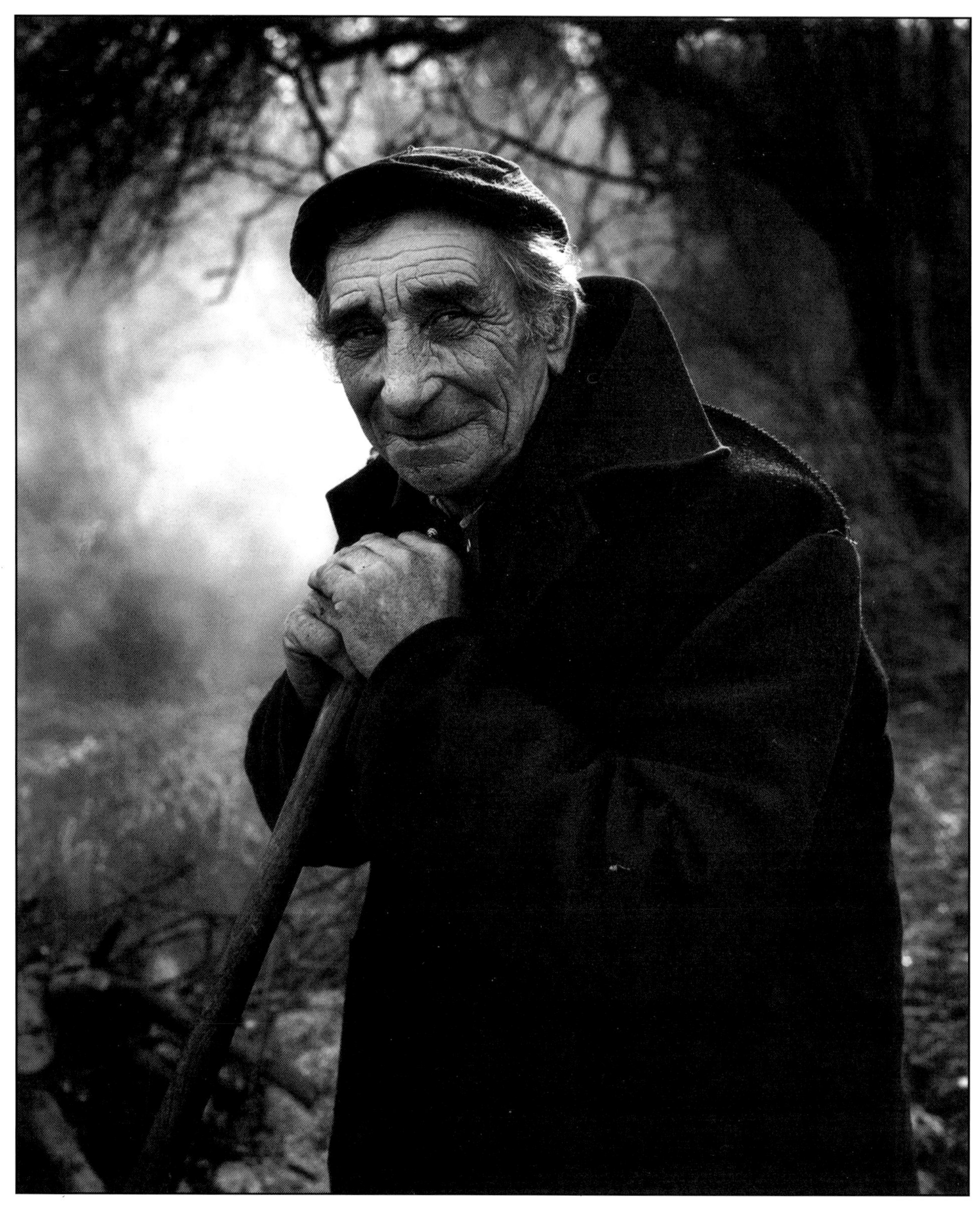

22
Woodsman
Trevor Fry

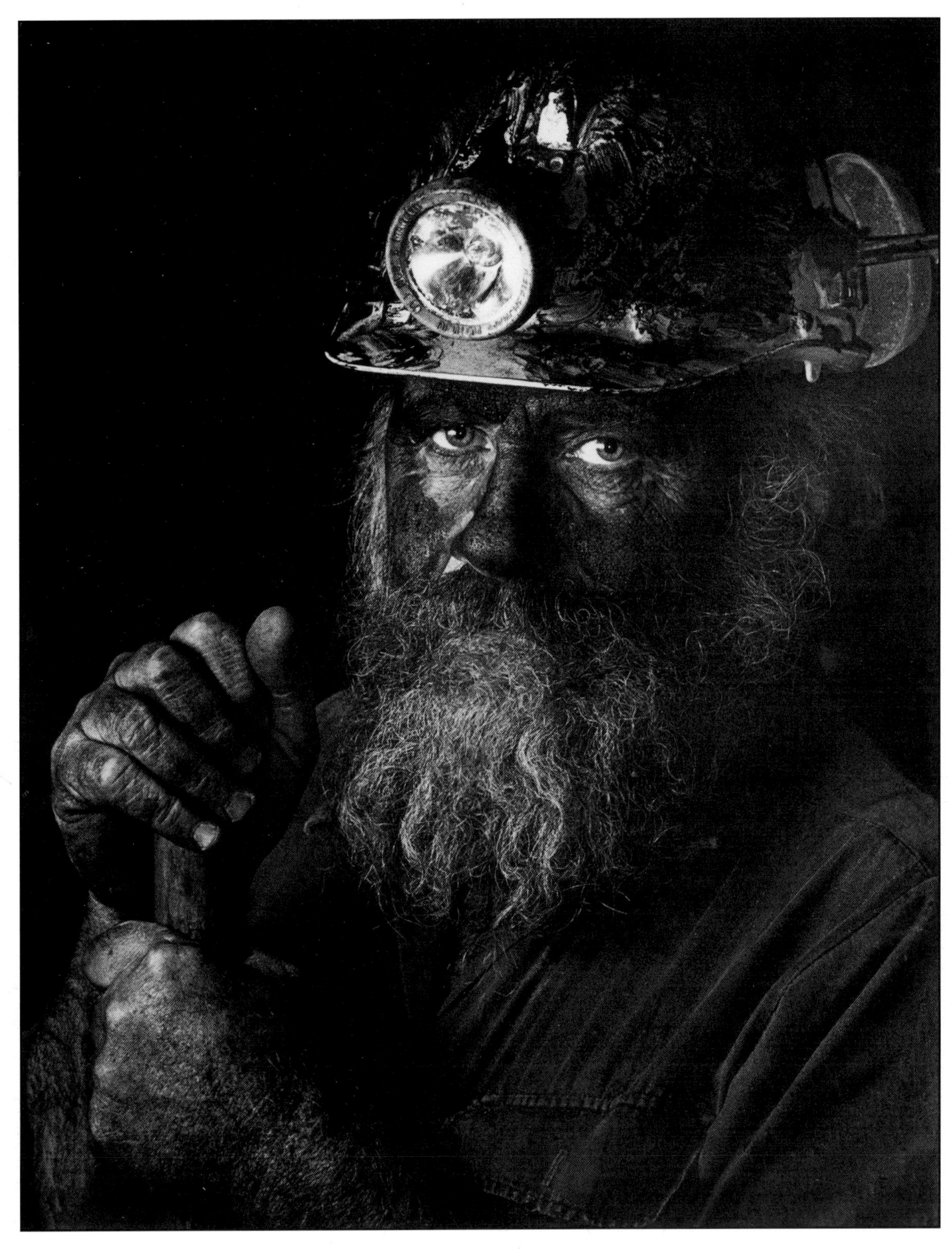

23
Master of the pit
David Mahony

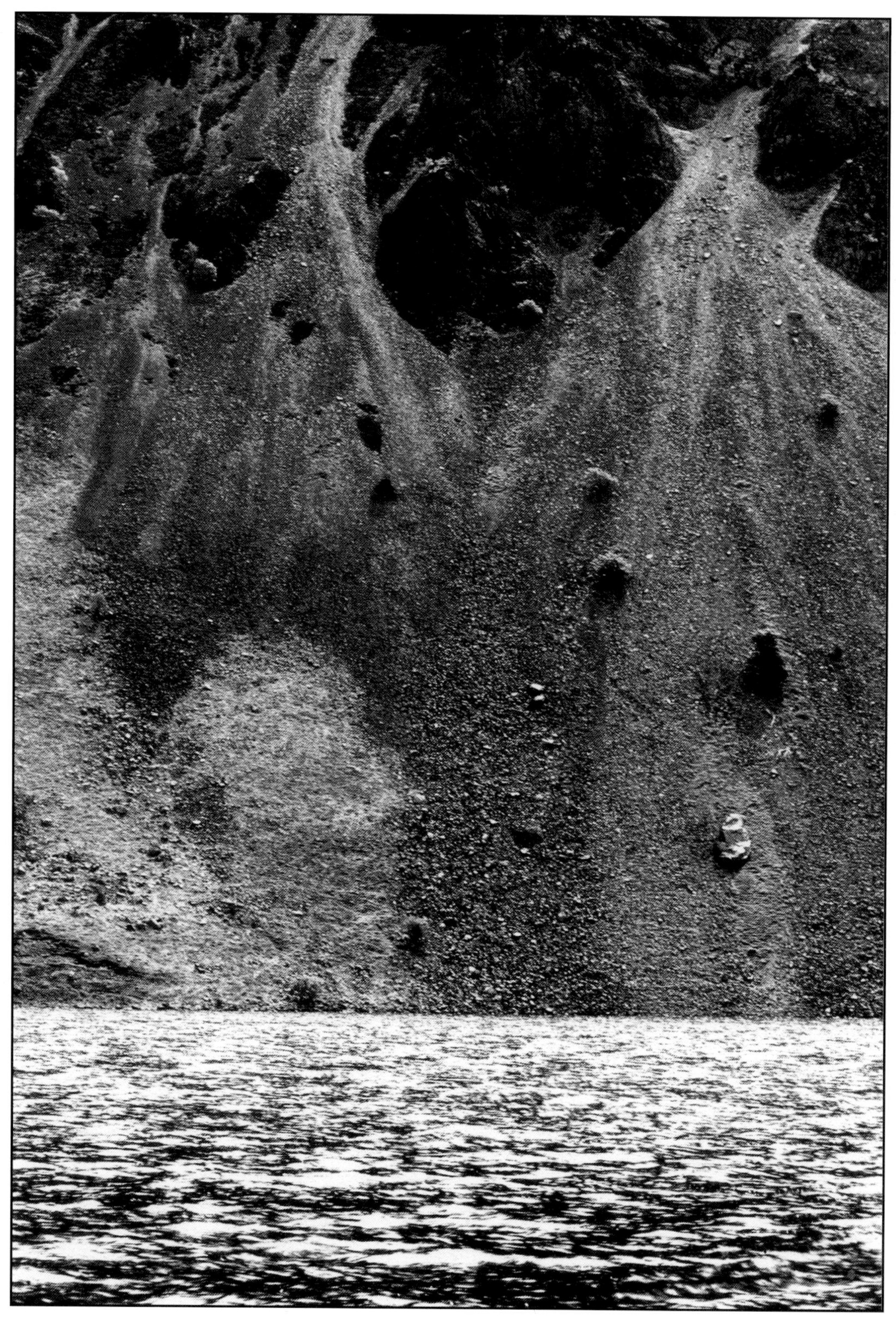

24
Scree
Roy Morgan

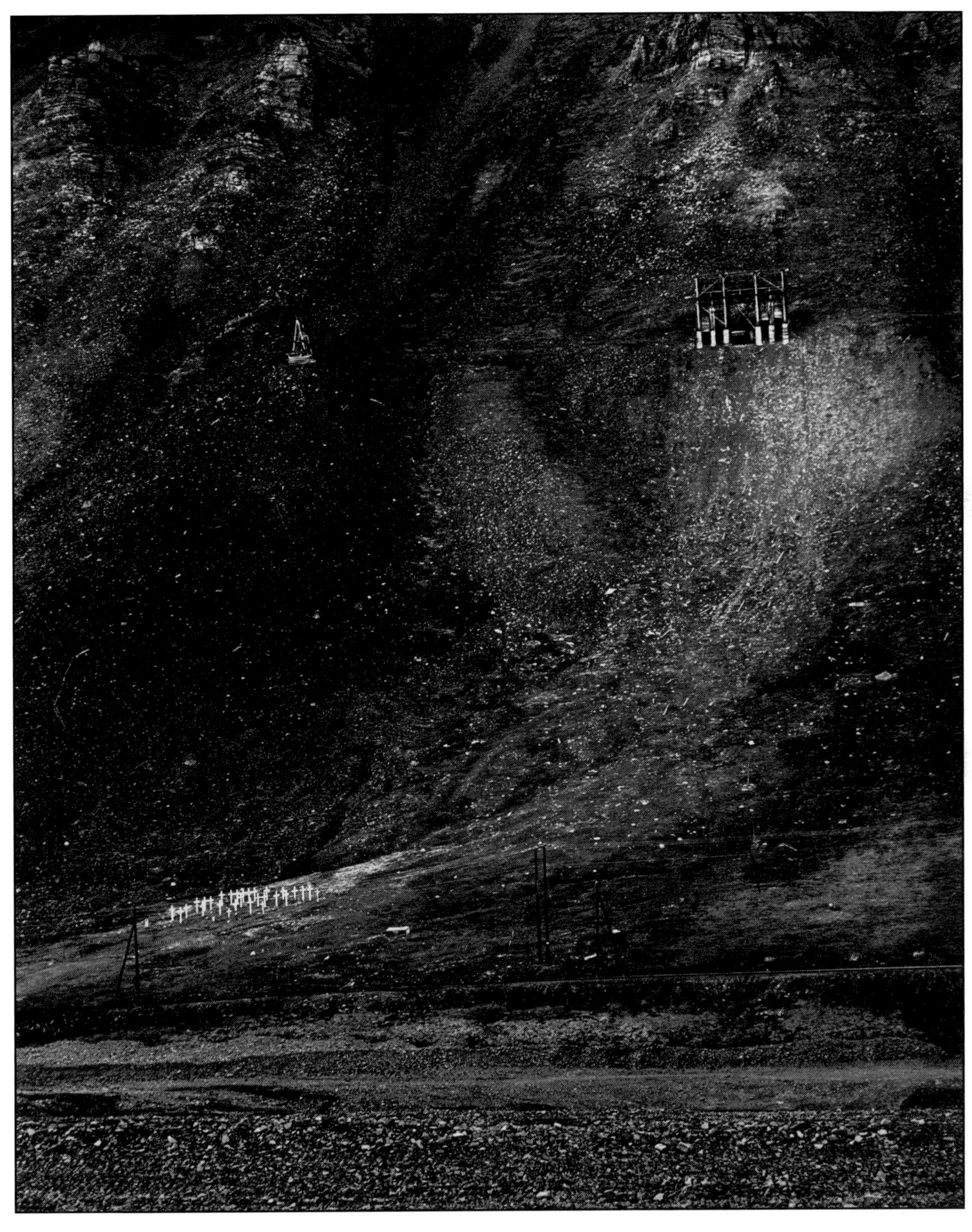

25
Cost of coal
David Conway

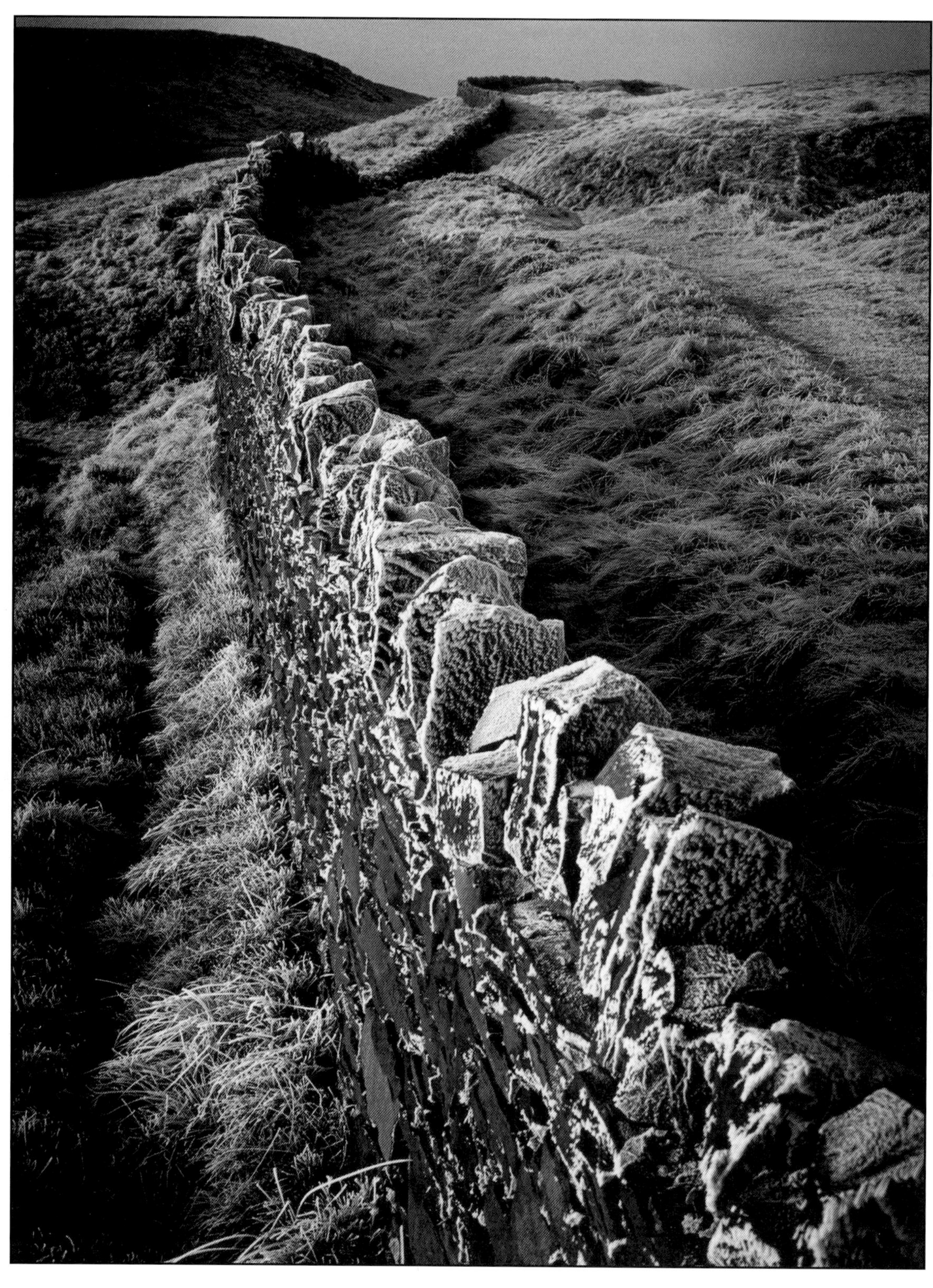

26
Wall o'er the moor
Alfred Hoole

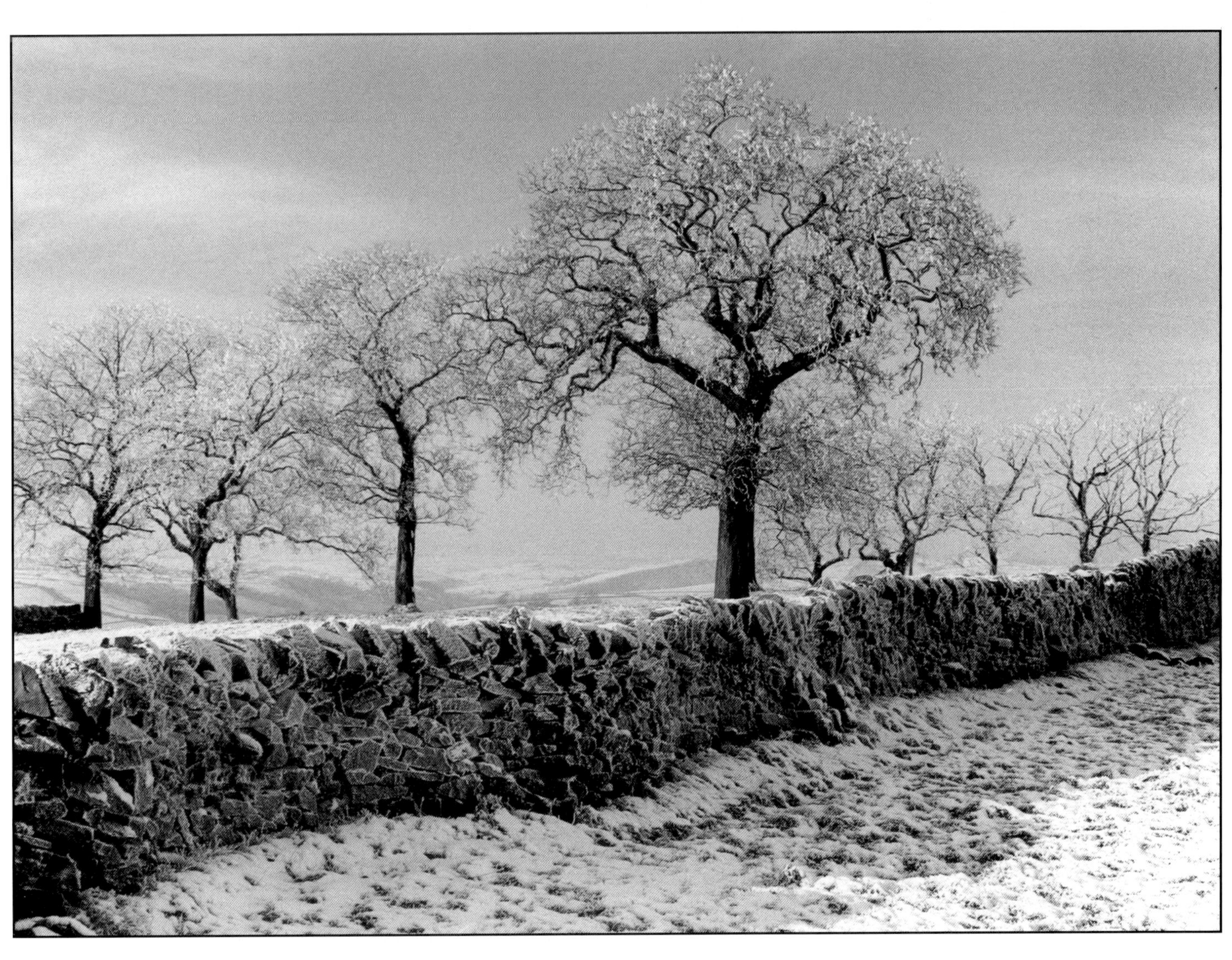

27
Simply winter
Kevin Bridgwood

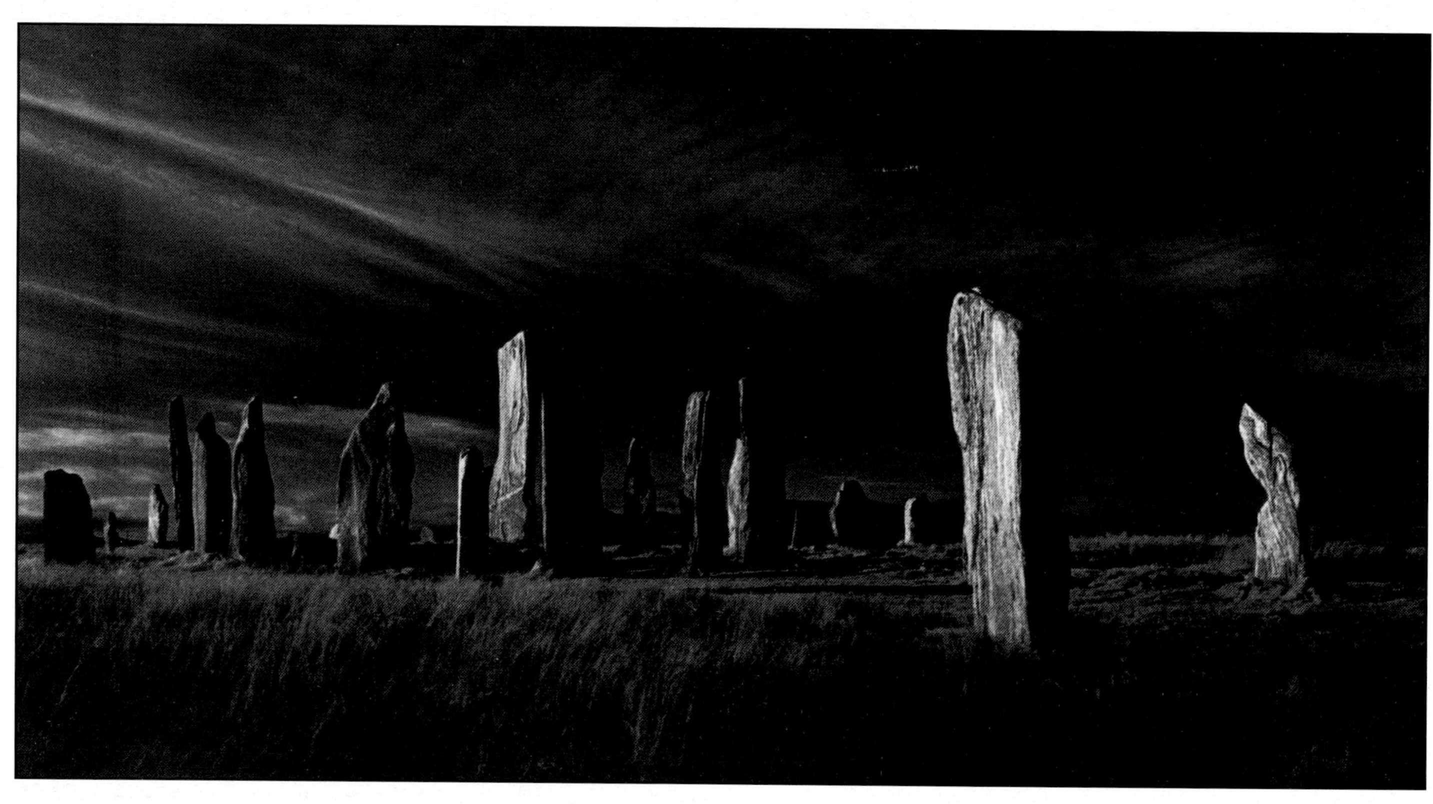

28
Callanish
Peter Clark

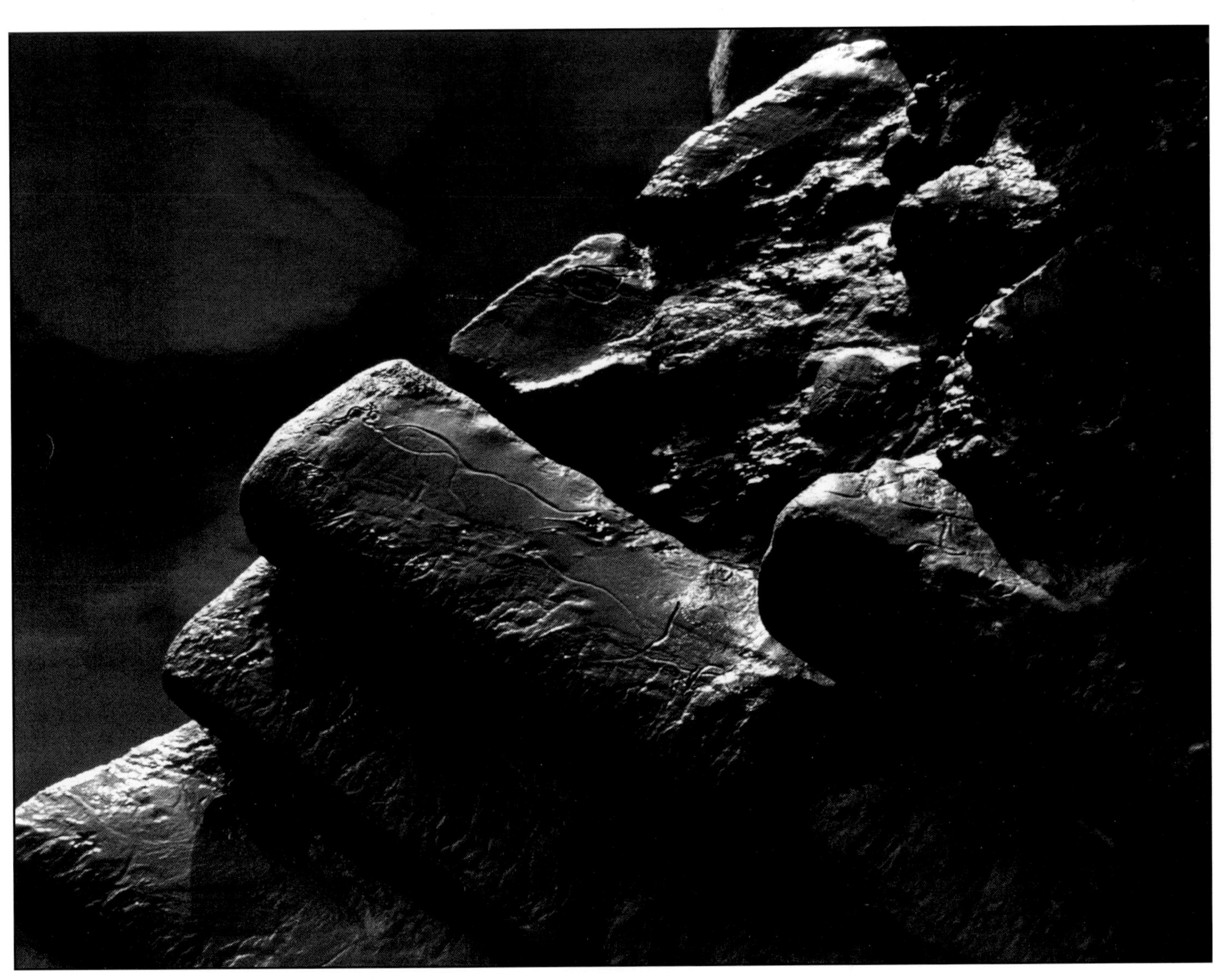

29
Time and tide
George Coupe

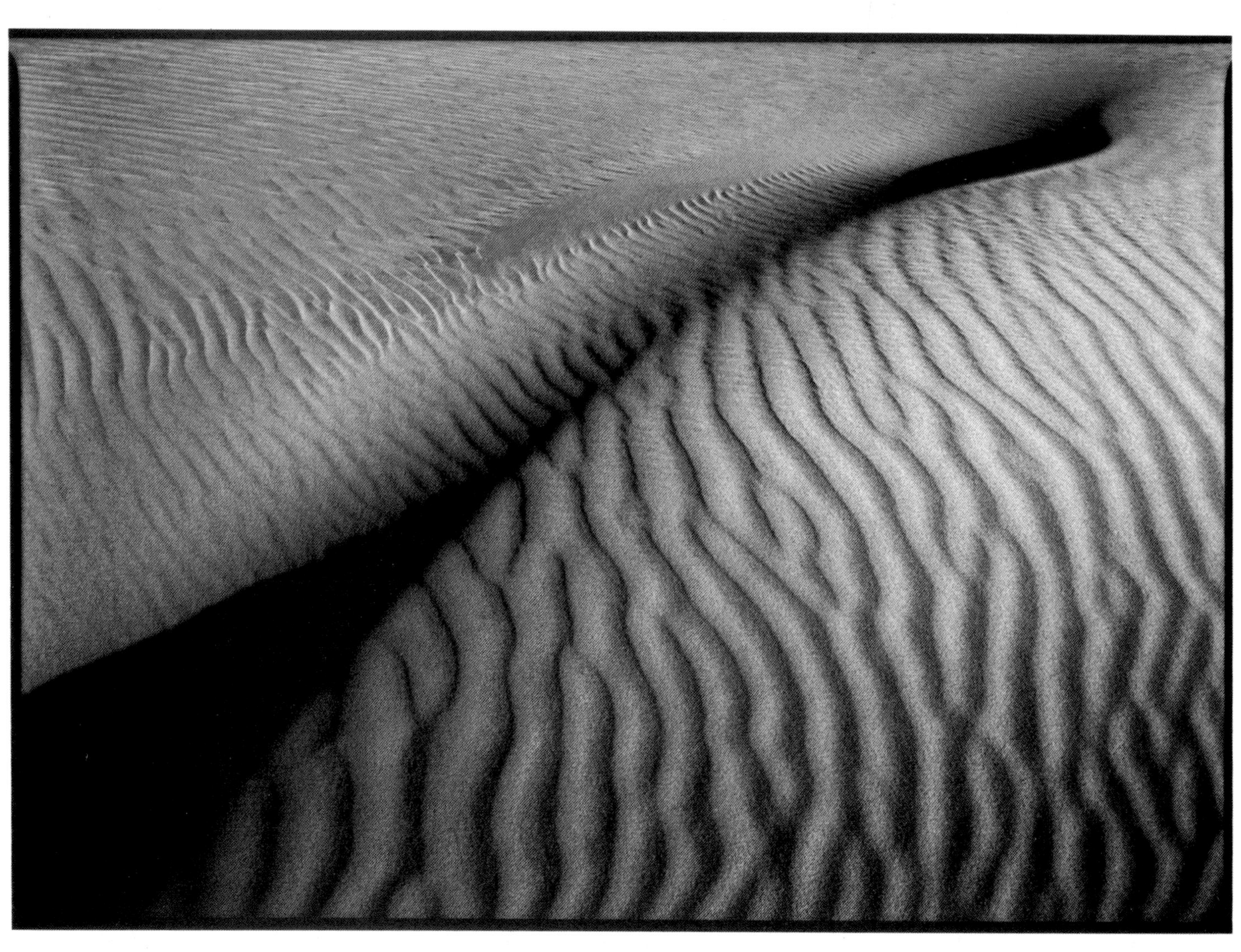

30
Dunes
Göran Stenberg

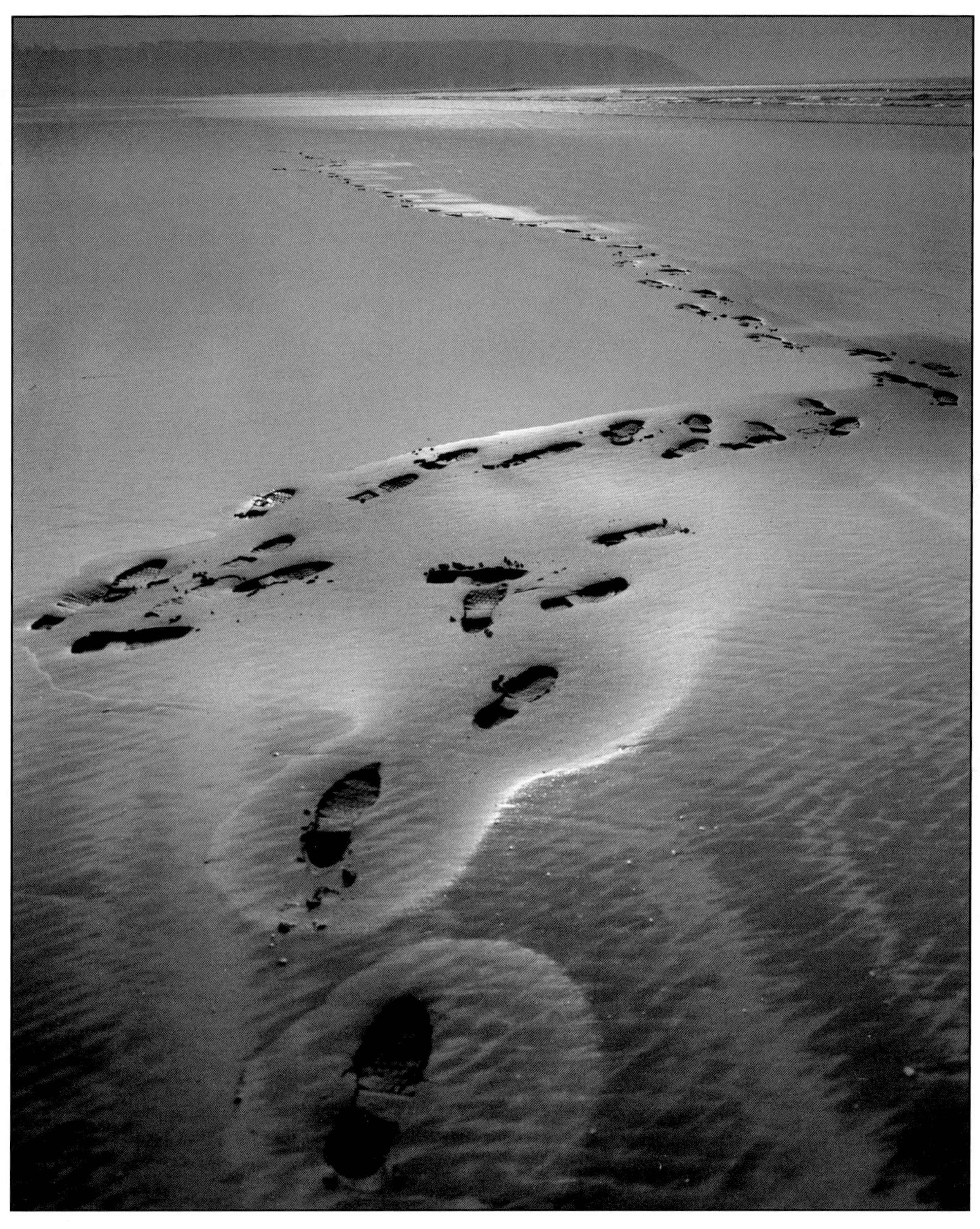

31
Footsteps
Dick Jones

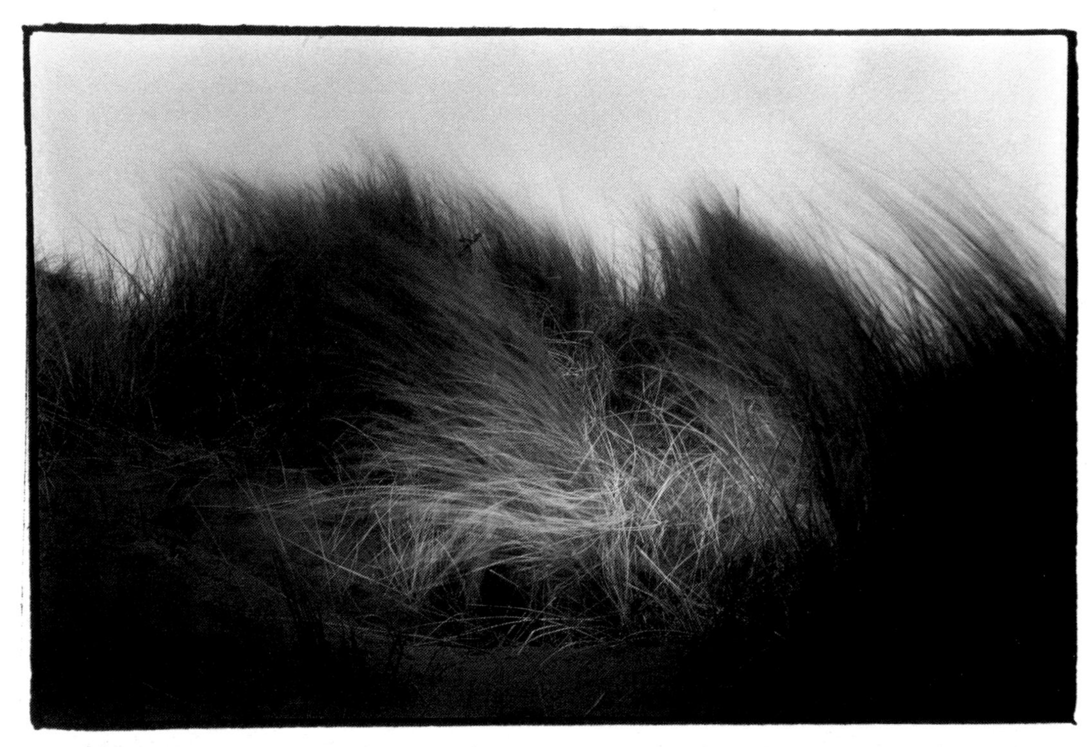

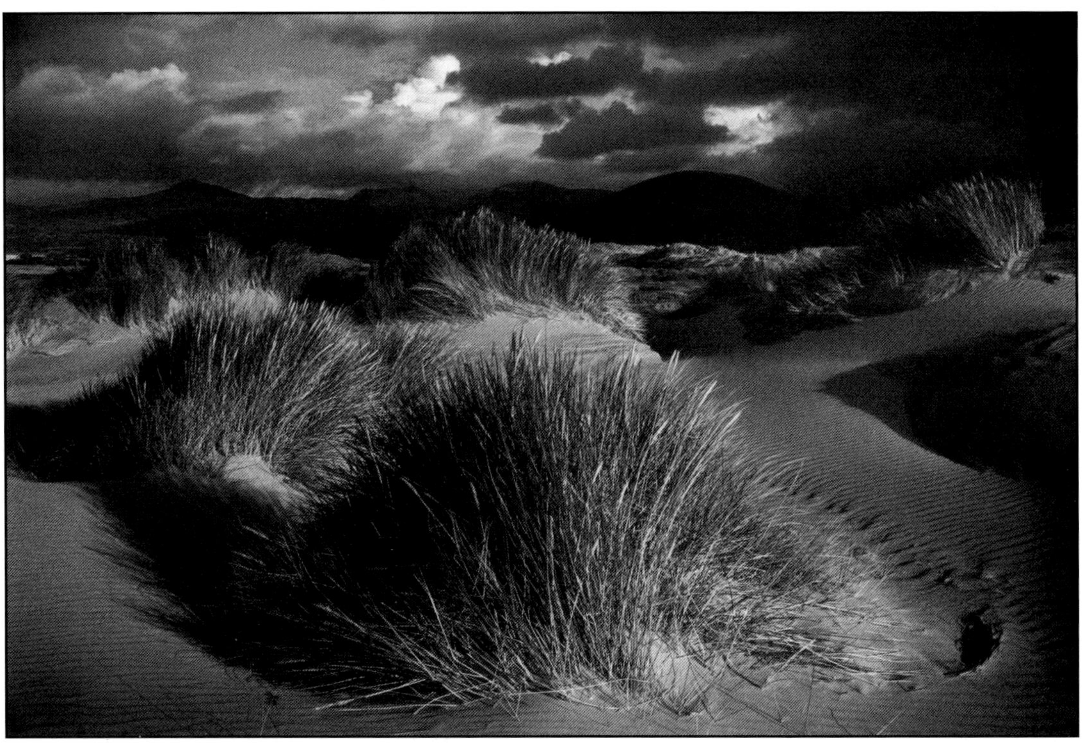

(top) 32, **October winds**, *Ian King*

(below) 33, **Dune storm**, *Peter Williams*

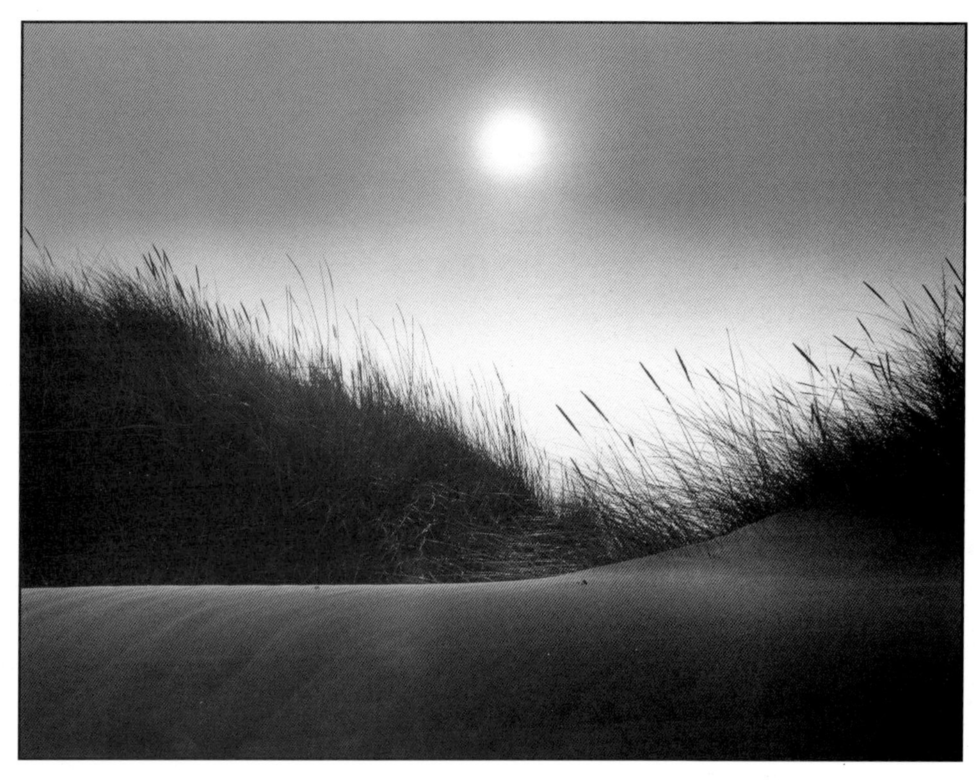

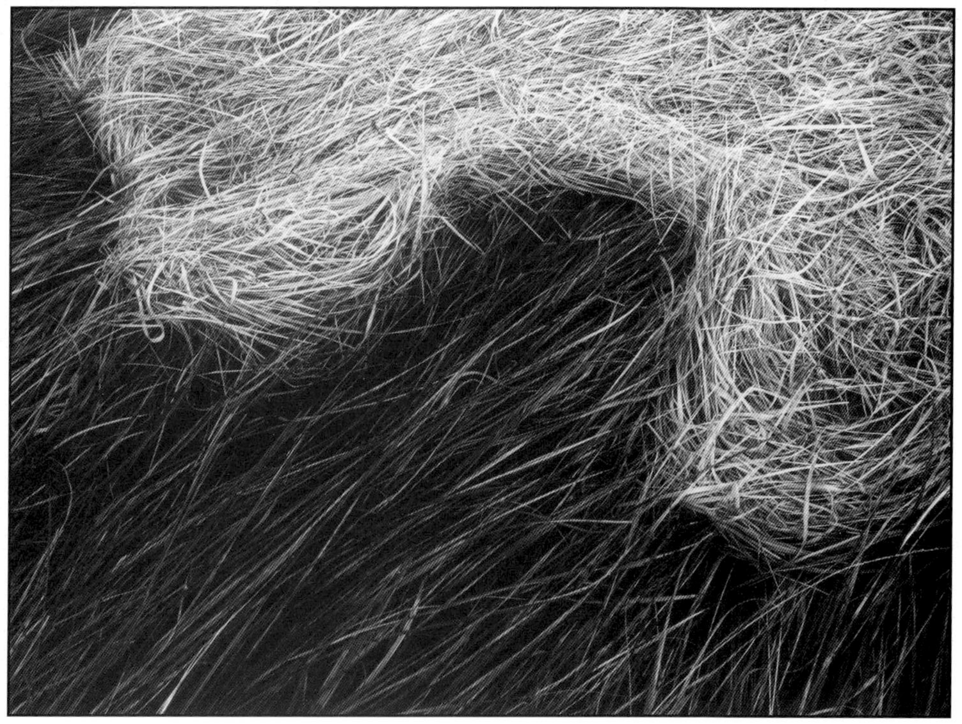

(top) 34, **Dunes 1**, *Alan Fowler*

(below) 35, **Grass wave after flood, Snowdonia**, *David Miller*

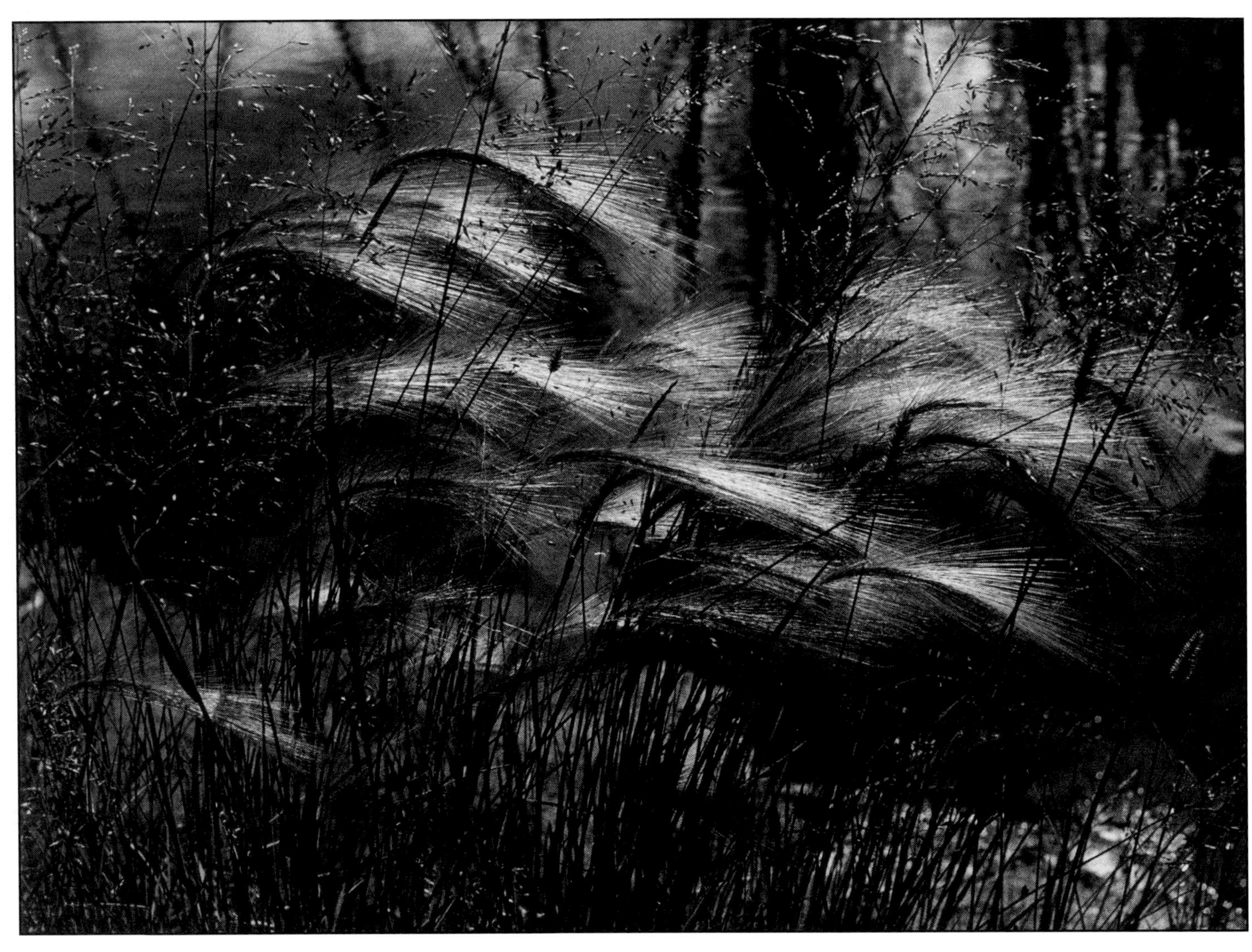

36
Grasses
David Pearce

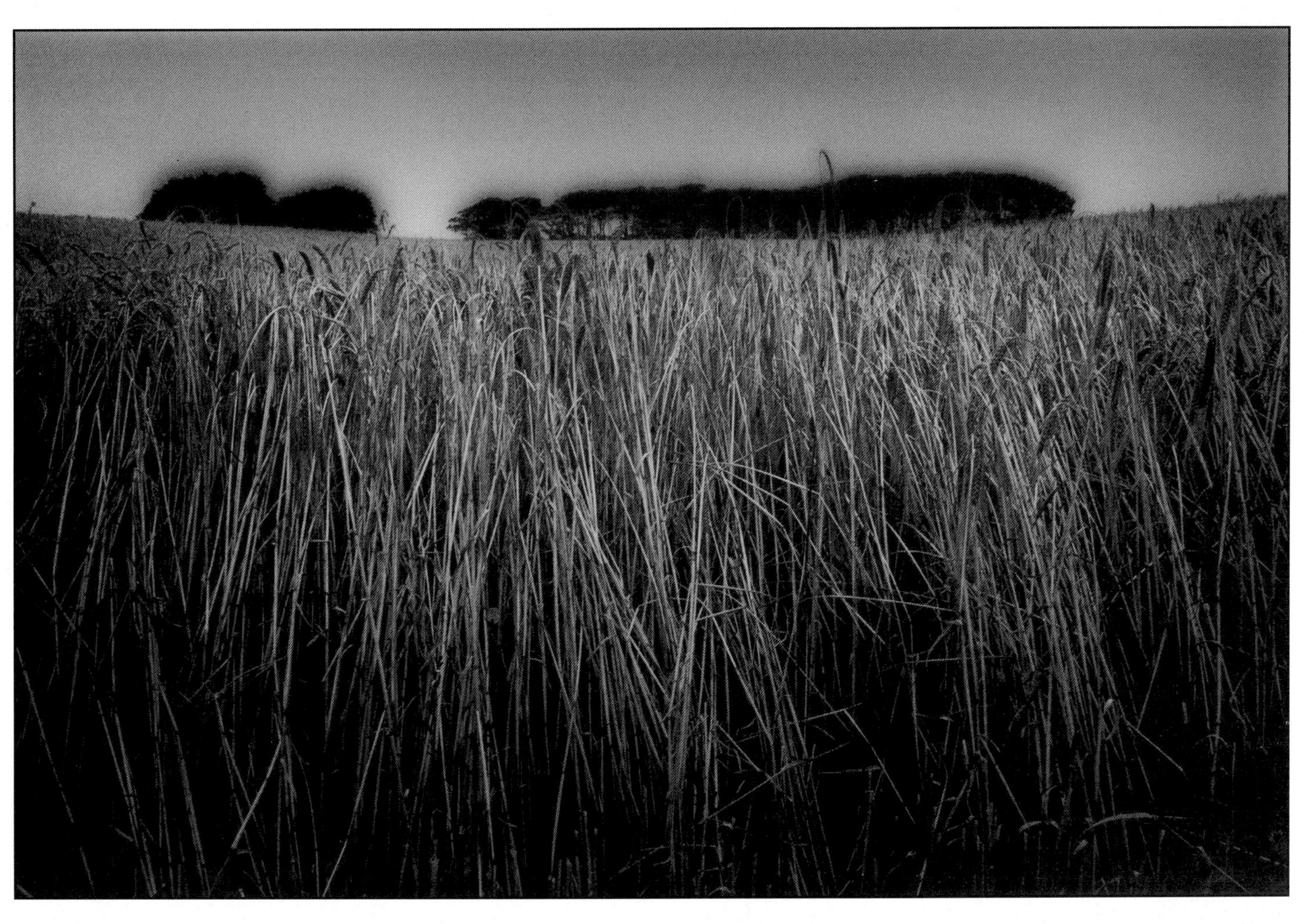

37
The tall fields
Neil Bedwell

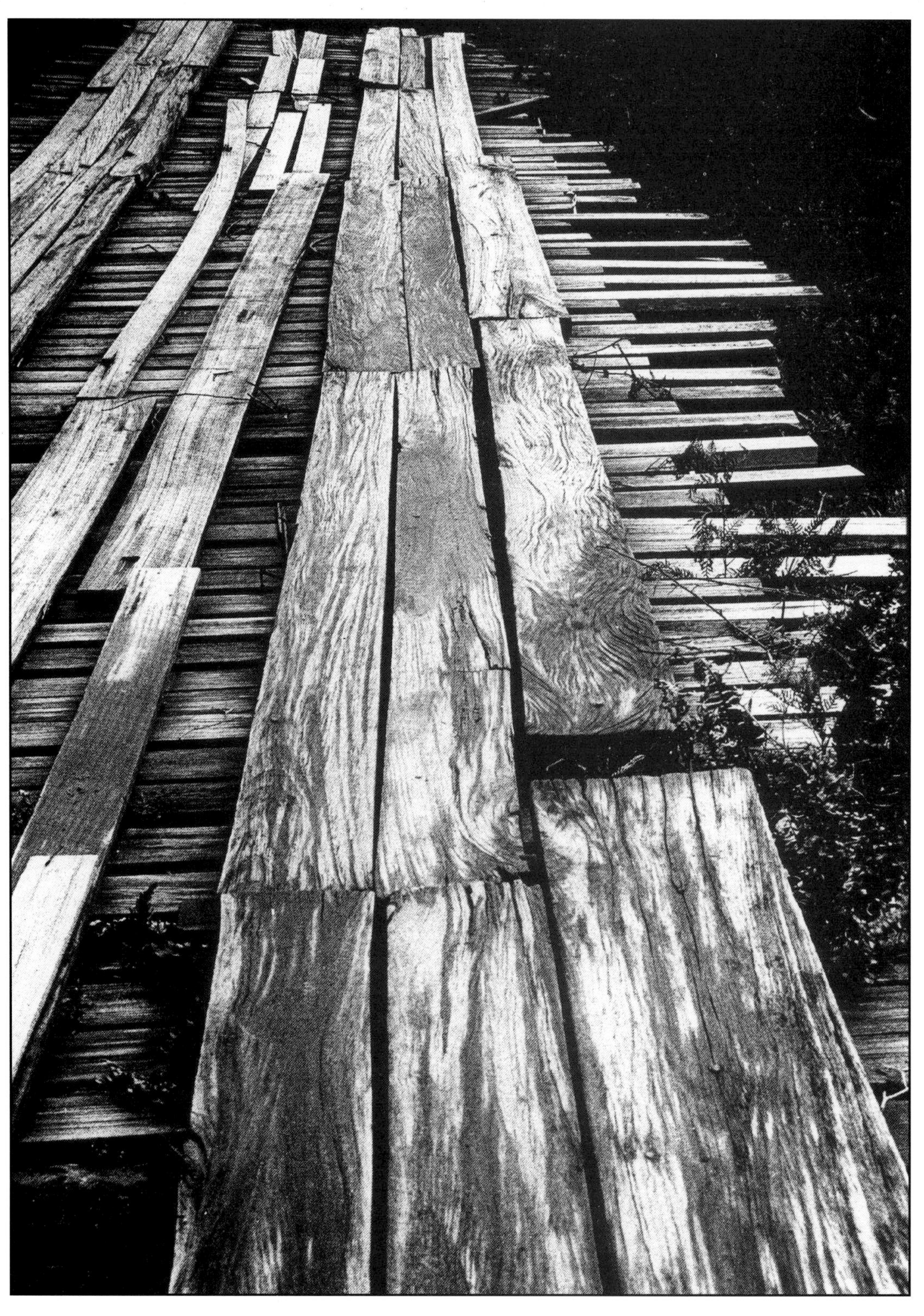

38
Xylophone bridge
Peter Motton

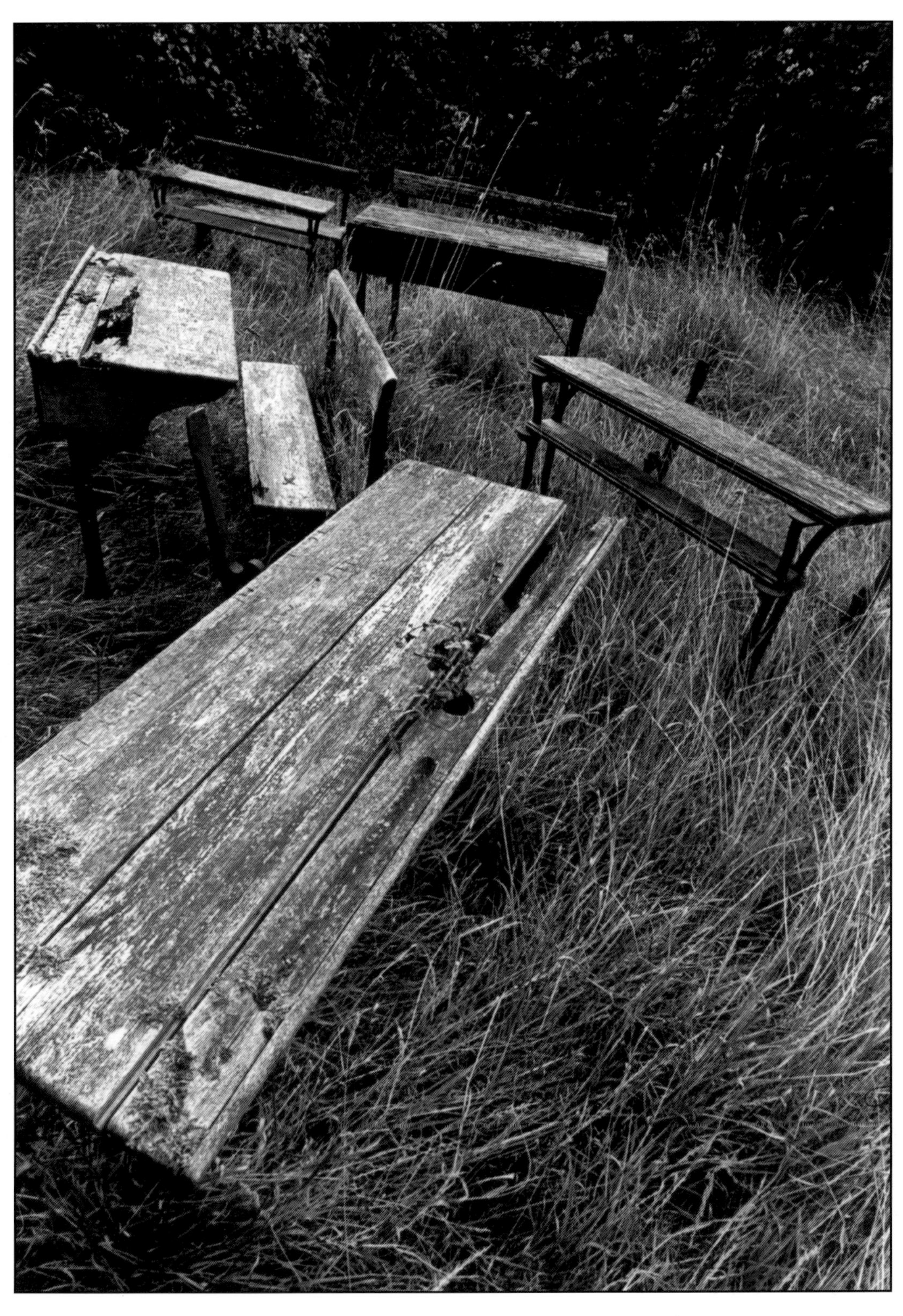

39
Abandoned desks
Patrick Reilly

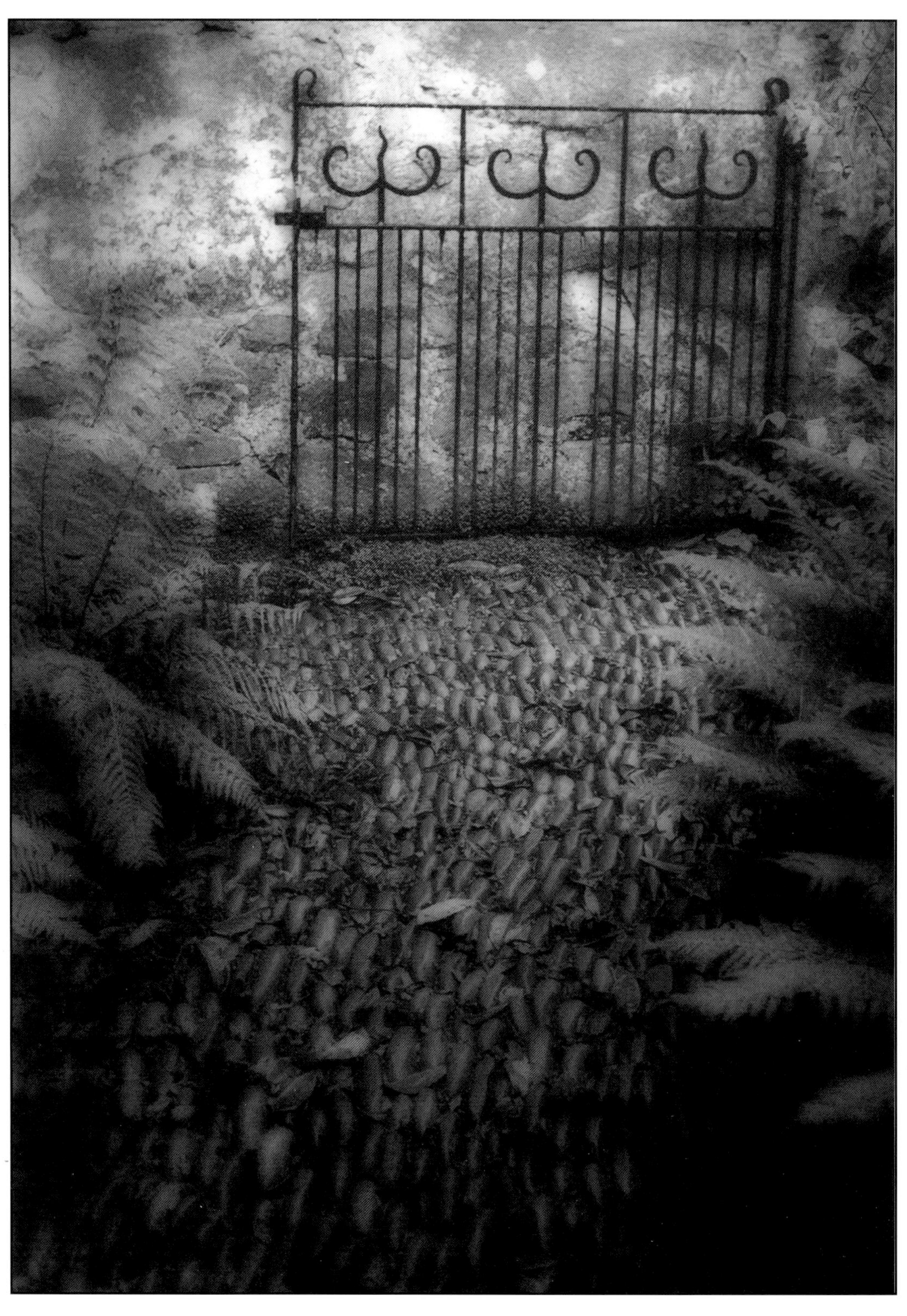

40
Gate, Rhiw
Neil Bedwell

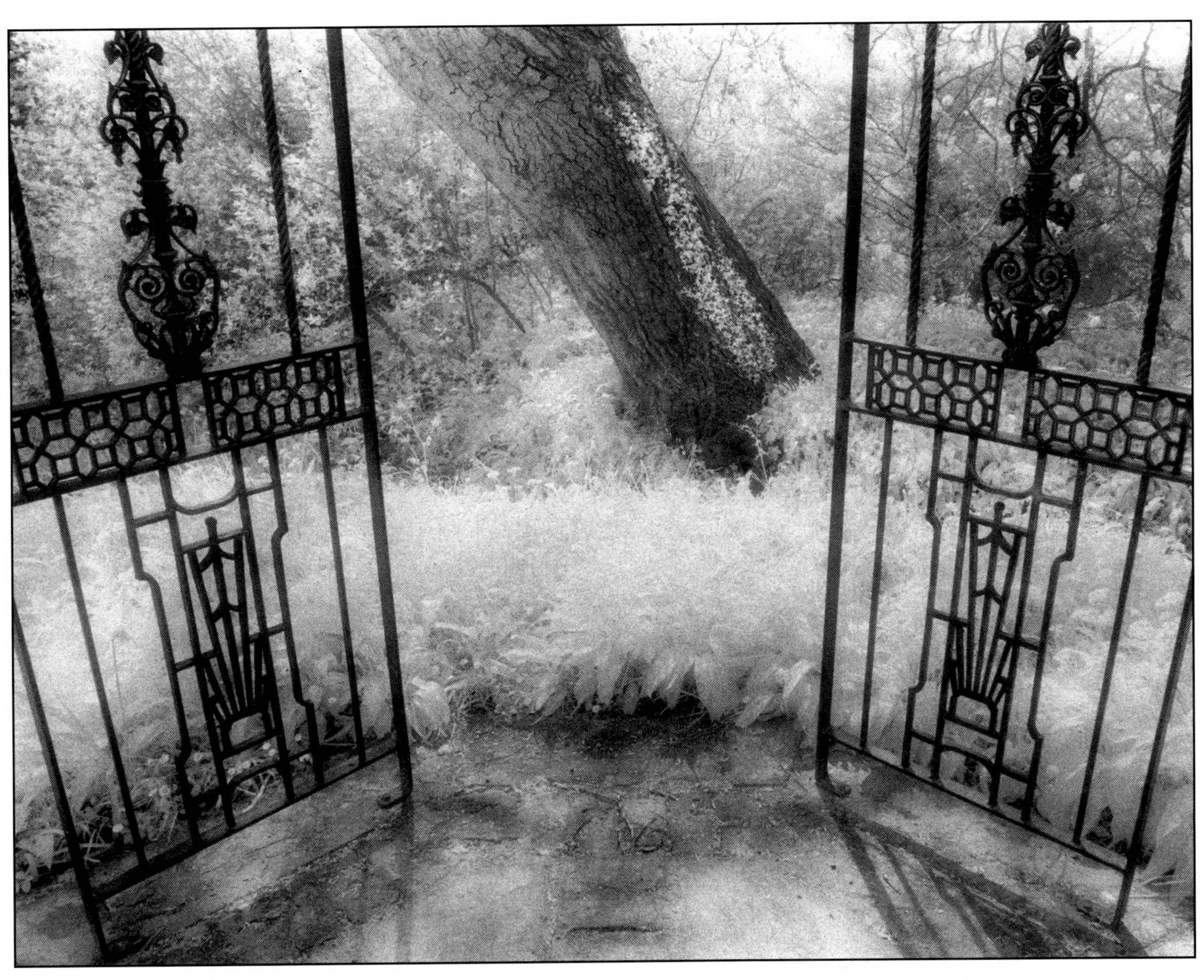

41
Tree and iron
John Reed

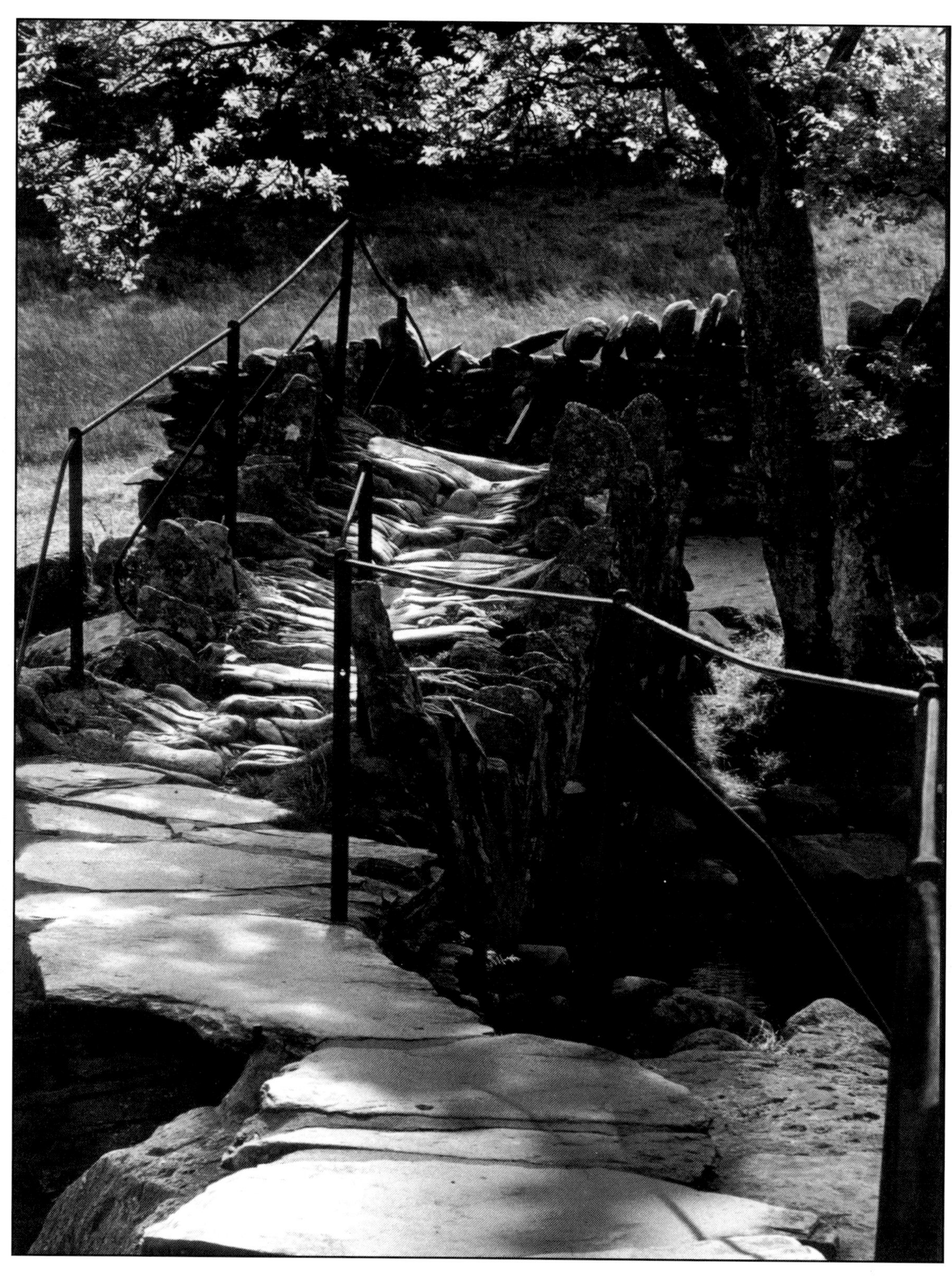

42
Slater Bridge, Little Langdale
John Fairclough

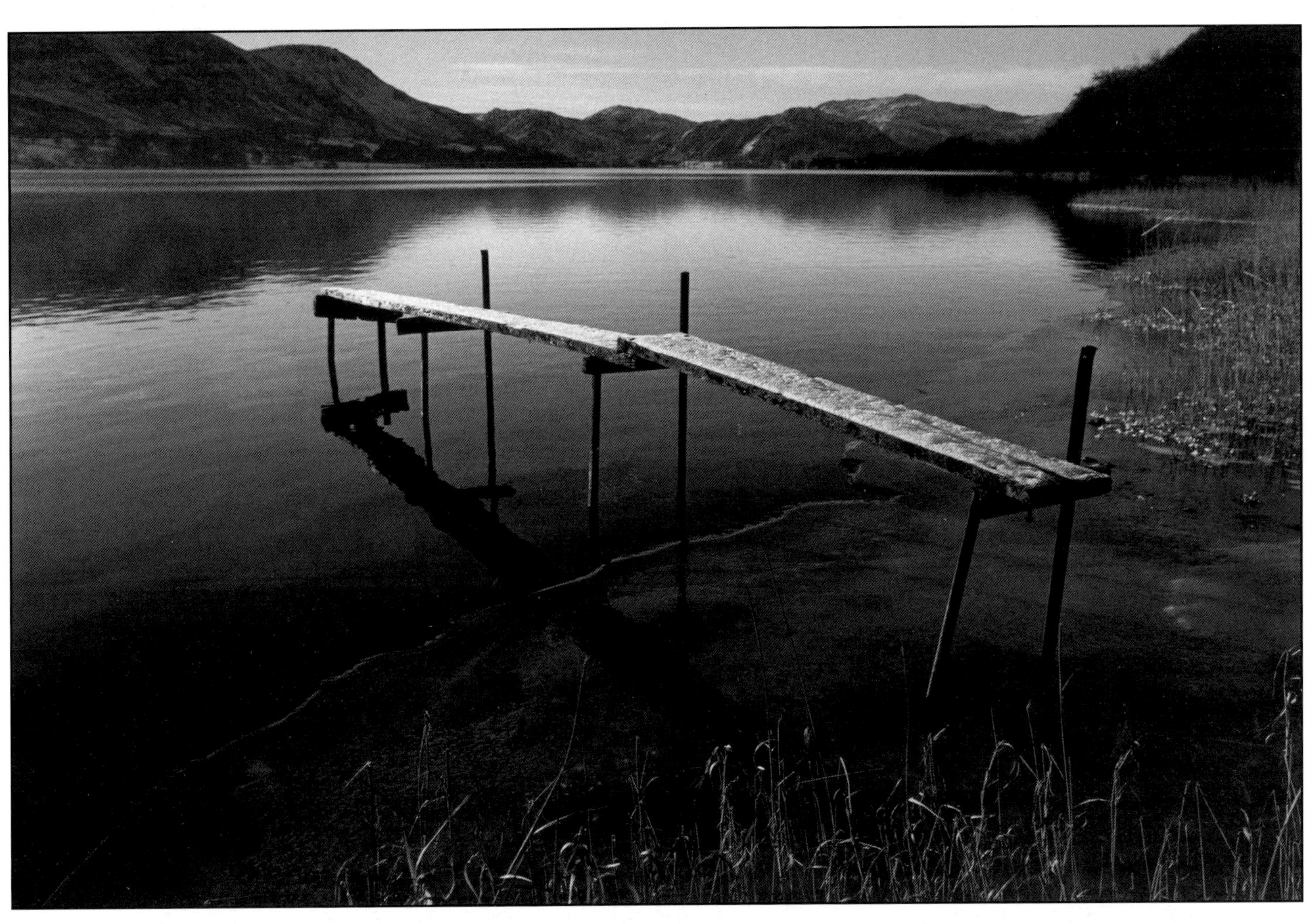

43
Landing stage
Chris Shore

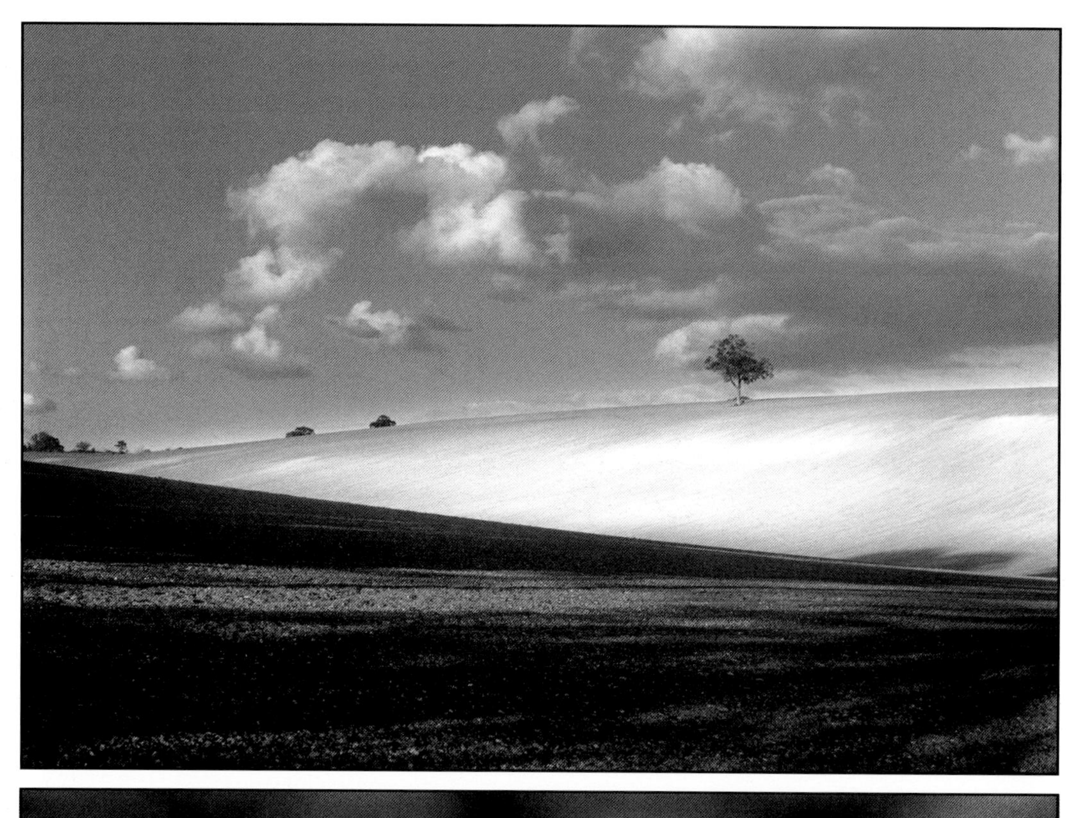

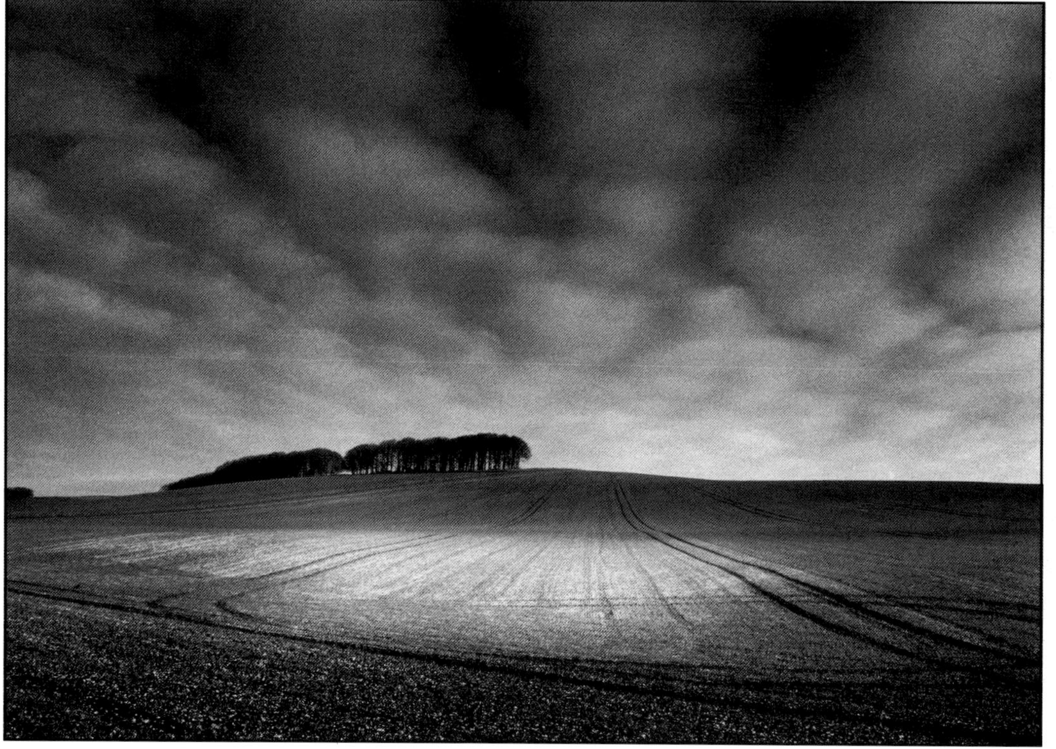

(top) 44, **Near Water End**, *John Winchcomb*
(below) 45, **Space to breathe**, *Ted Richards*

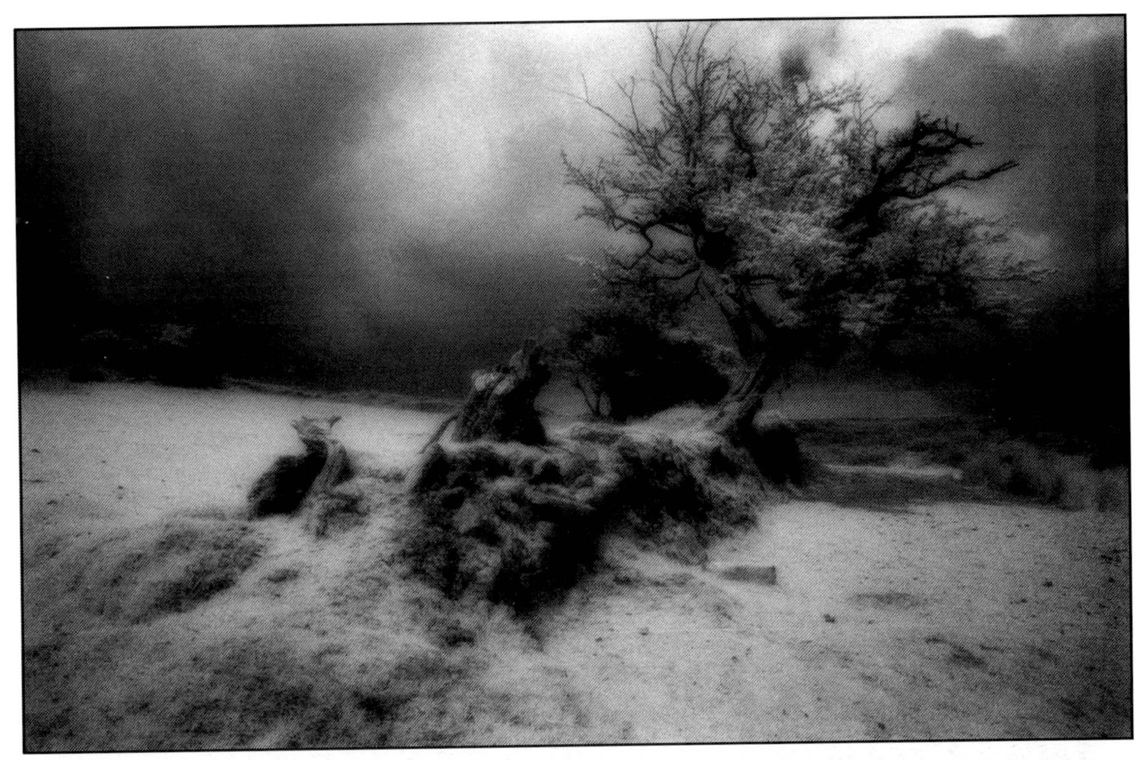

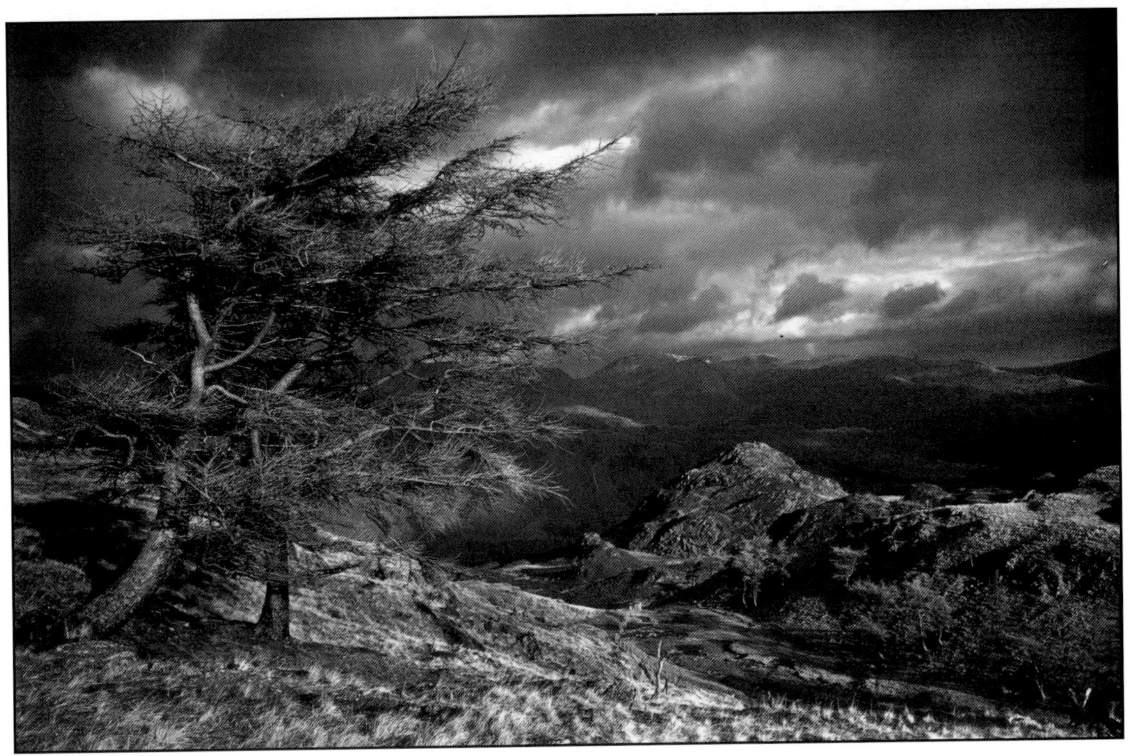

(top) 46, **Blasted heath,** *Clive Vincent*
(below) 47, **Weathered larches,** *Keith Launchbury*

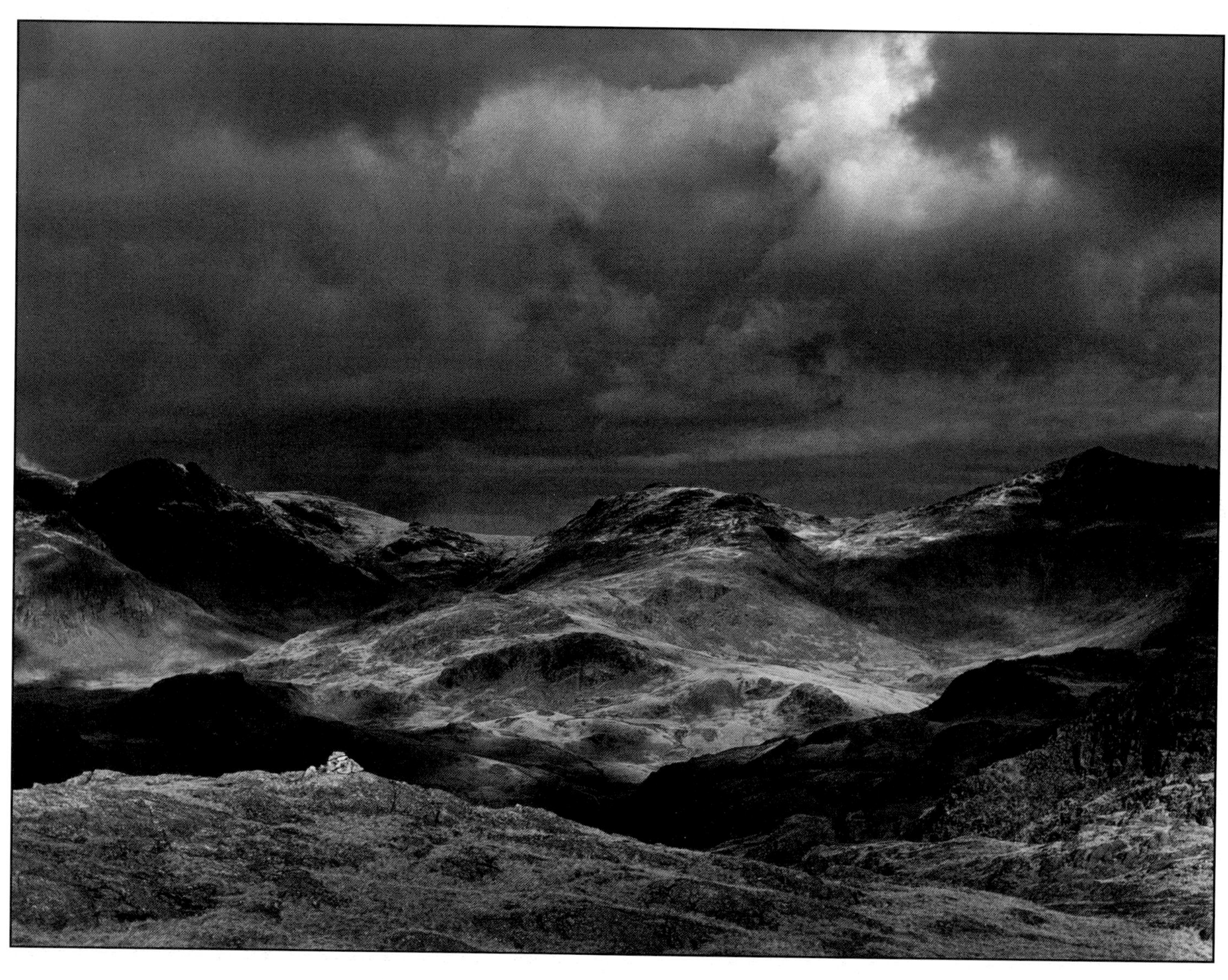

48
Winter in the hills
Derek Singleton

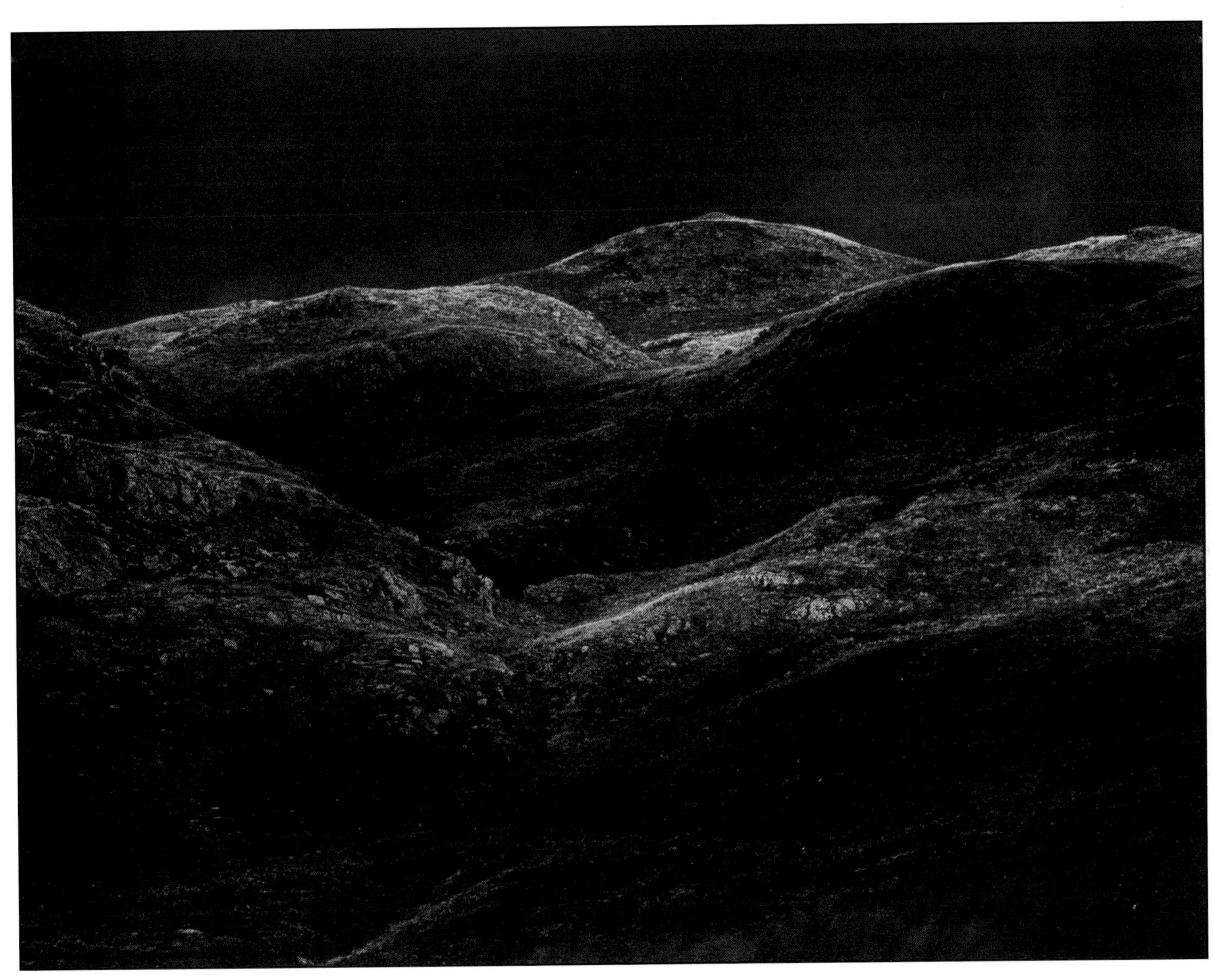

49
Moonscape
Baron Woods

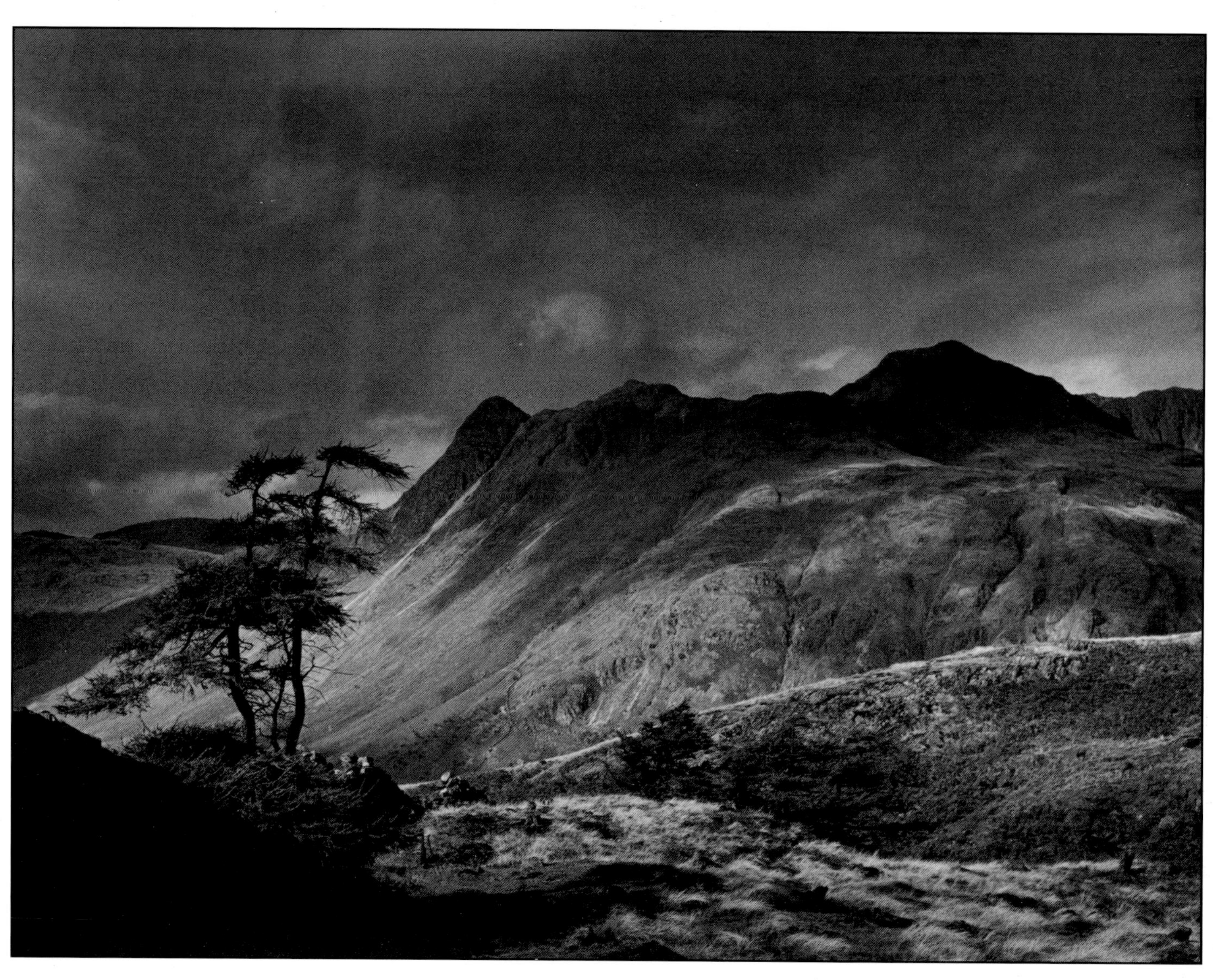

50
Langdale
Derek Singleton

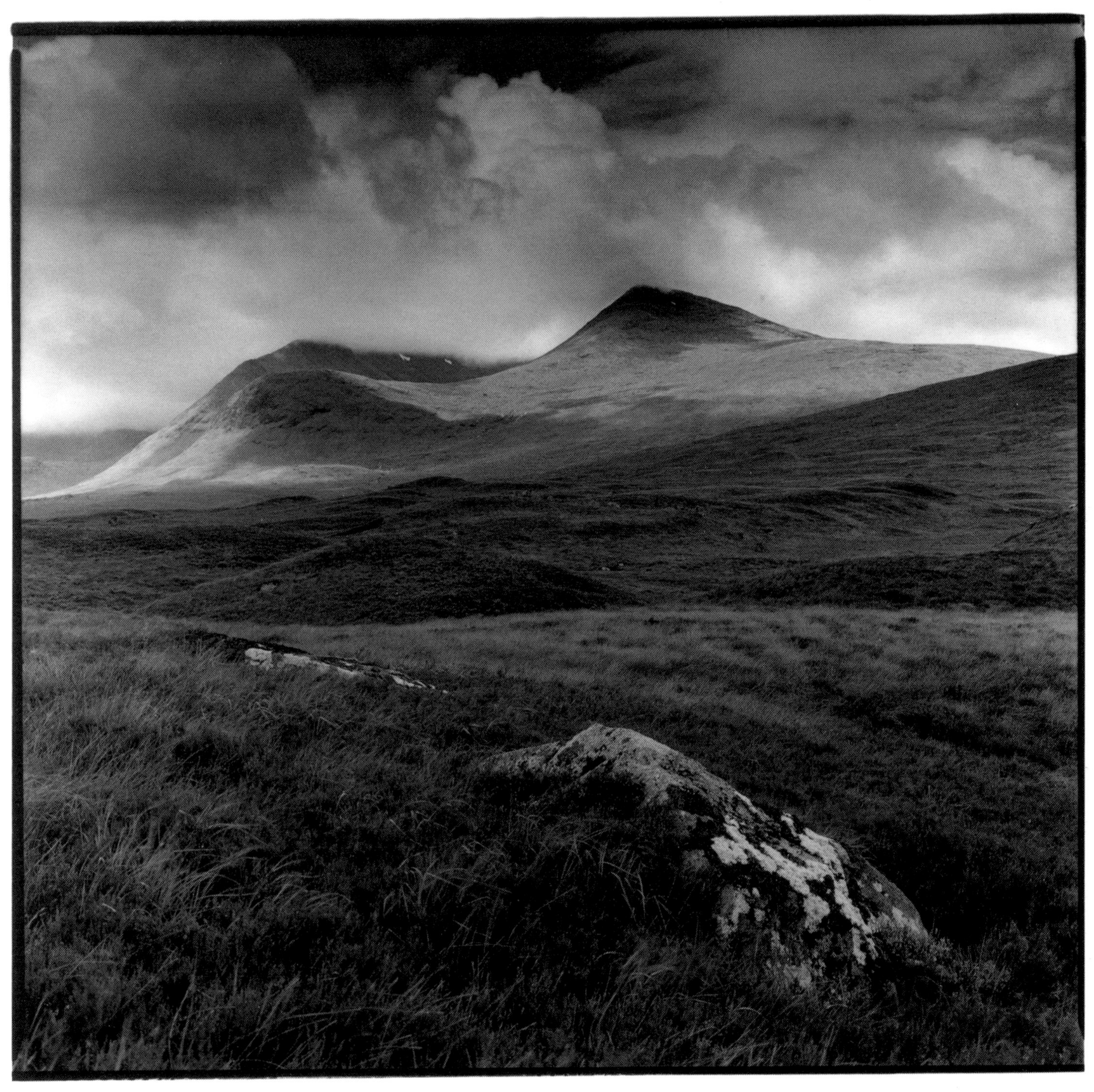

51
Rannoch moor 1
Julie Woodhouse

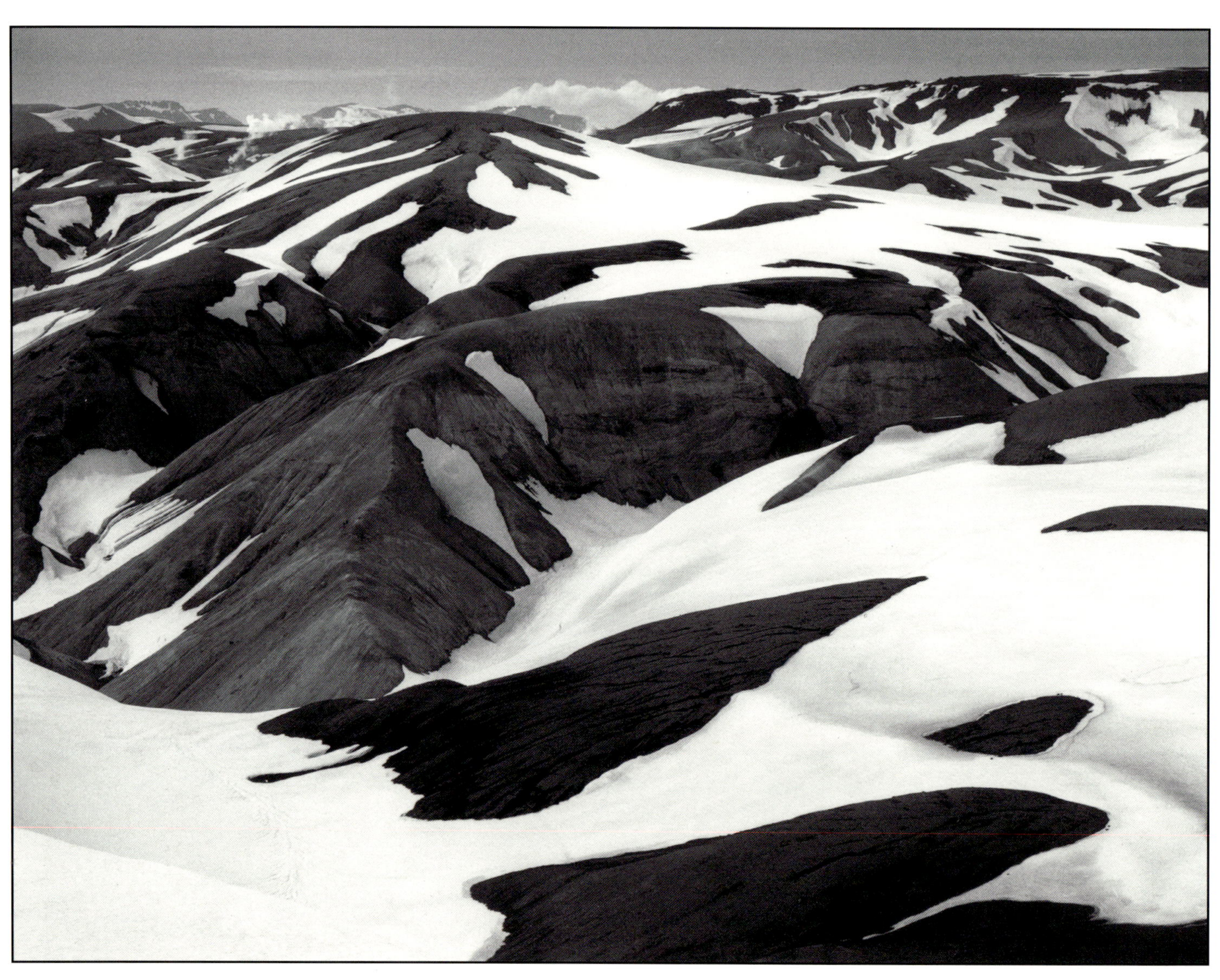

52
Mountains of Carva
Roger Crane

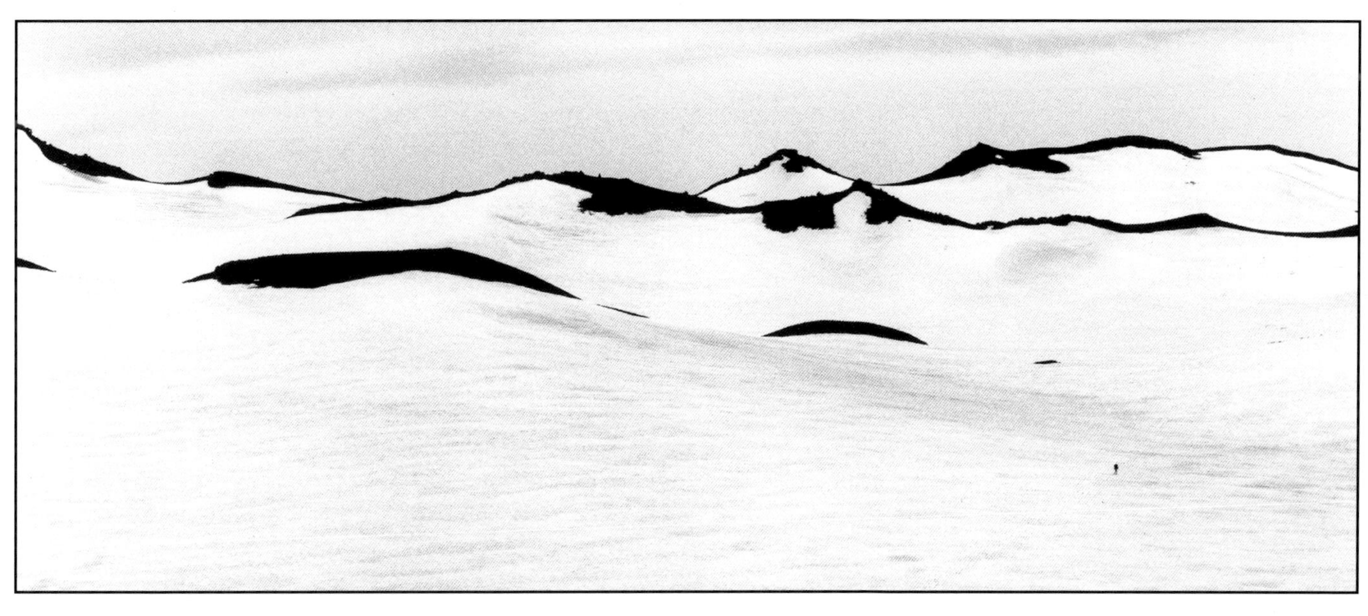

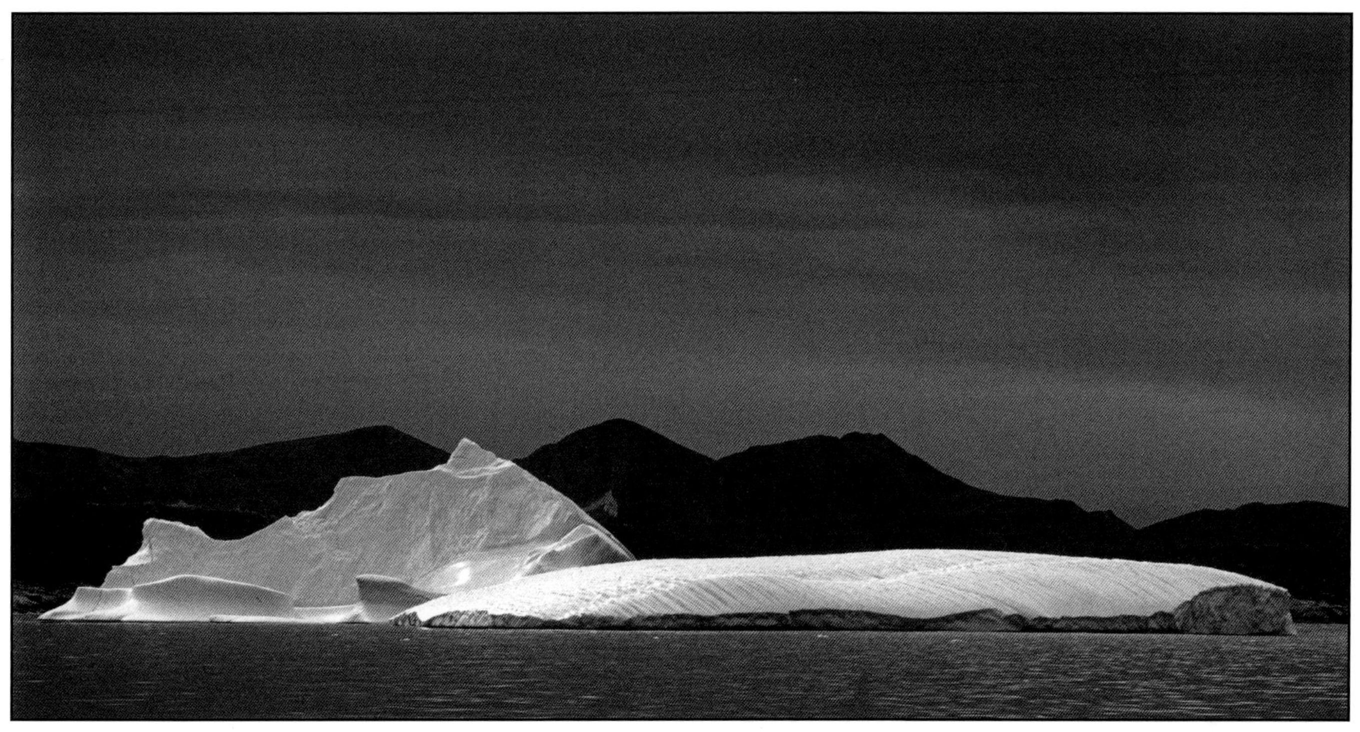

(top) 53, **Myralsjokull, Iceland**, *John Reed*
(below) 54, **Arctic seascape**, *Mike Chambers*

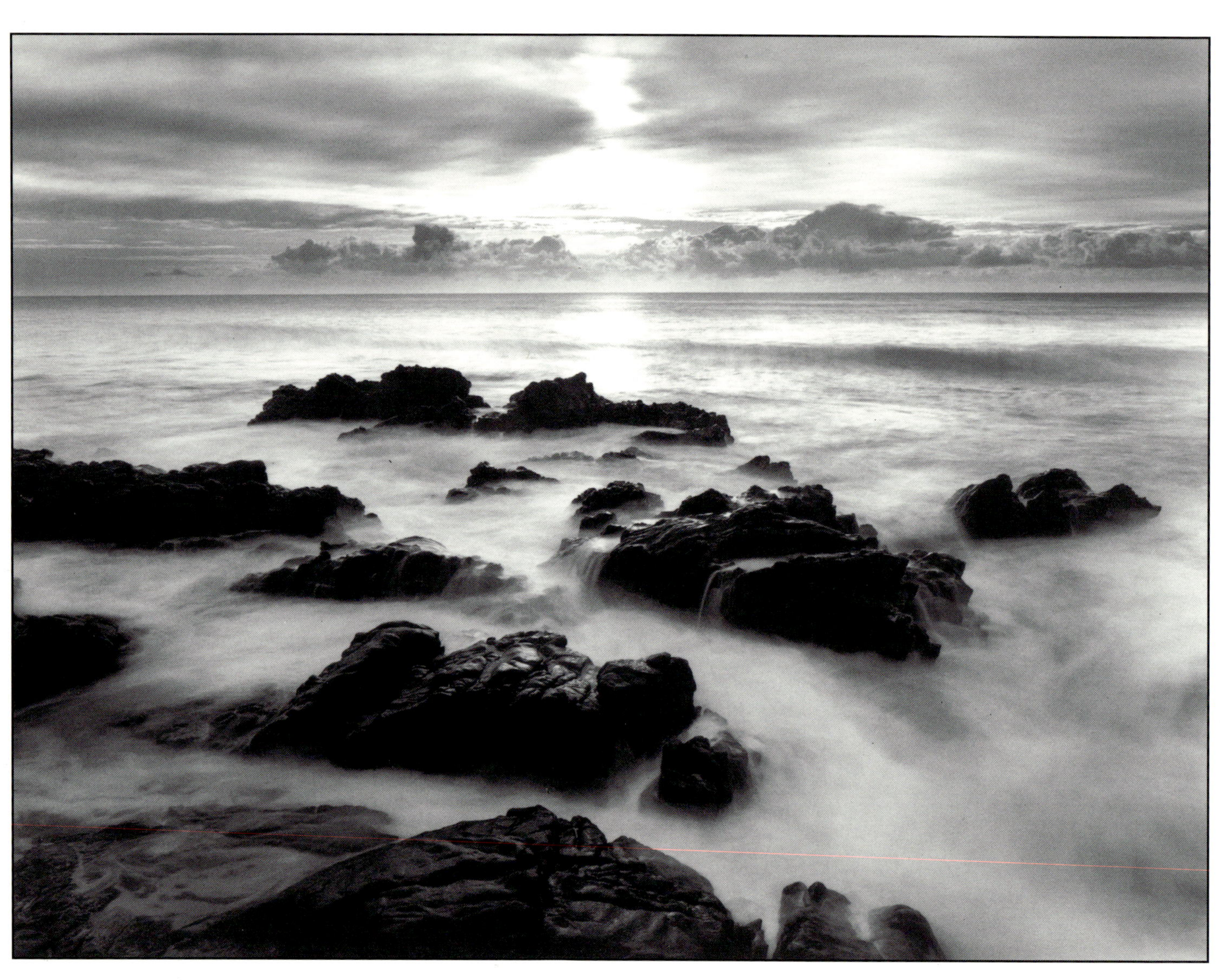

55
Millennium dawn
Rob Gray

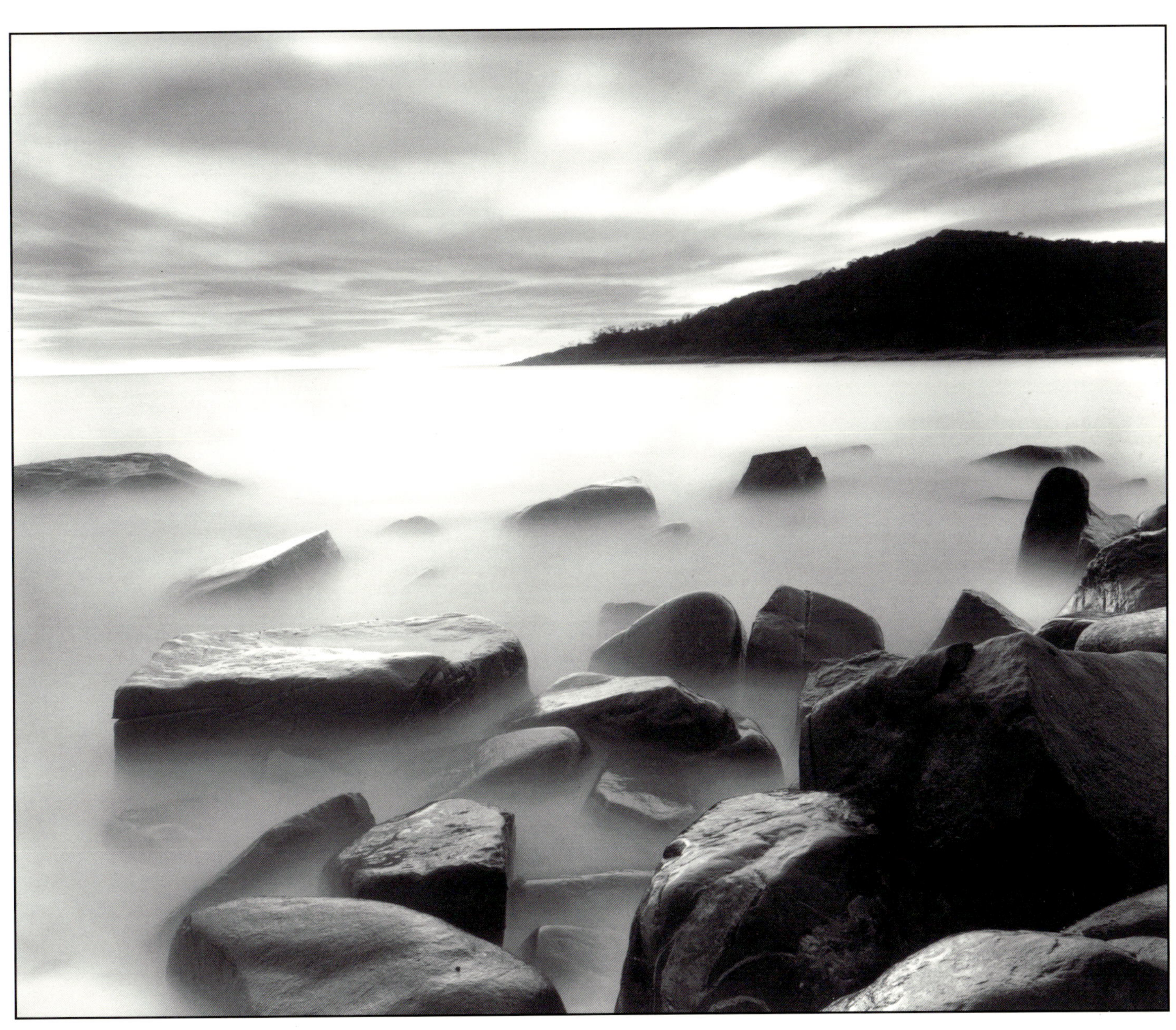

56
Noosa dawn
Rob Gray

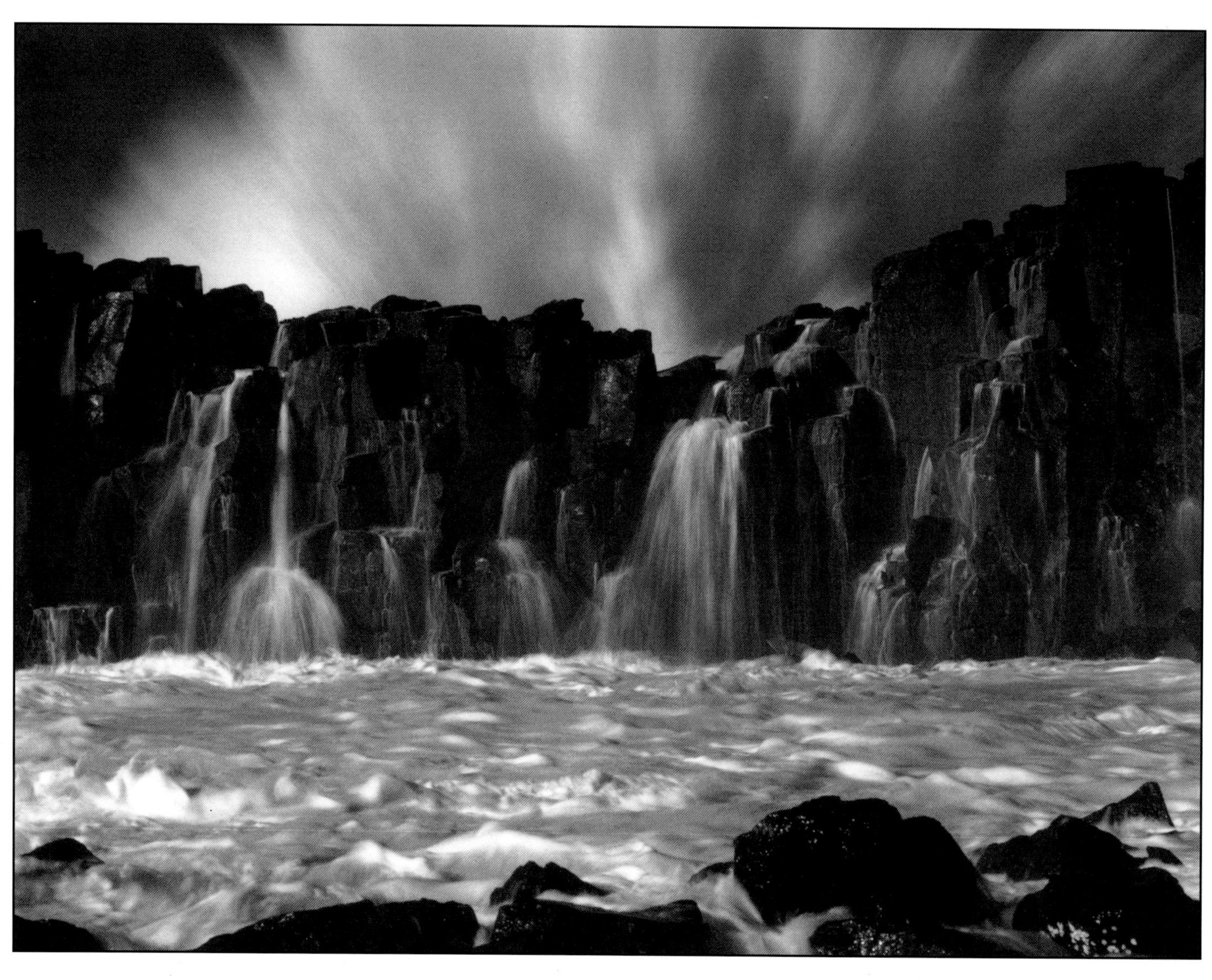

57
Here comes the next wave
Brian Scott

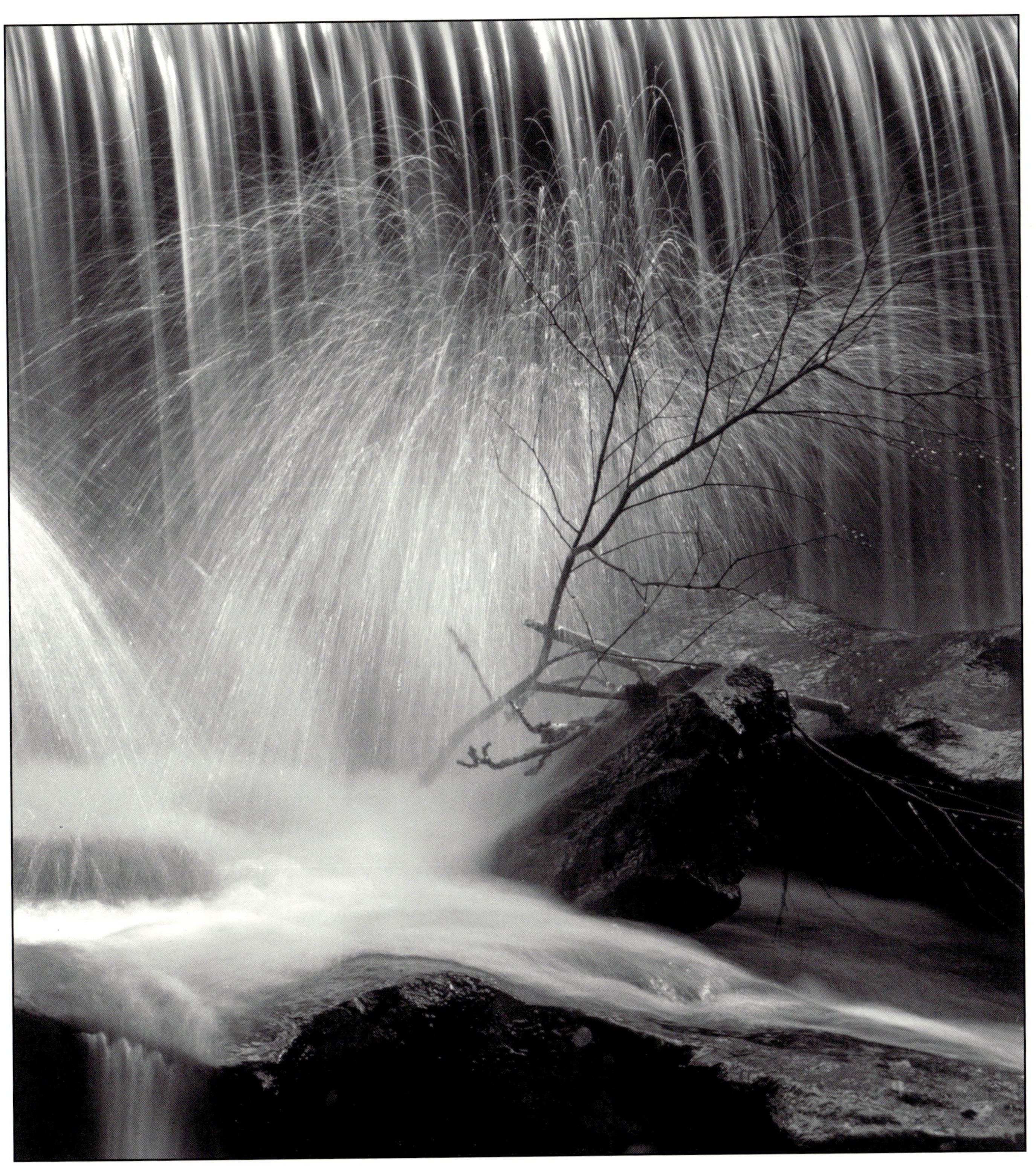

58
Cascade
Ken Huscroft

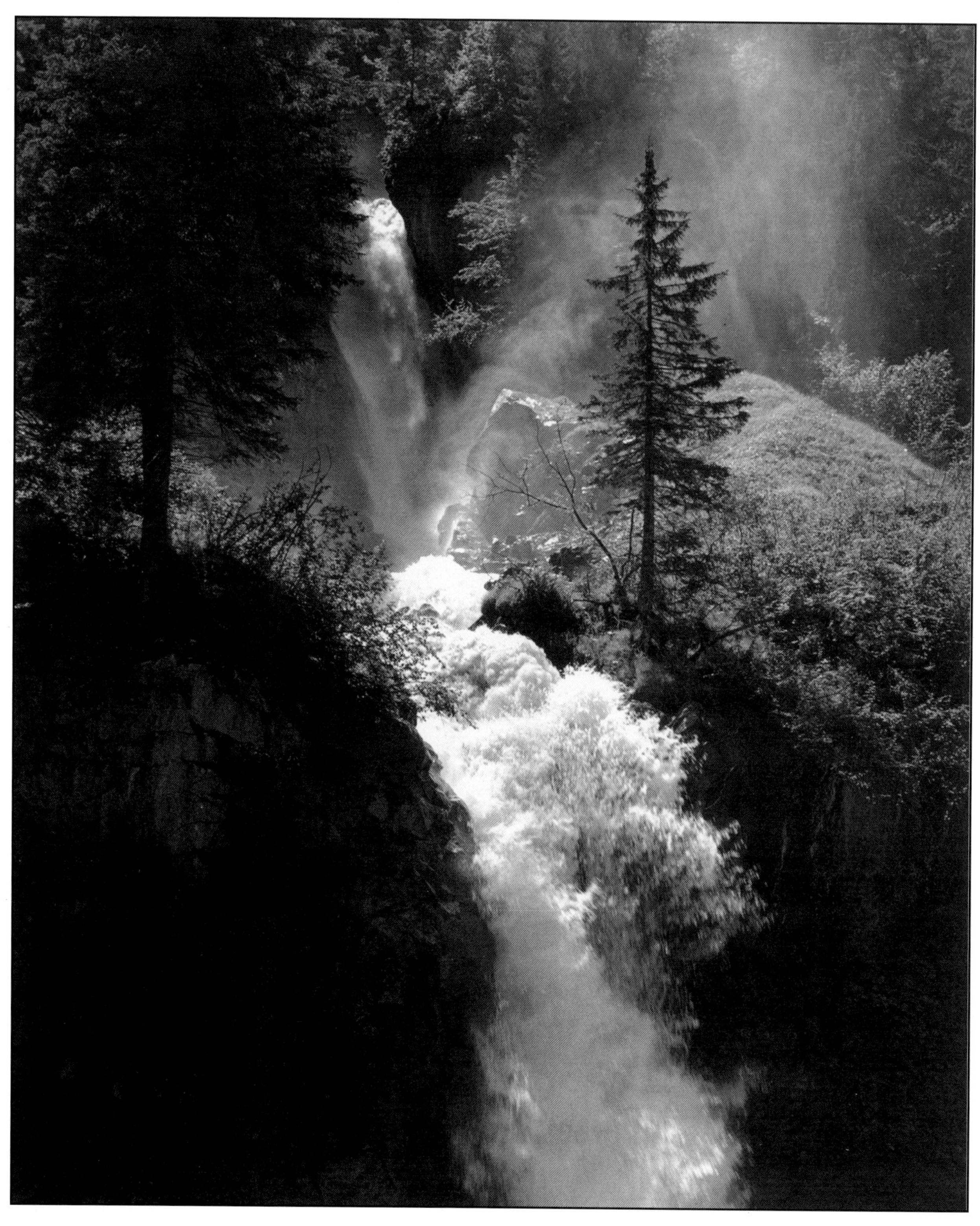

59
Schmadribach
Mike Farrow

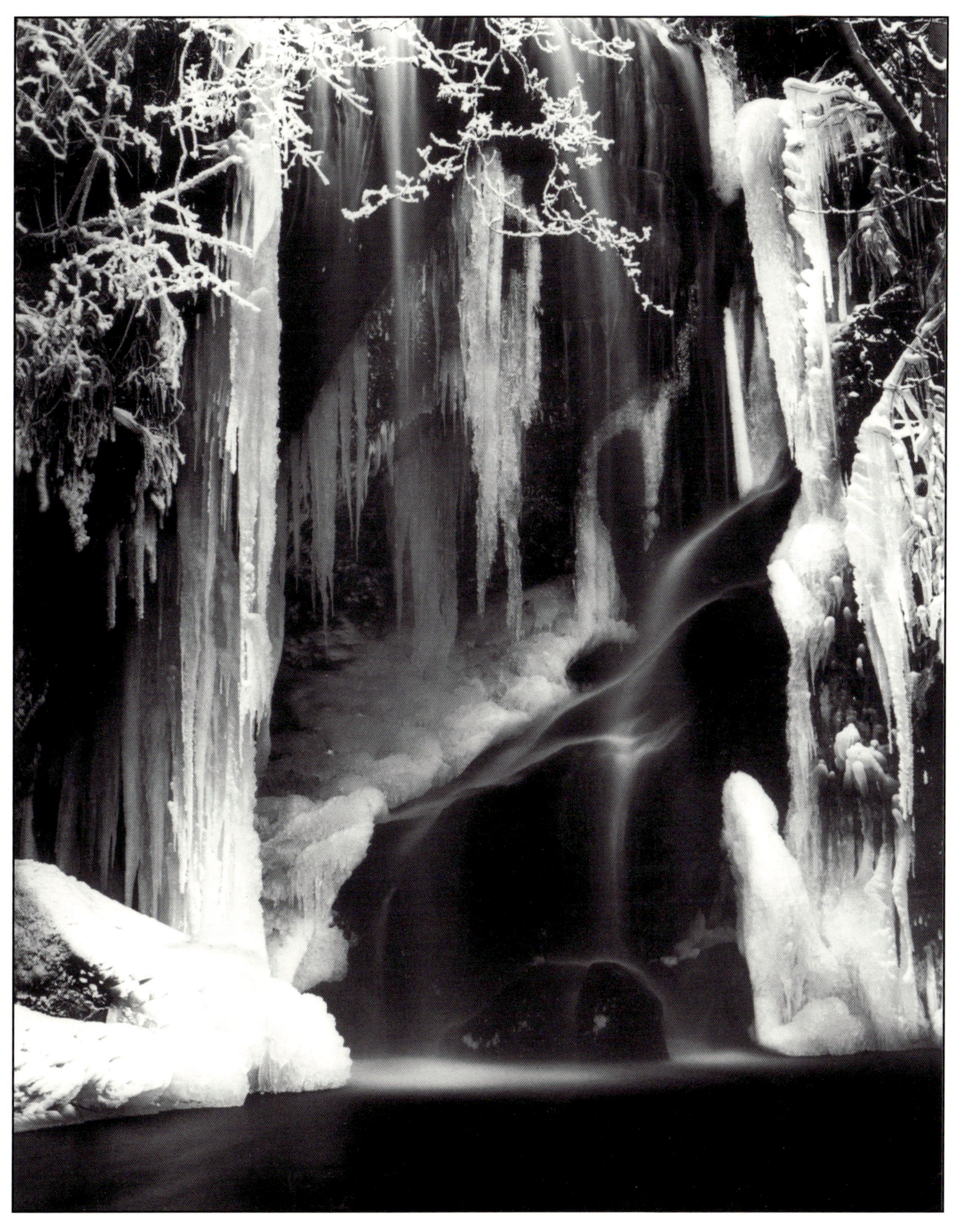

60
Roughting Linn in winter
Peter Dixon

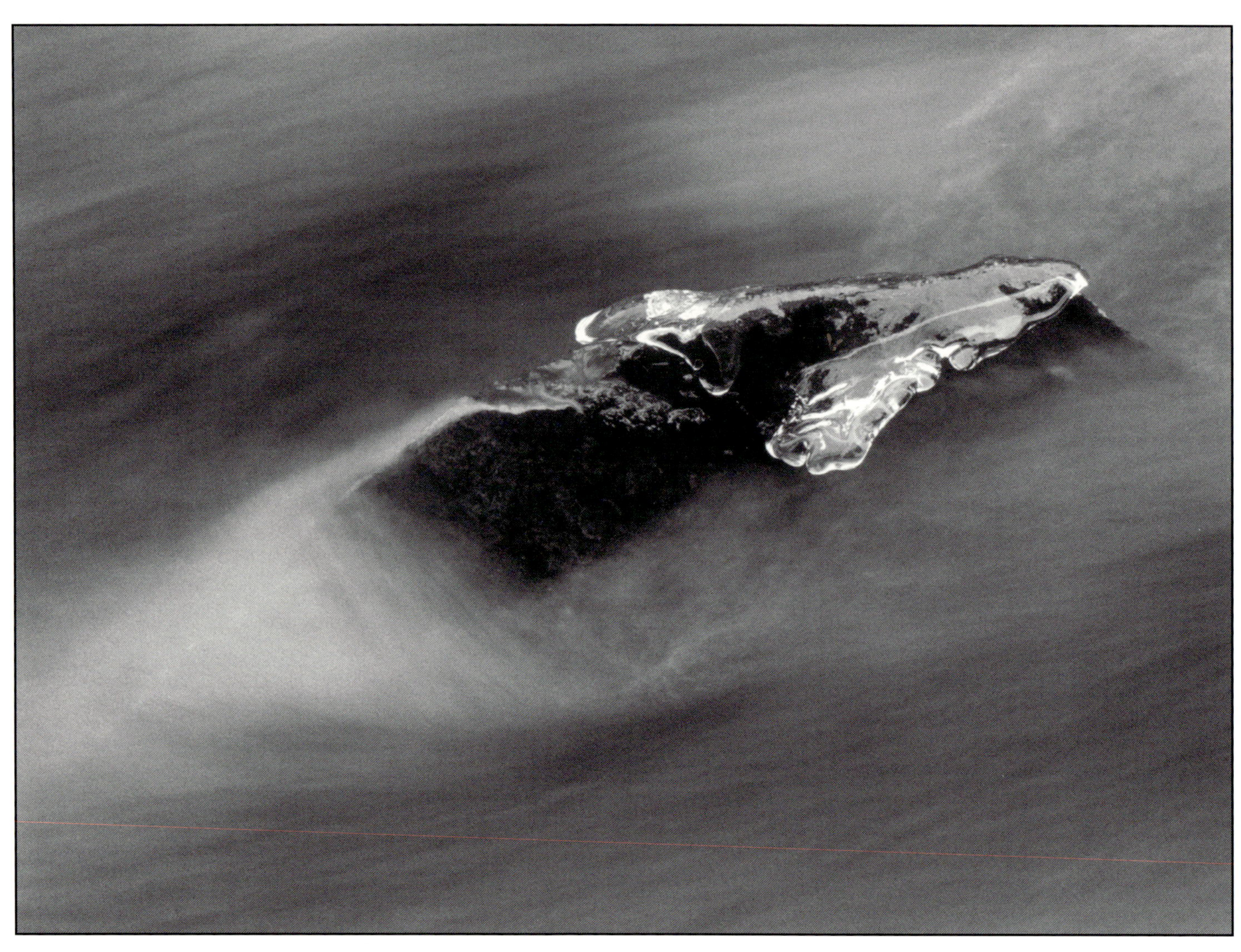

61
Ice rocket
Len Perkis

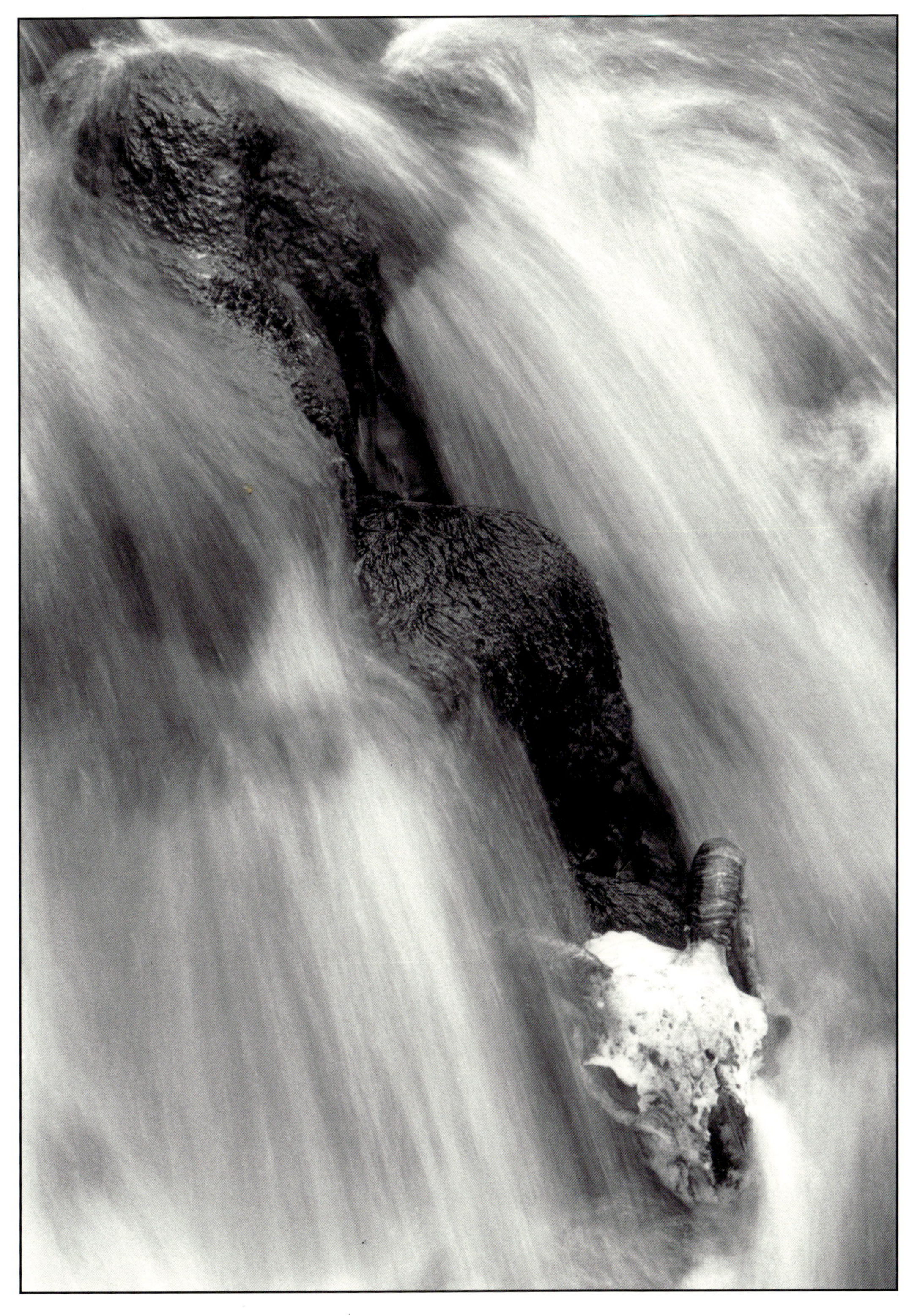

62
Rock and skull
David Gordon

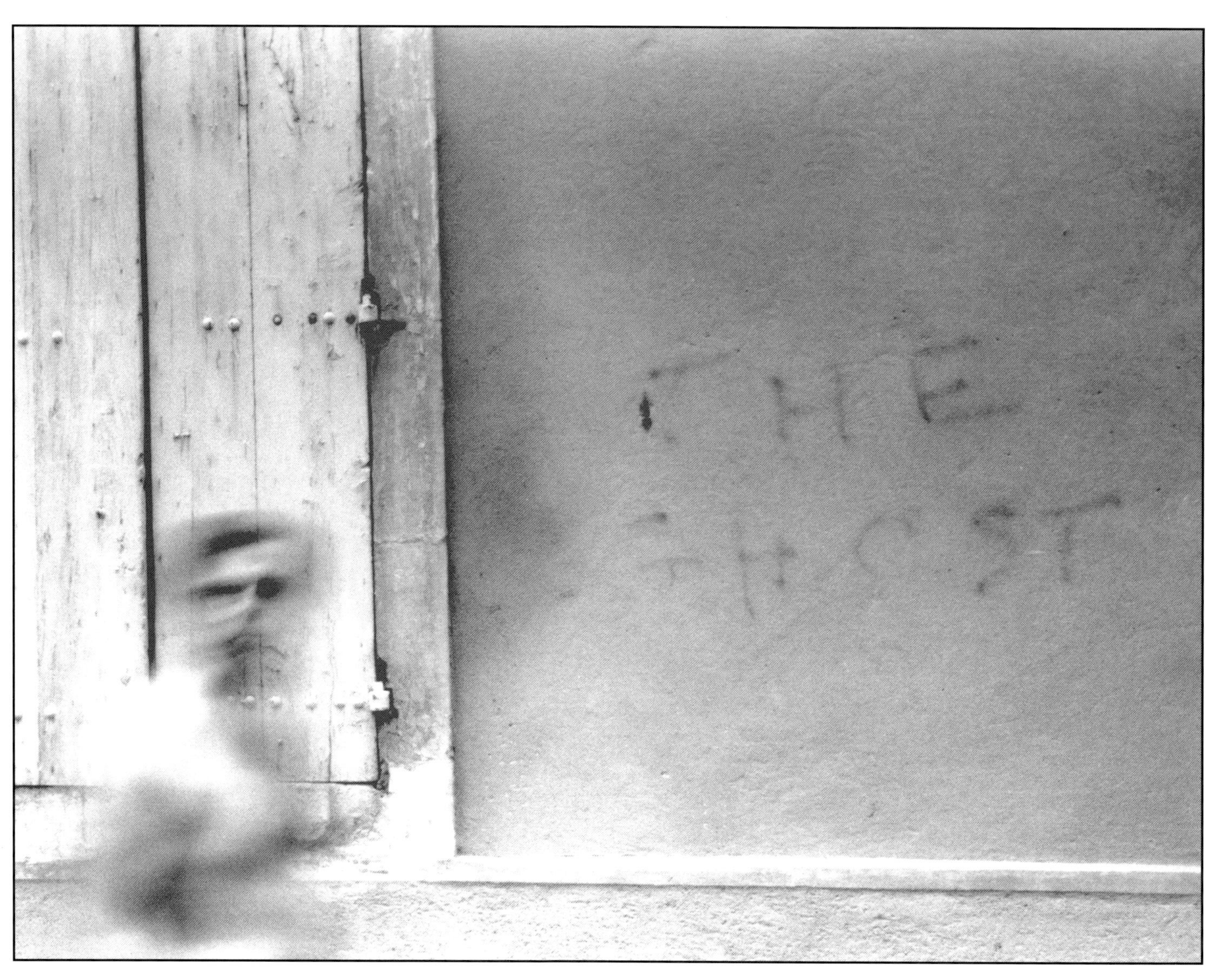

63
L'esprit d'Arles
Steve Francis

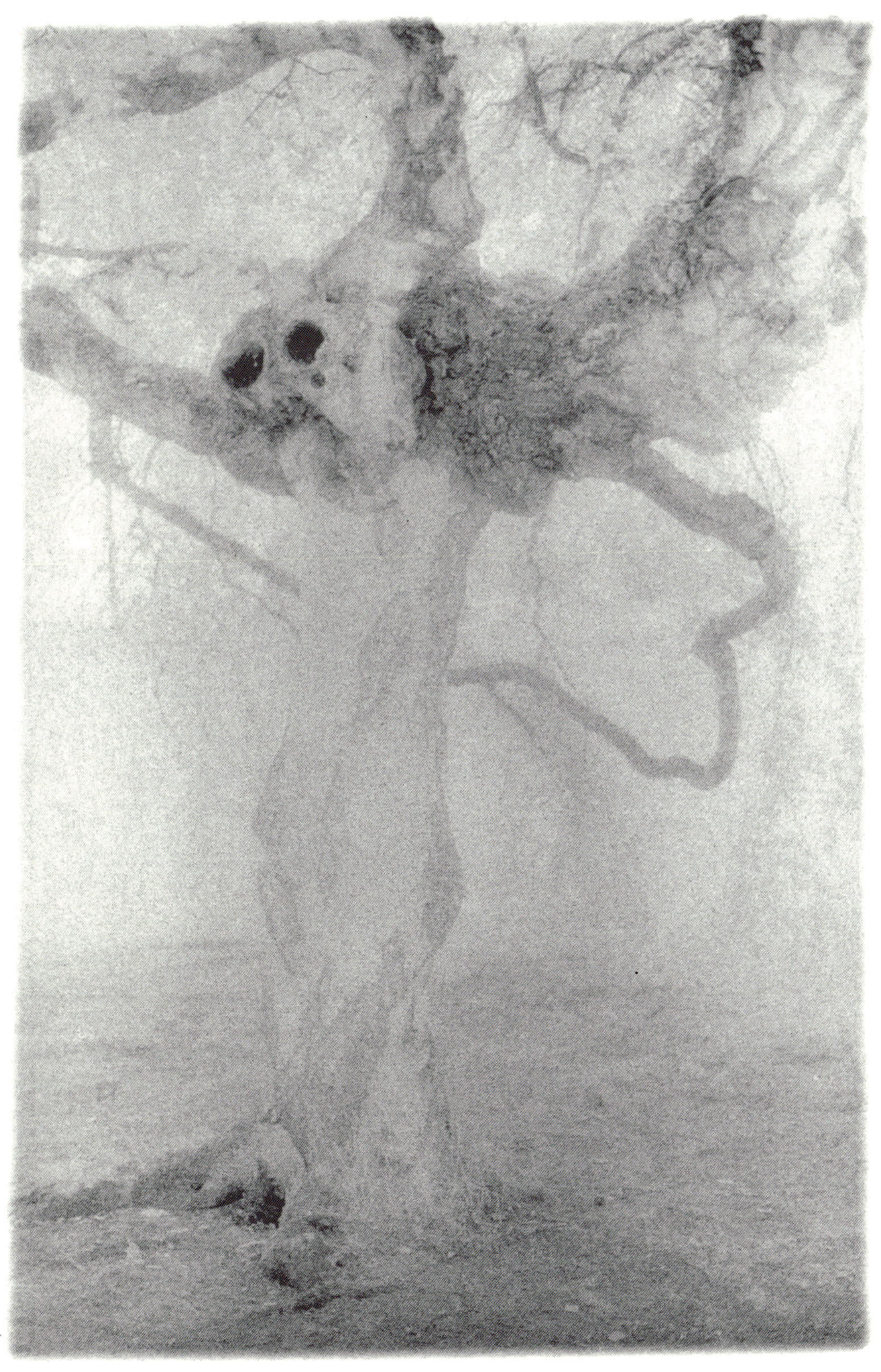

64
The bardo of becoming
Andrew Machon

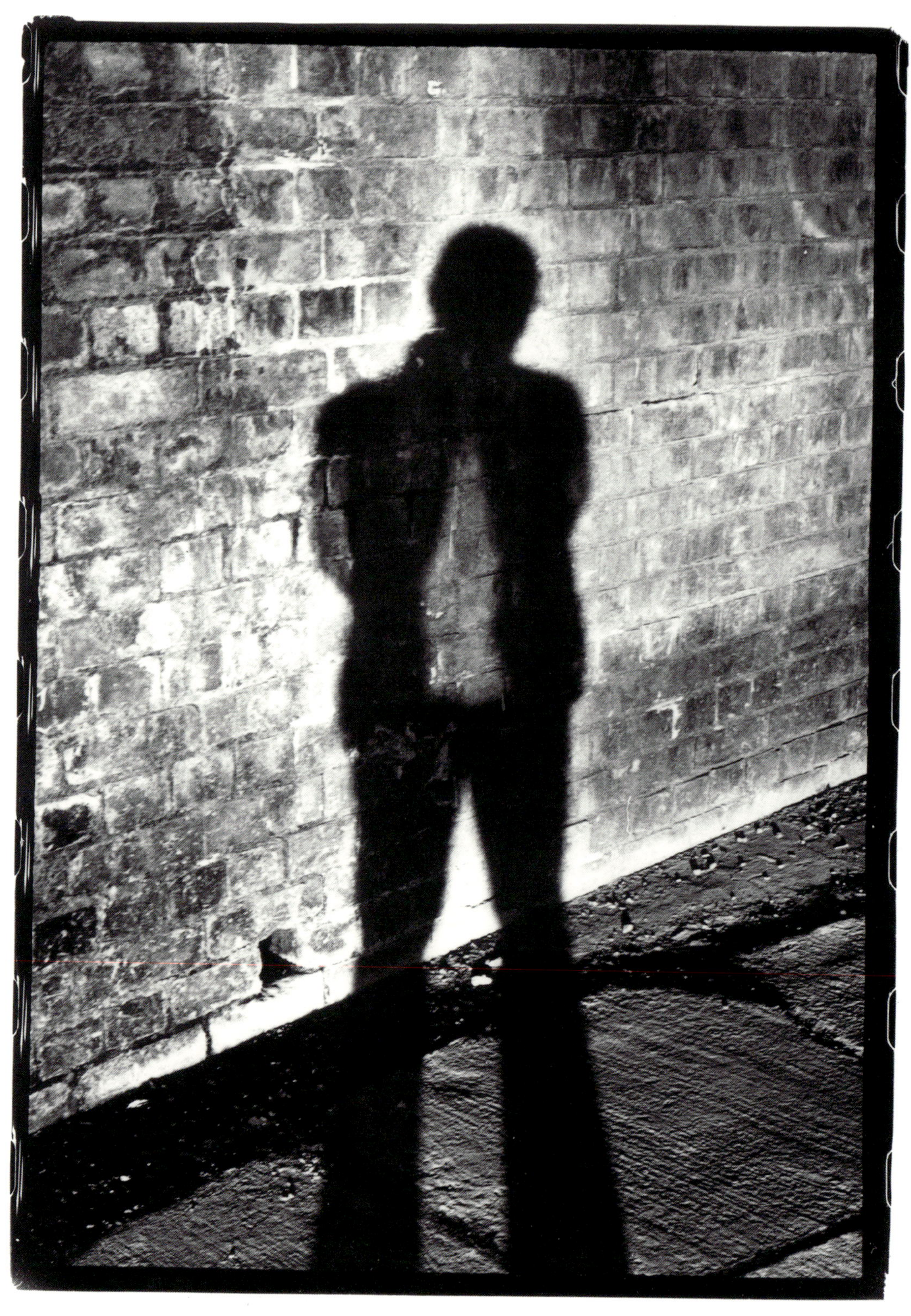

65
Untitled
Pavel Glebov

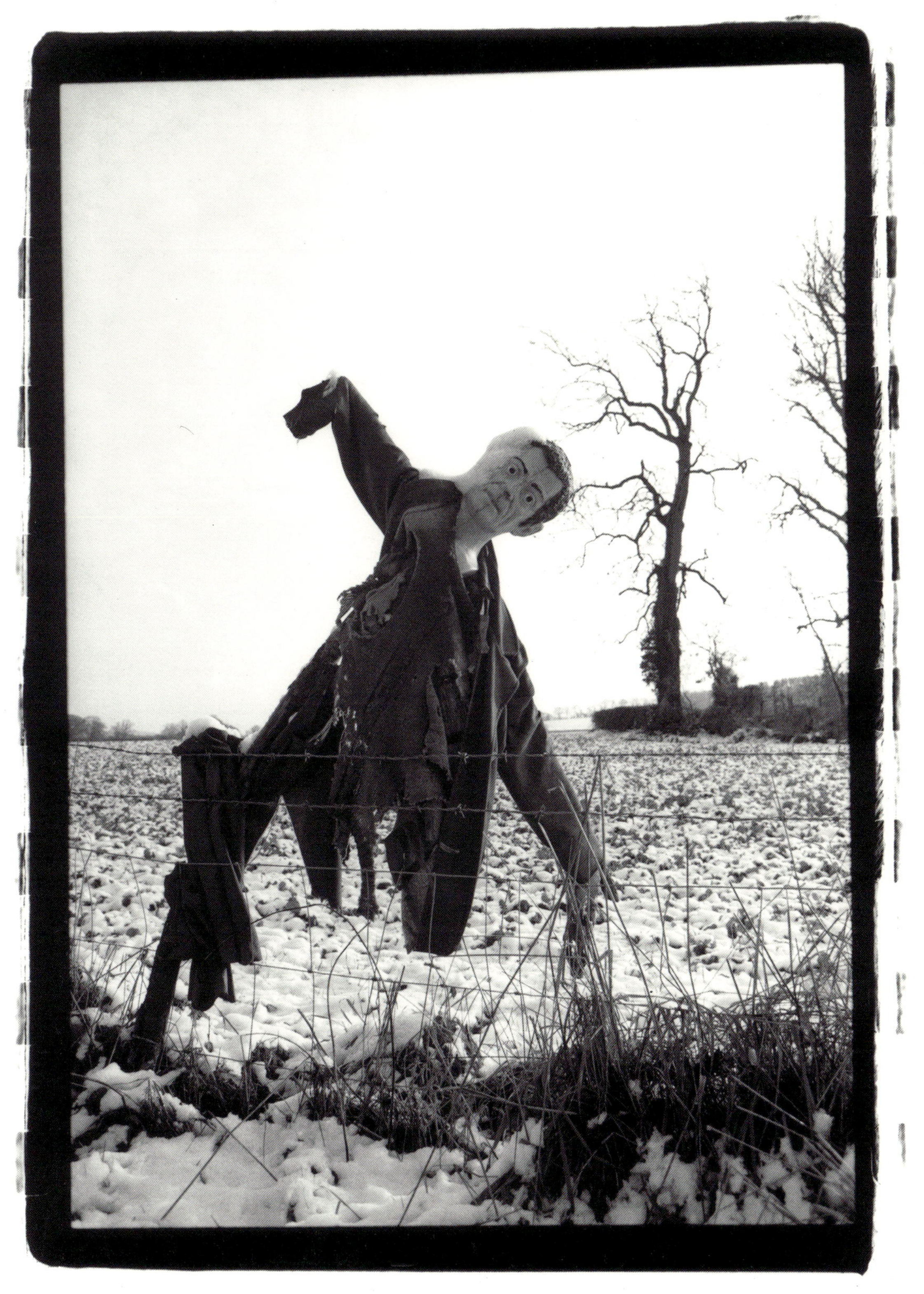

66
Scarecrow
Gary Freeman

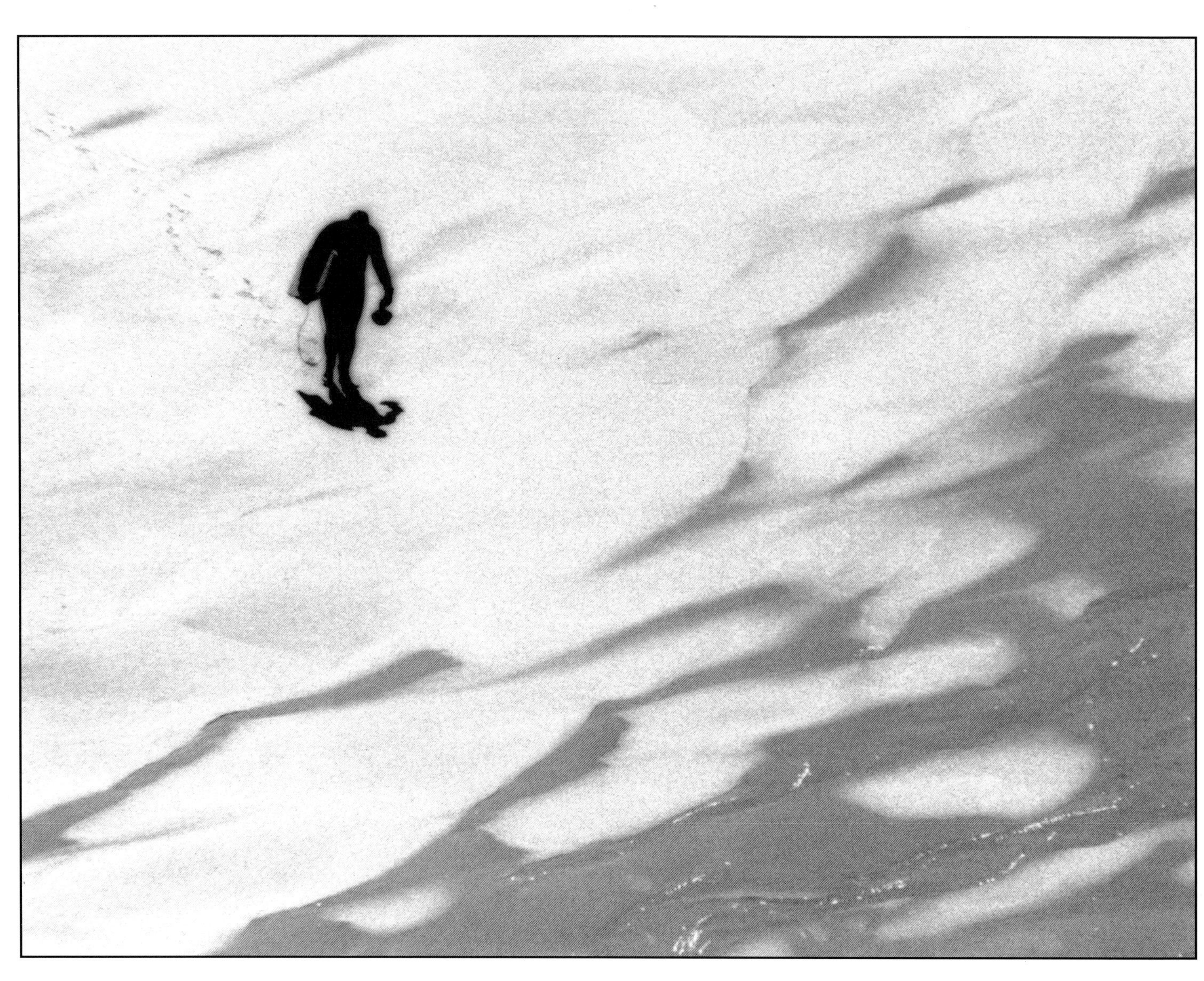

67
Spaceman
Mike Coles (Avon)

68
Estacaõ
Ernesto Tarnoczy Jr

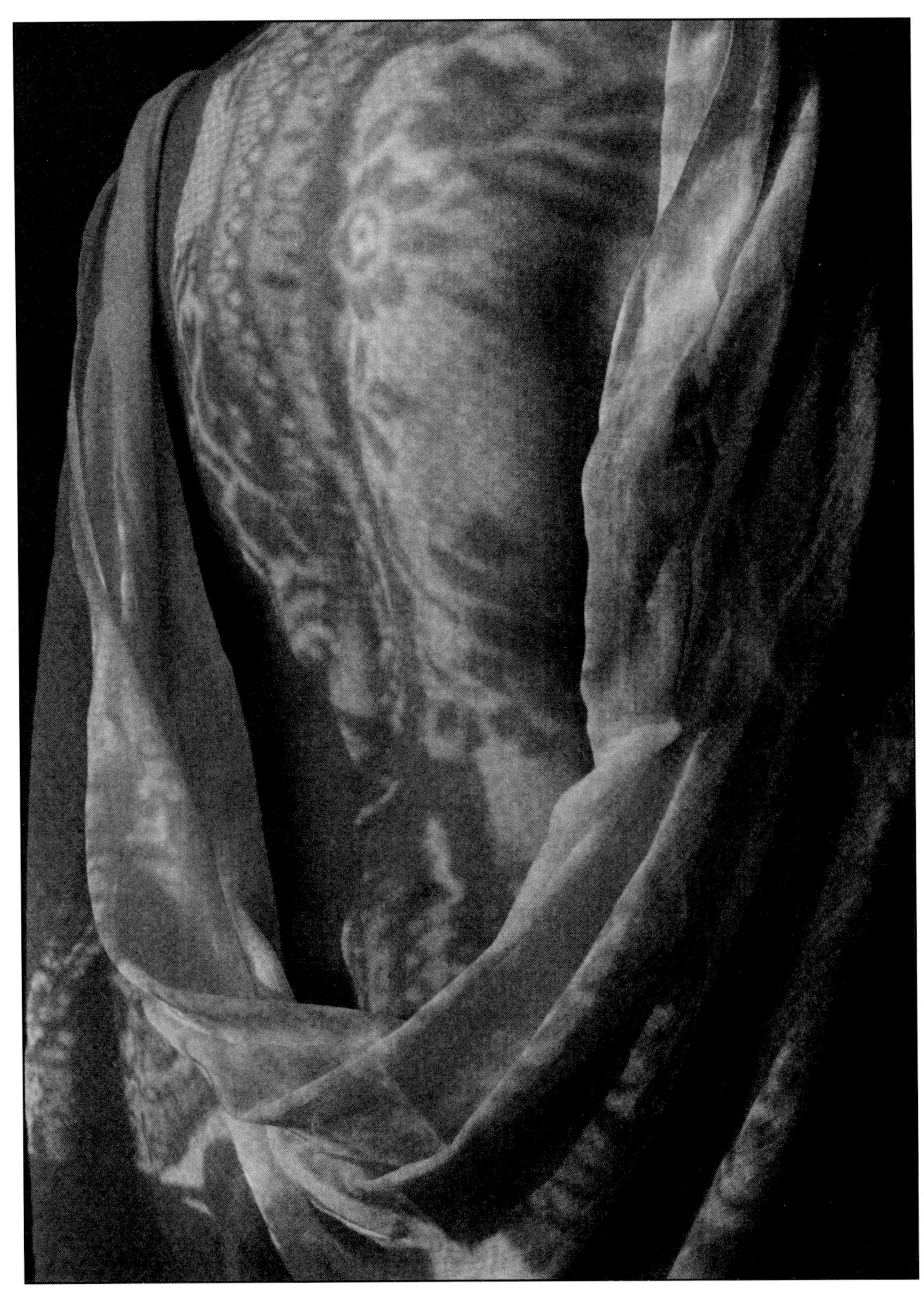

69
Shadowed figure #2
Mike Salter

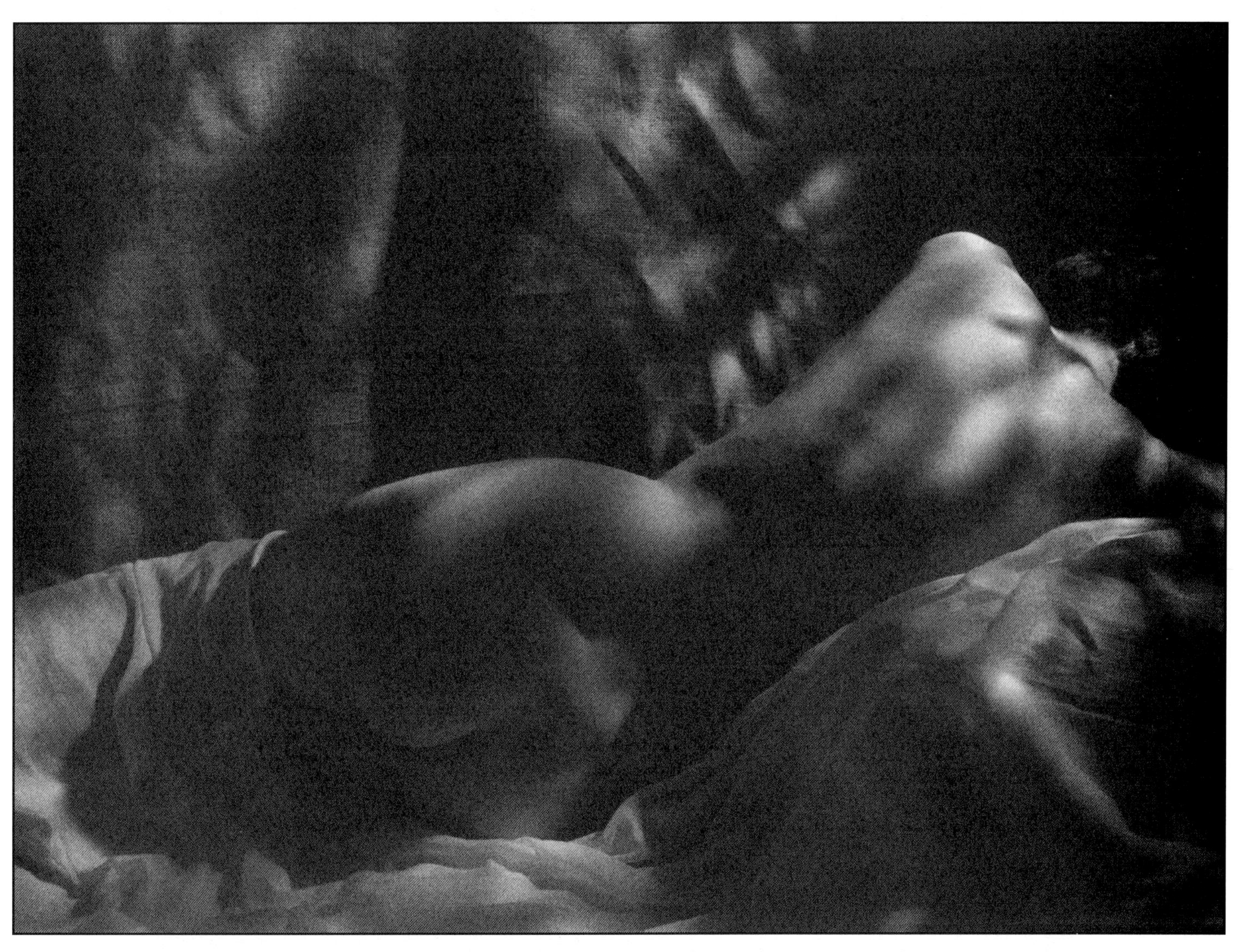

70
Study #5
Mike Salter

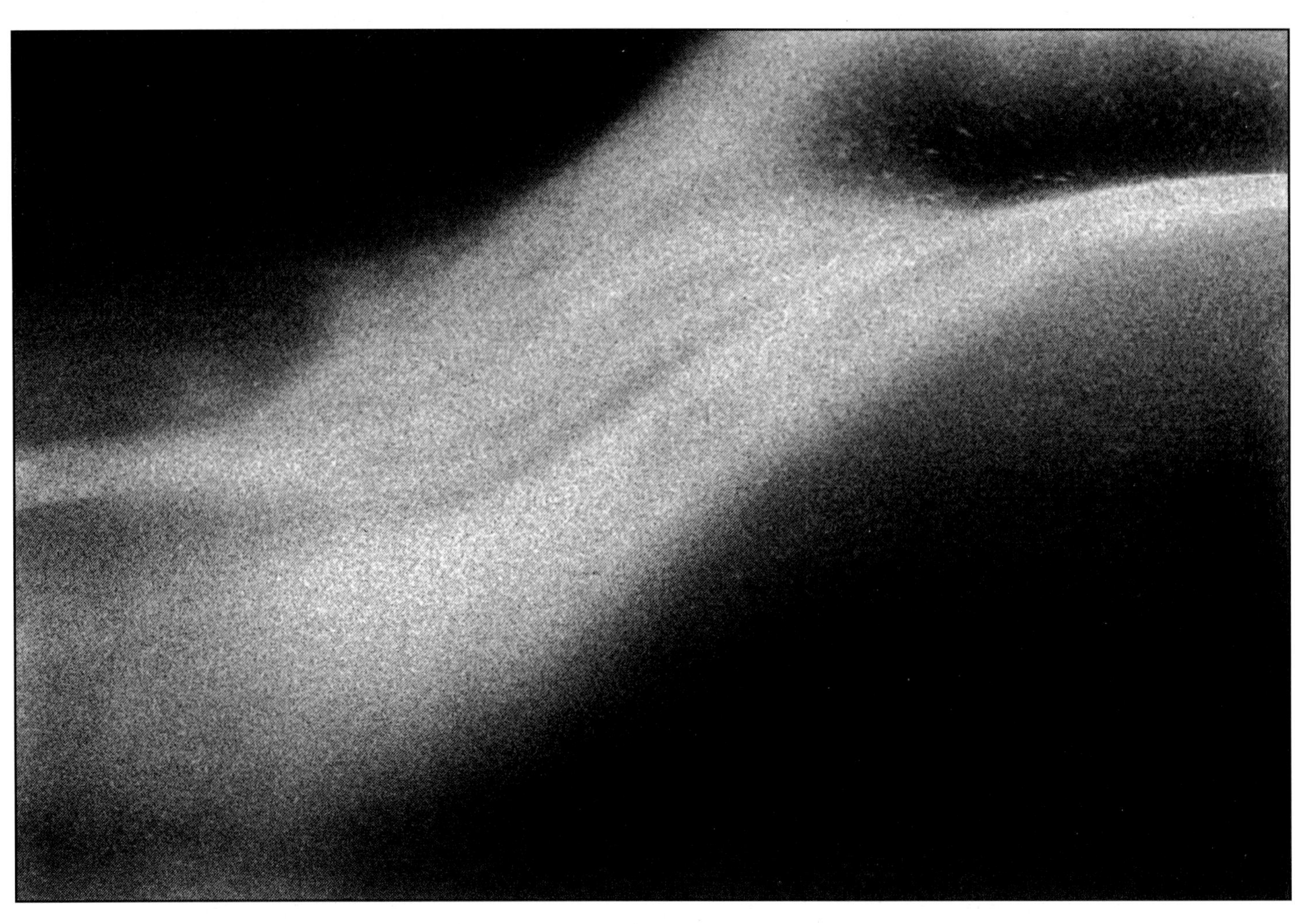

71
Graced with light
Andrew Machon

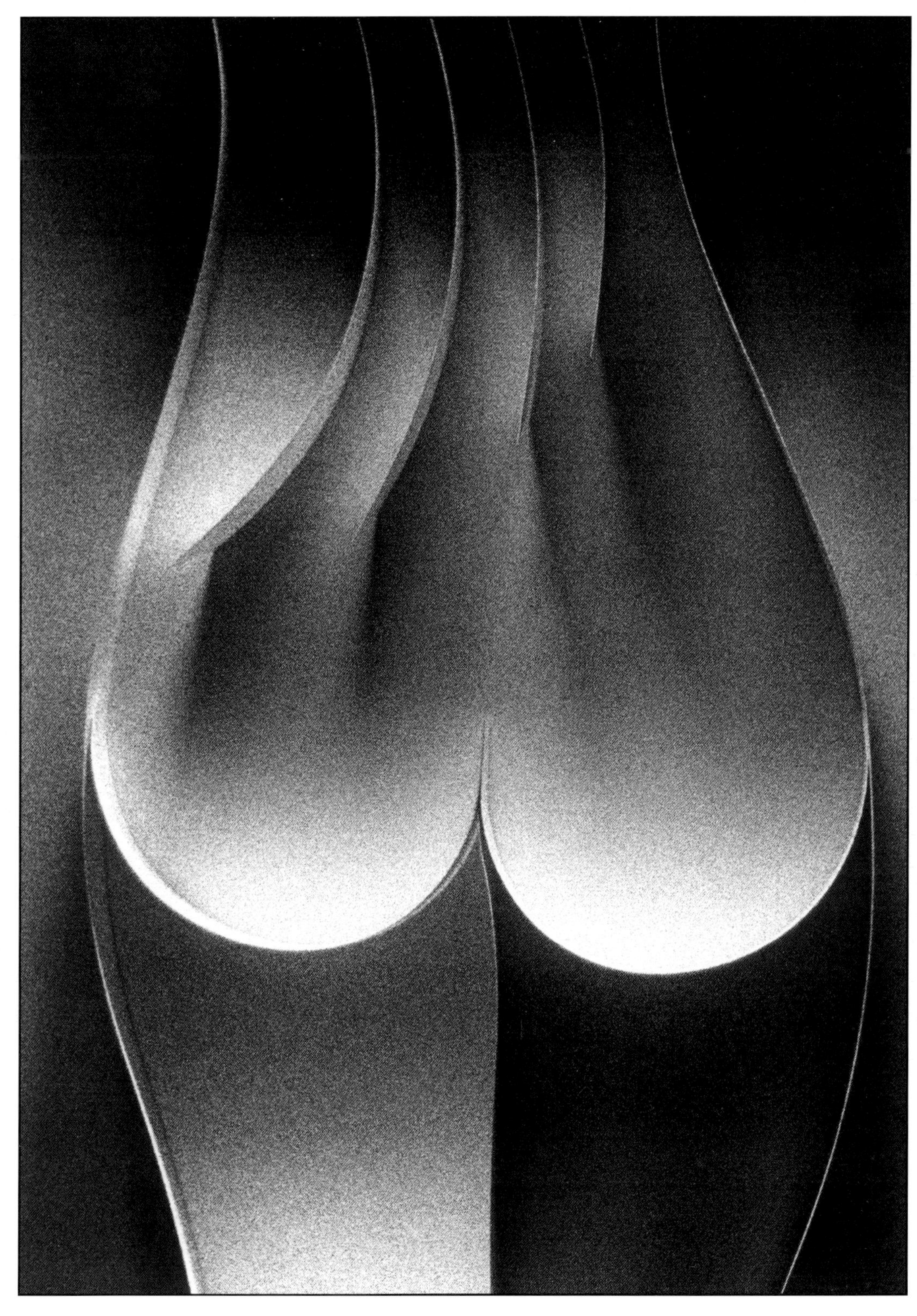

72
Figure (experimental)
Peter Motton

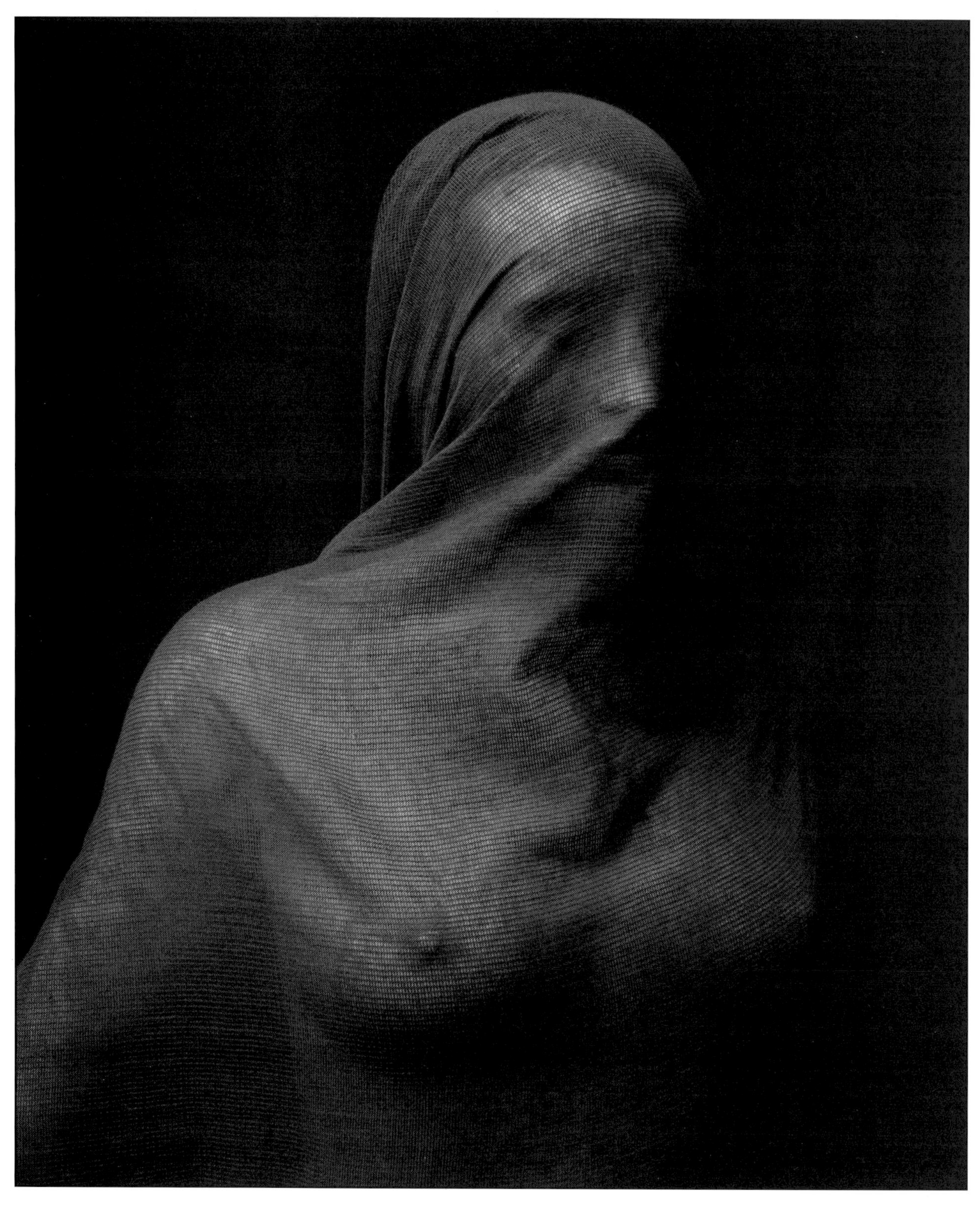

73
Veil 1
Ray Spence

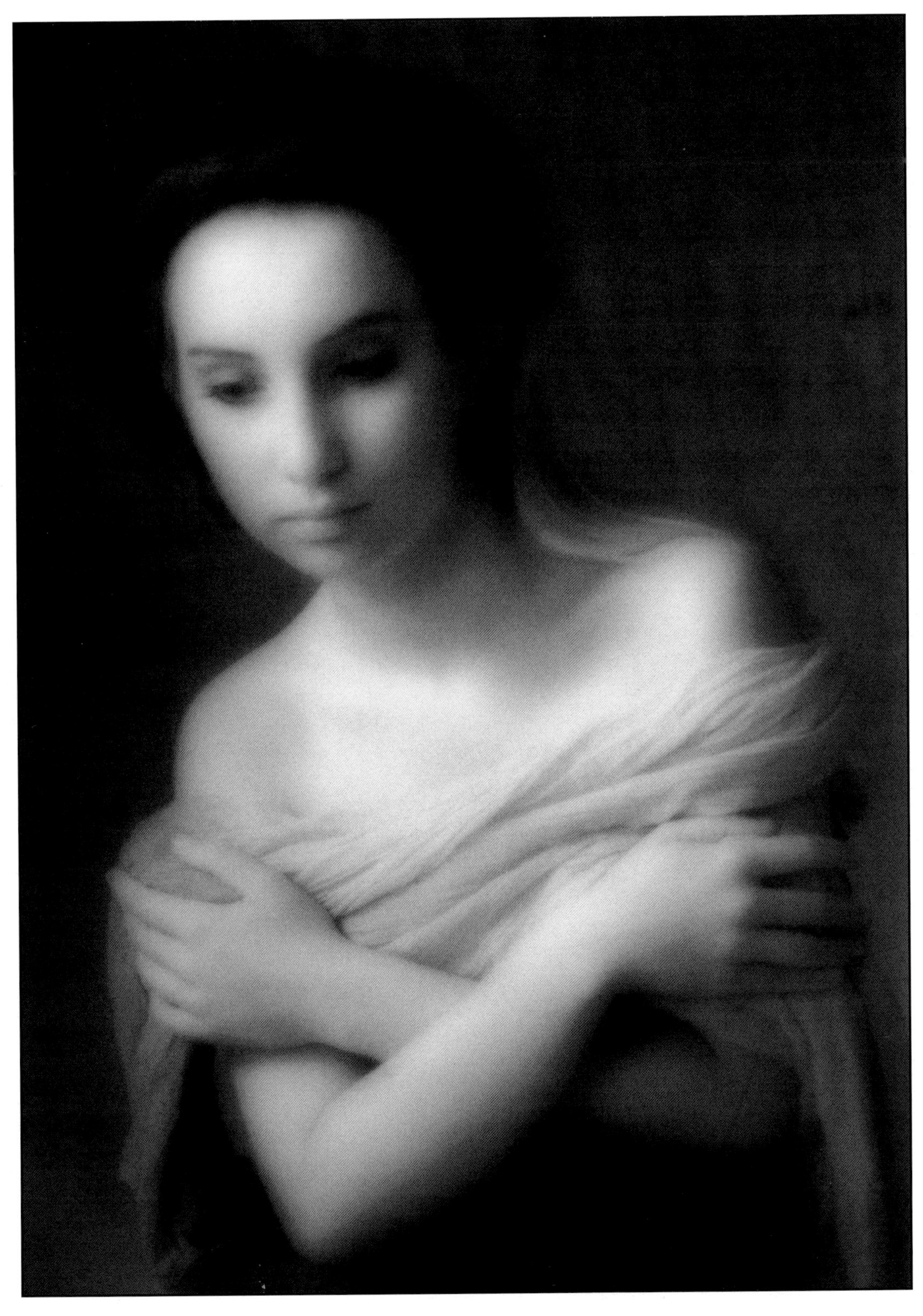

74
Katherine #1
Liz Williams

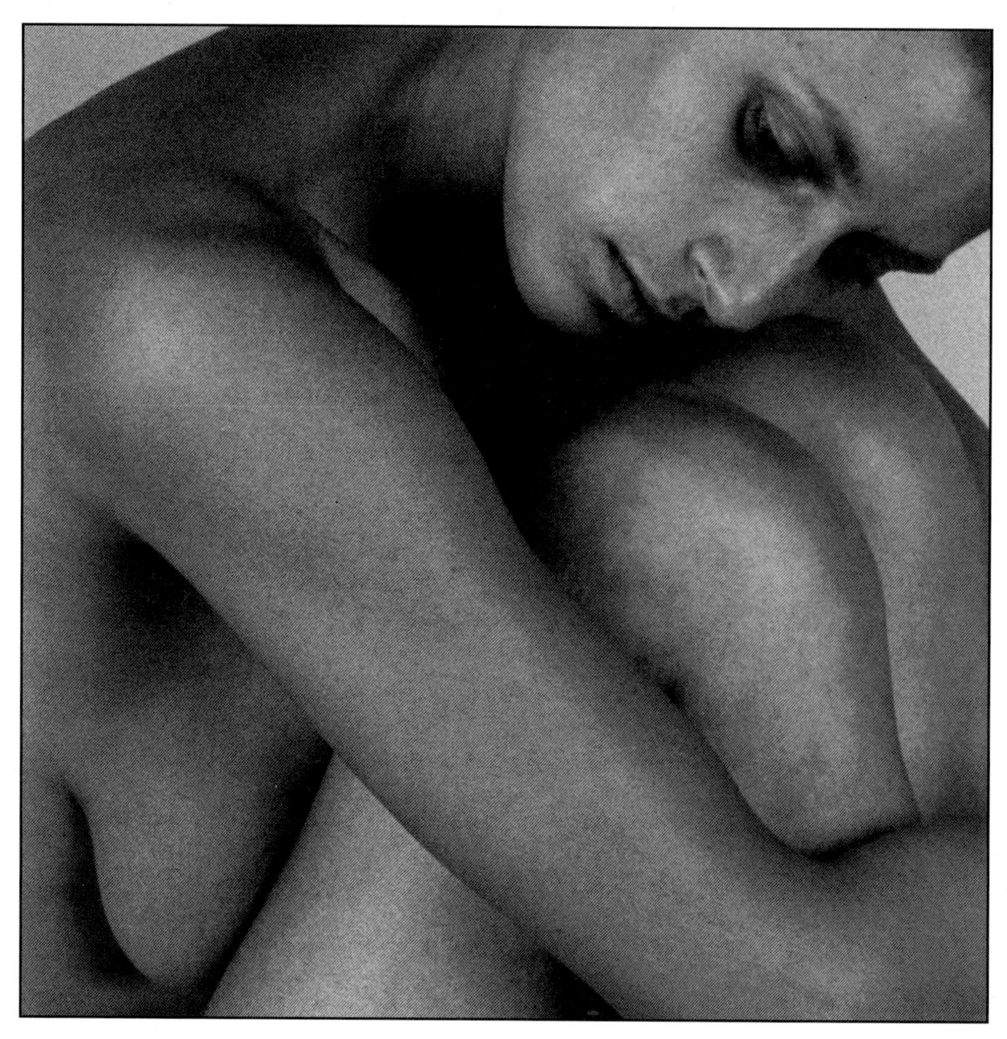

75
Tracey at rest (detail)
Glyn Edmunds

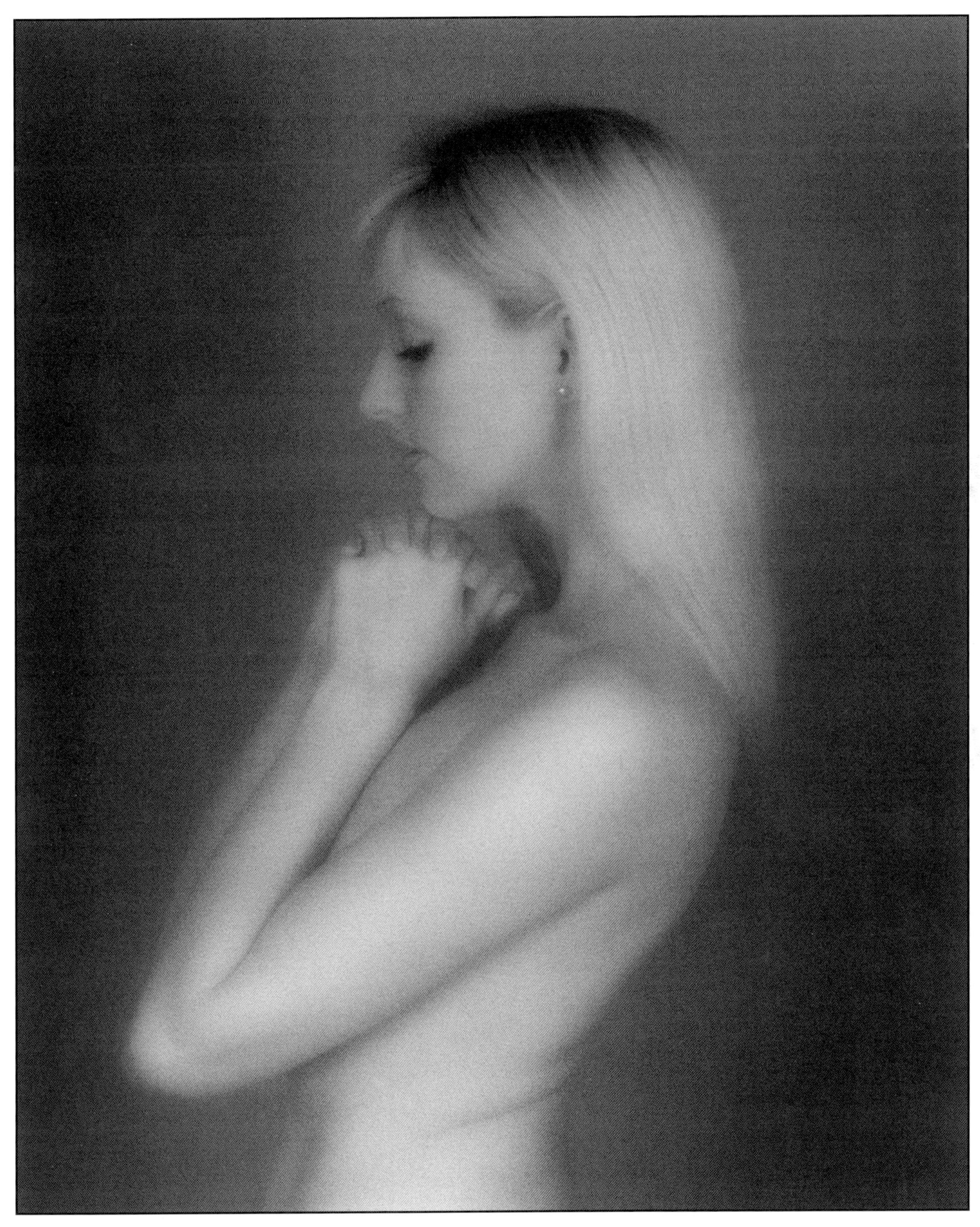

76
Donna
Ian Mellor

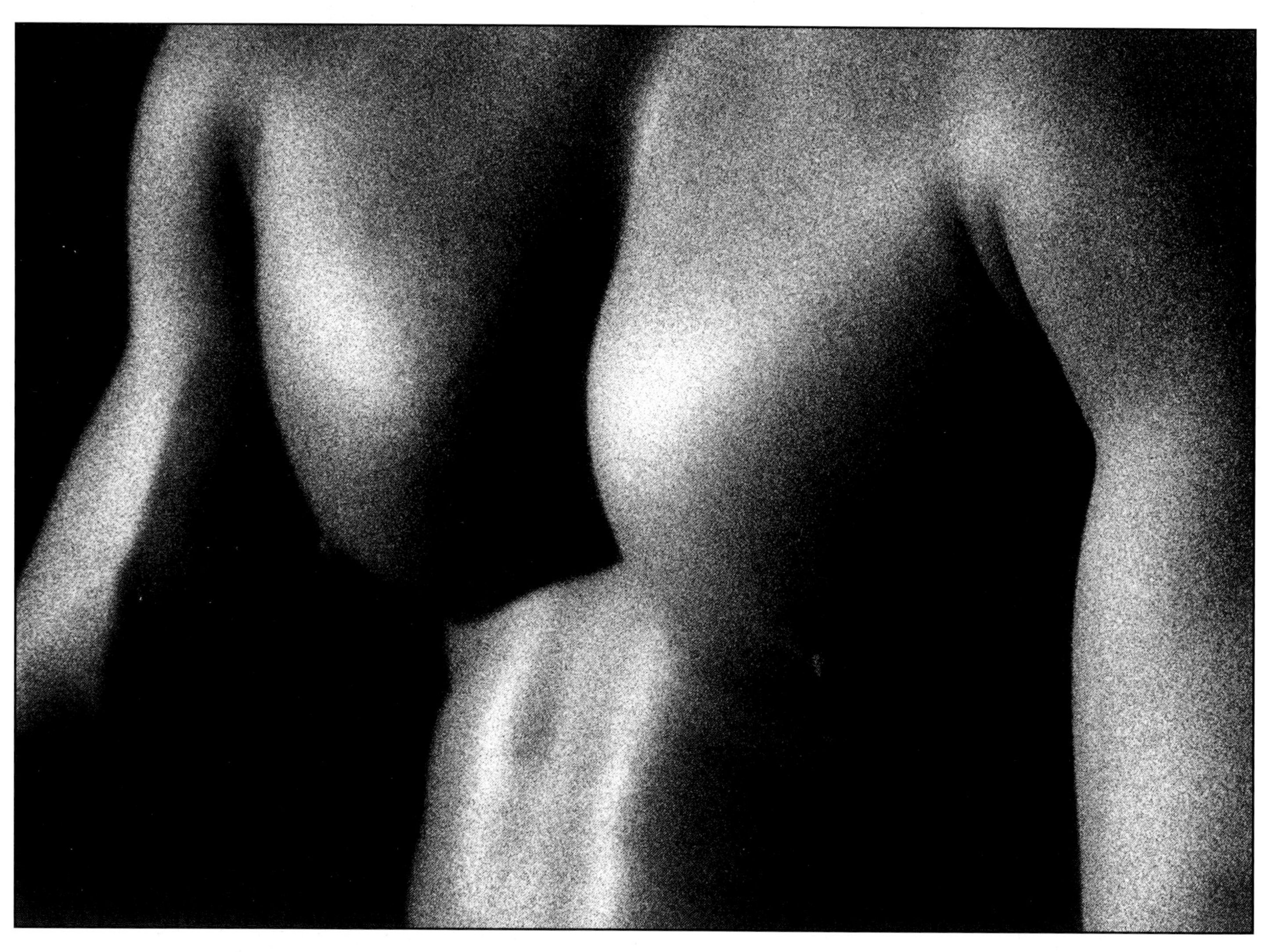

77
The shape of shadows #1
Jerry Keogh

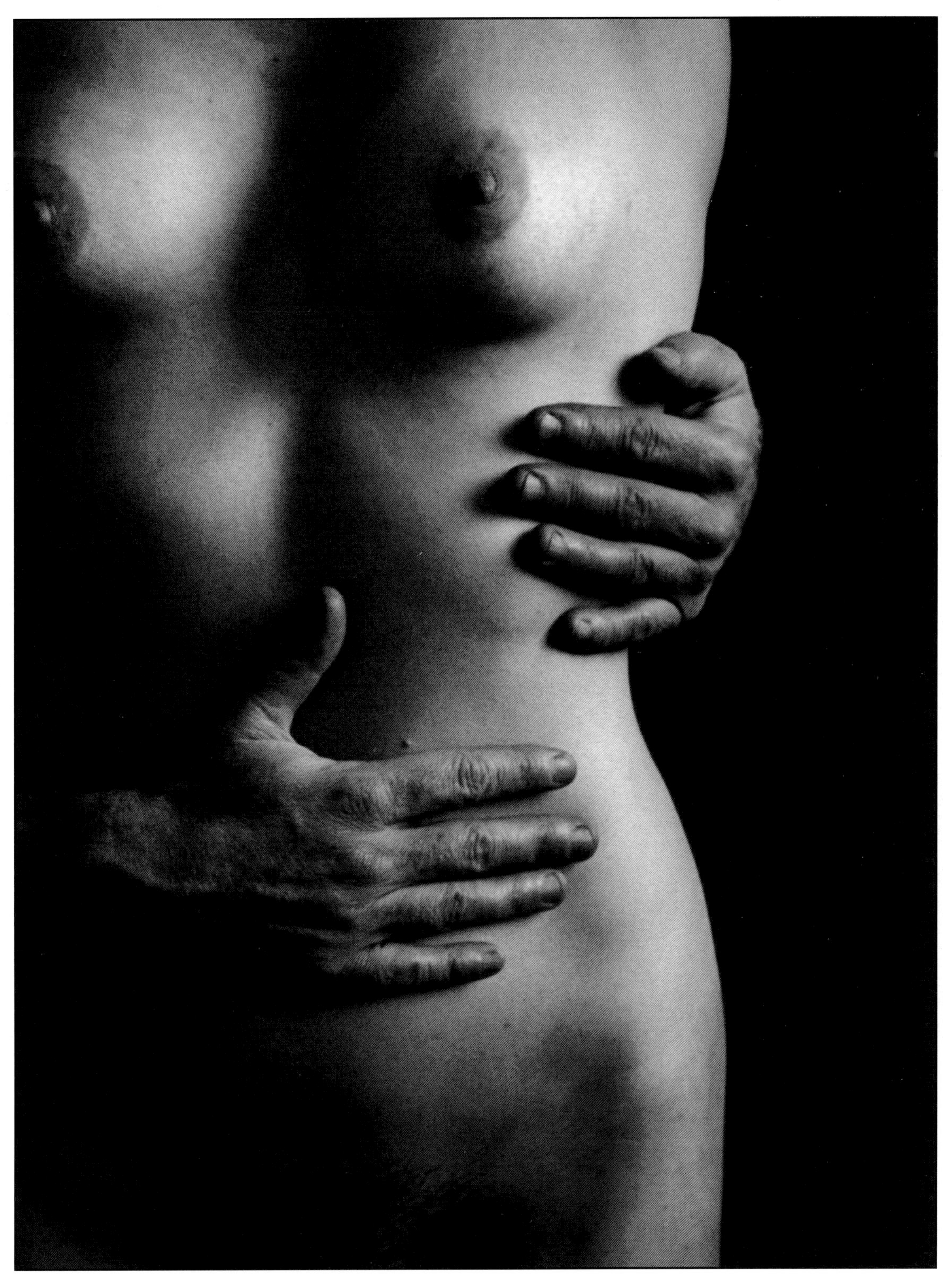

78
He and she
Roy Elwood

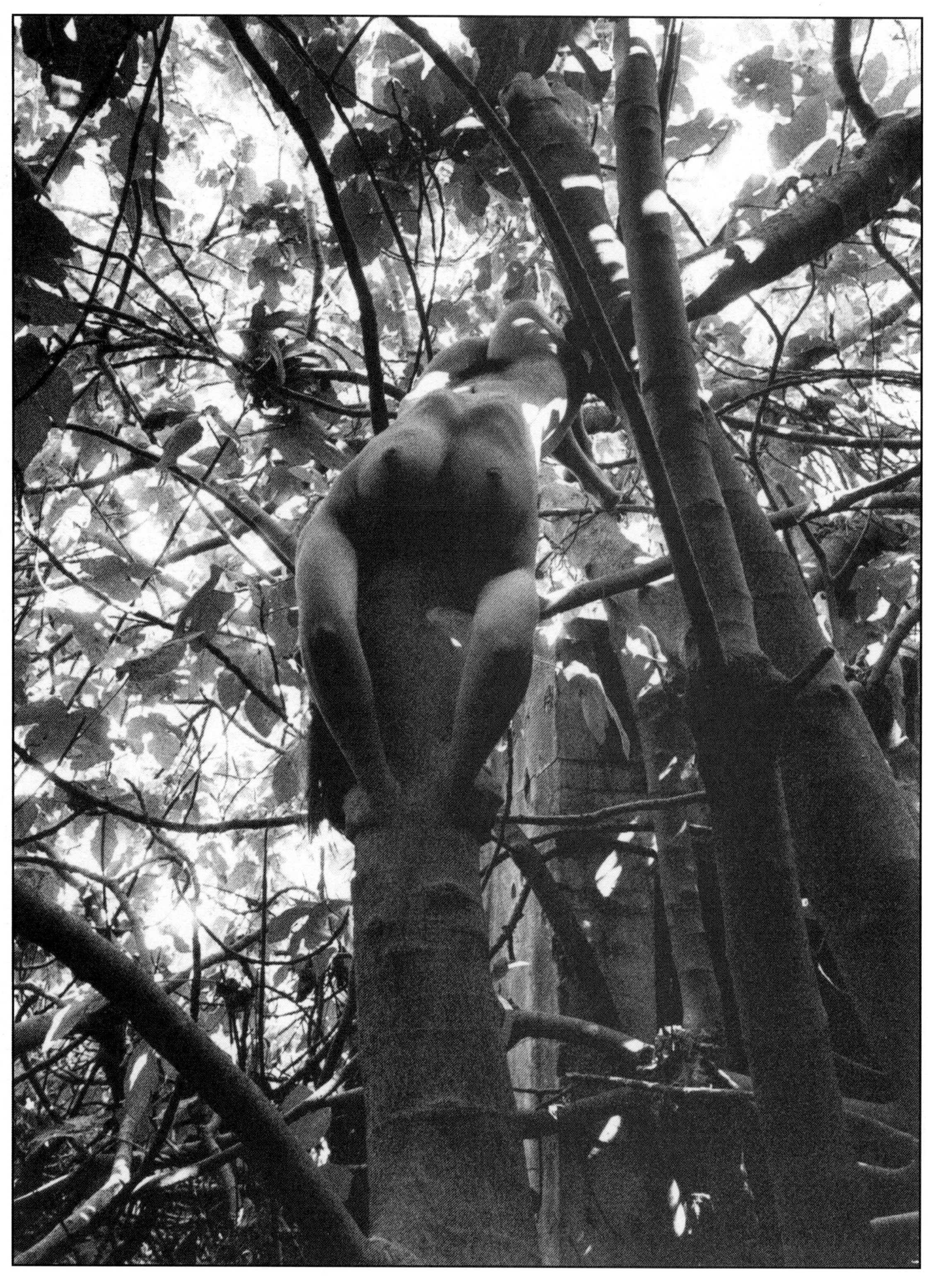

79
The fruit
Ron Abrahams

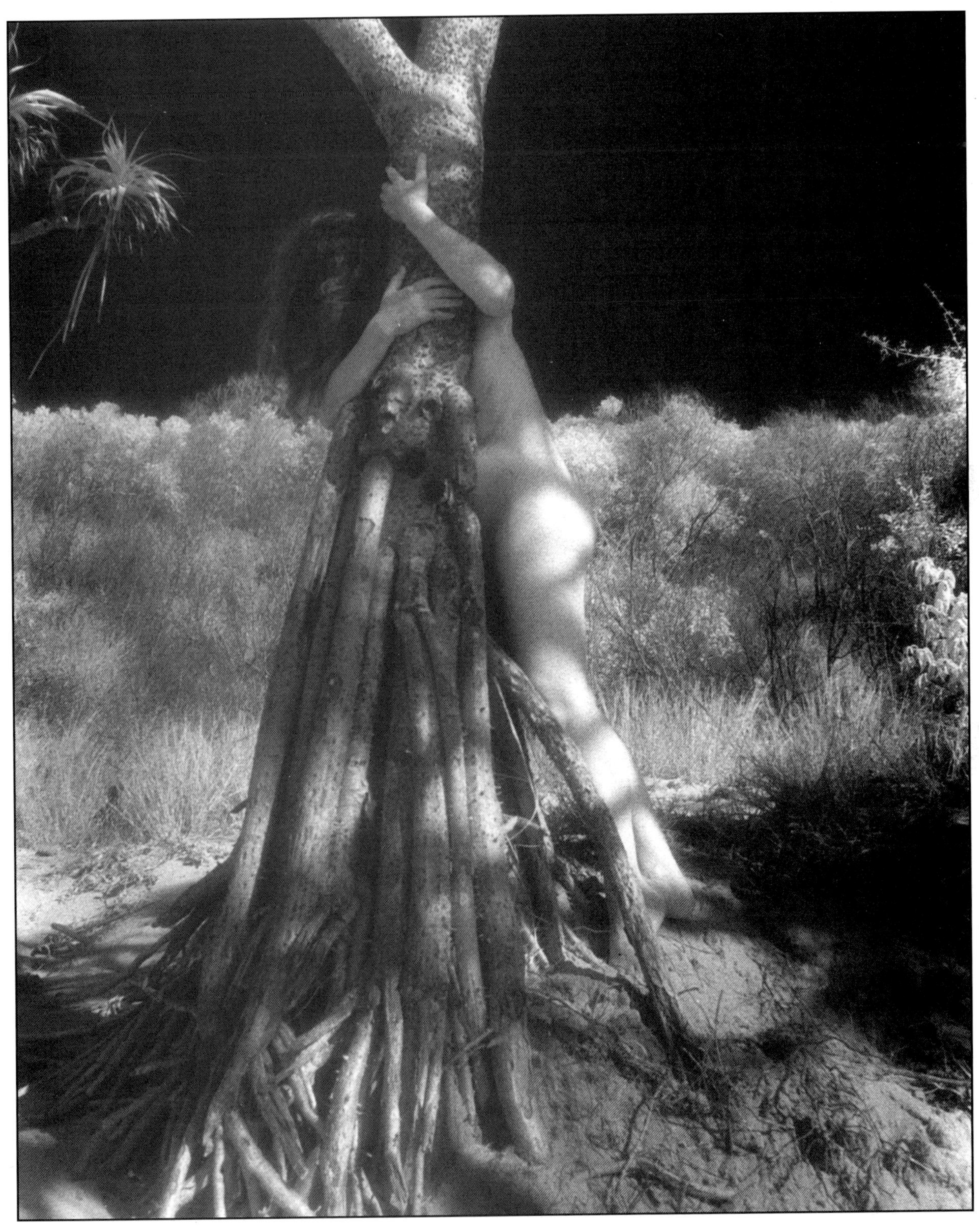

80
Pandanus roots
Derek Christy

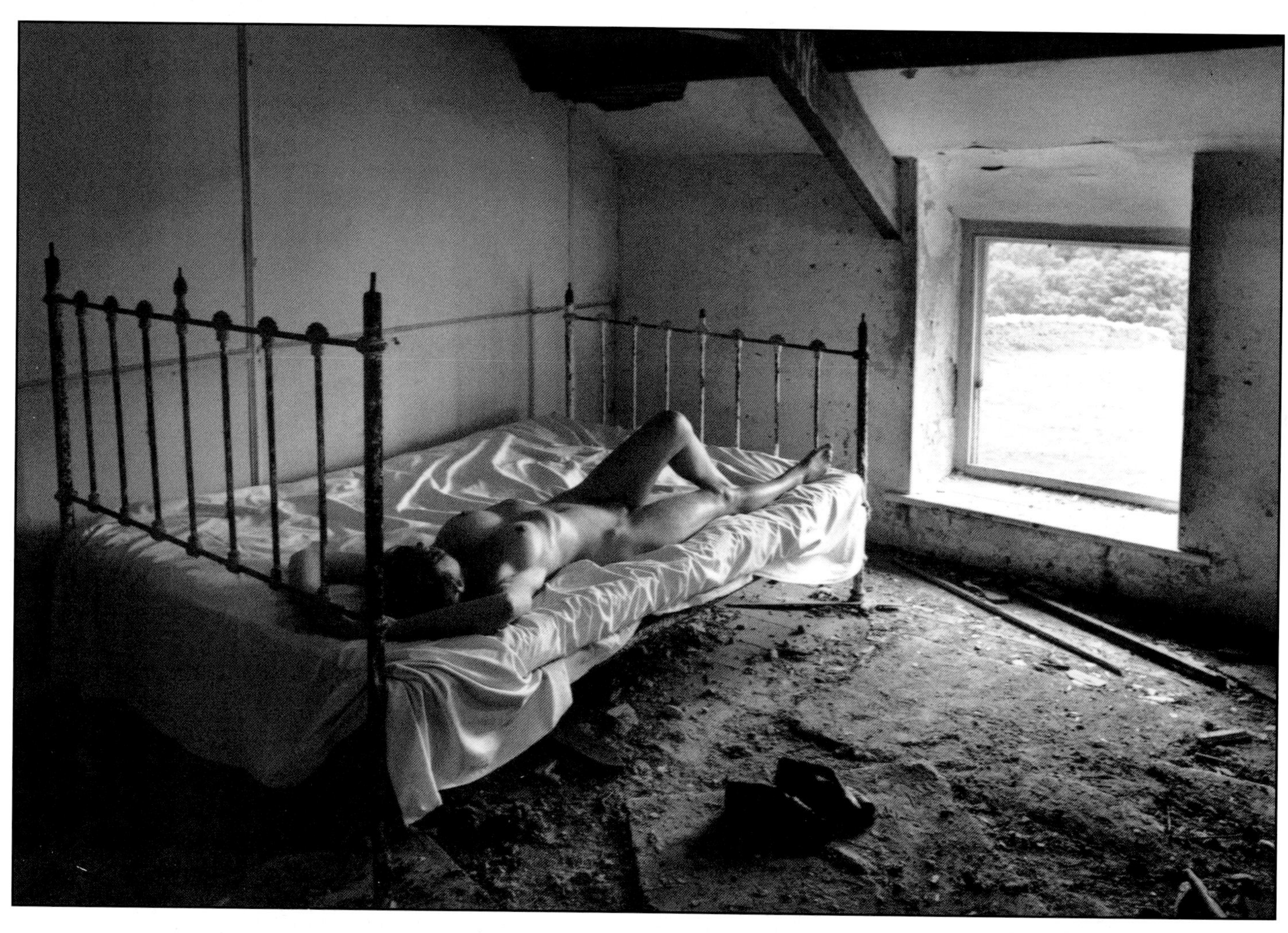

81
Cottage nude
Roy Elwood

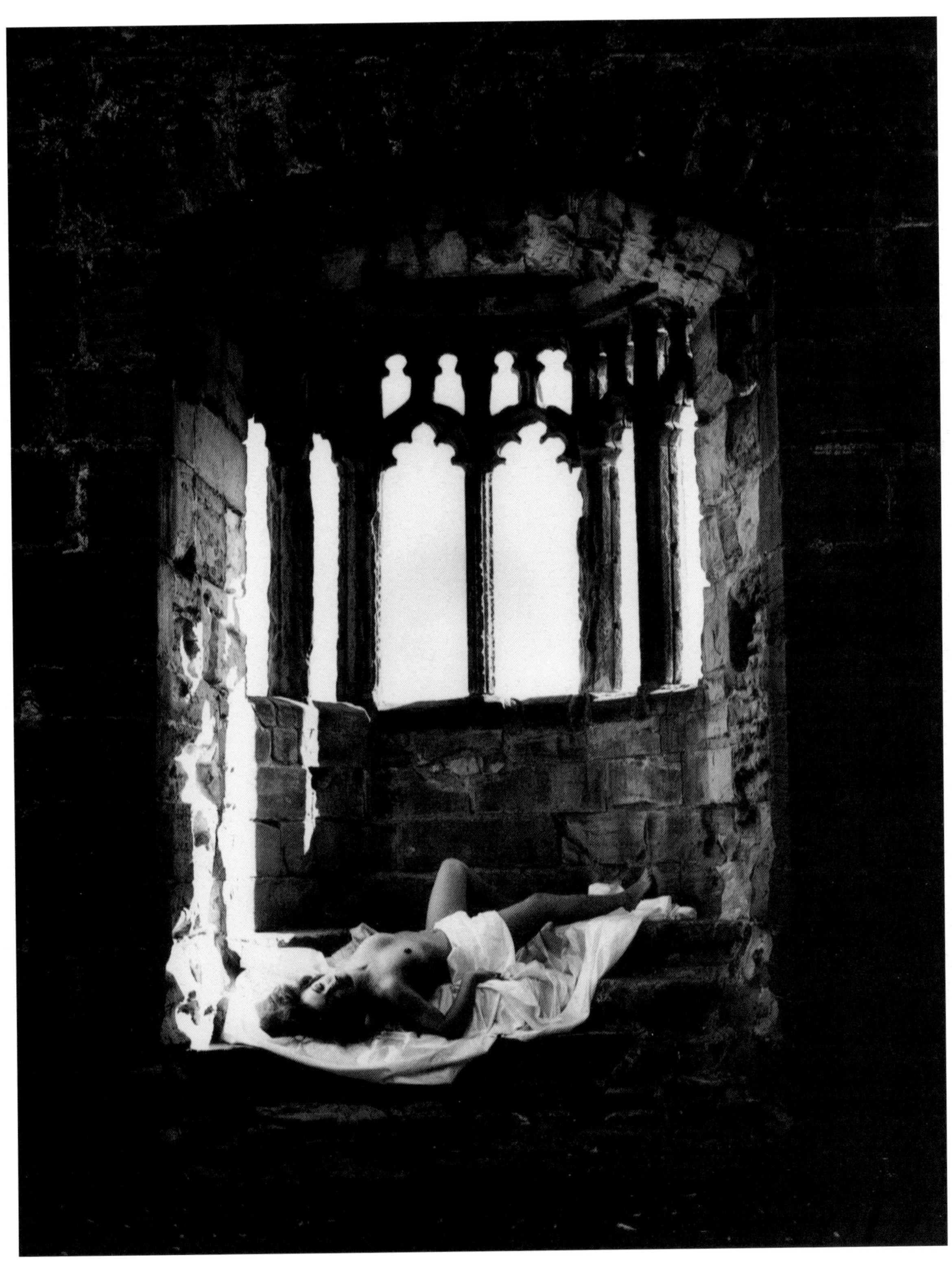

82
Fulfilled desires
Richard Egan

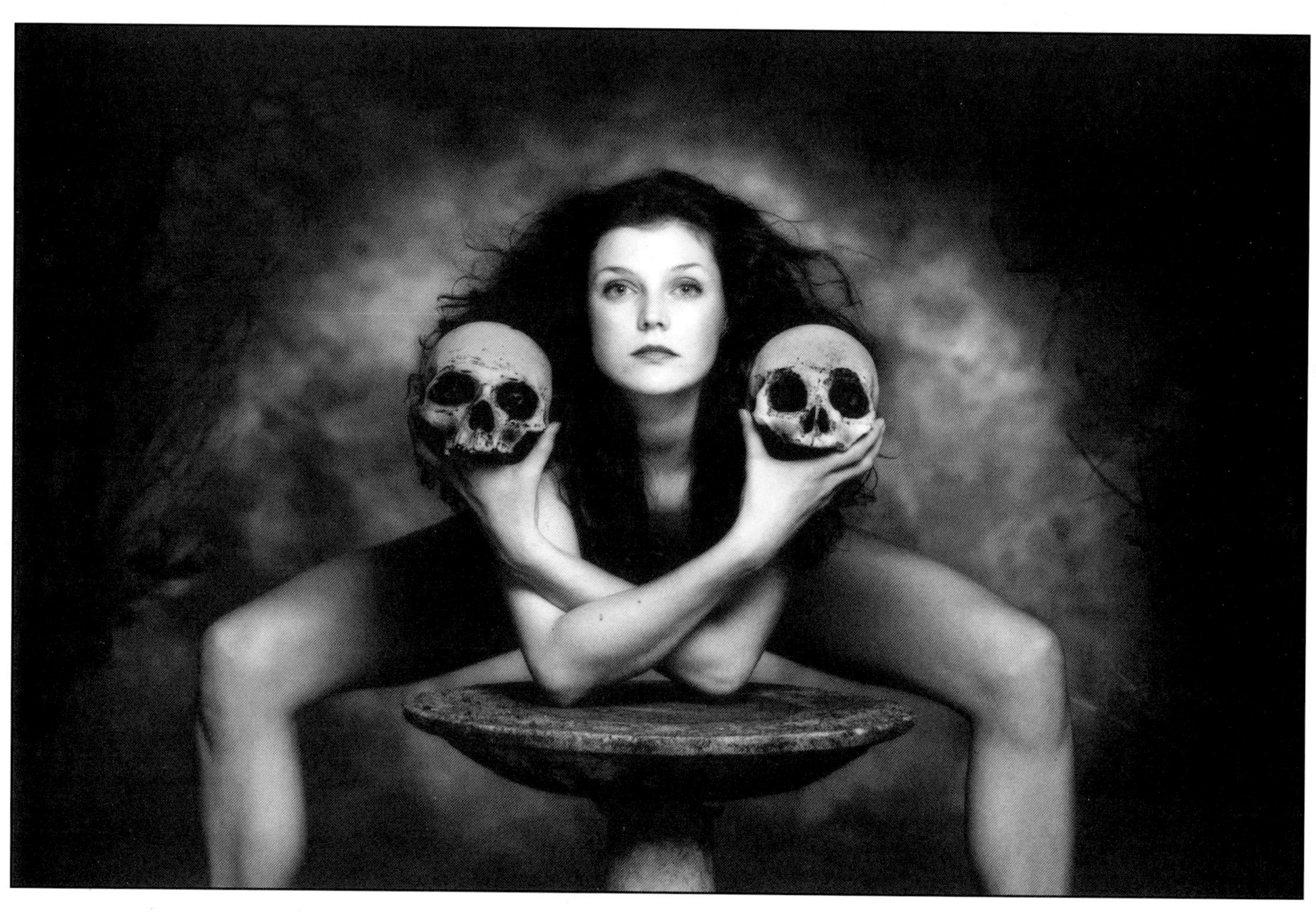

83
Sentinels #15
John Laurens

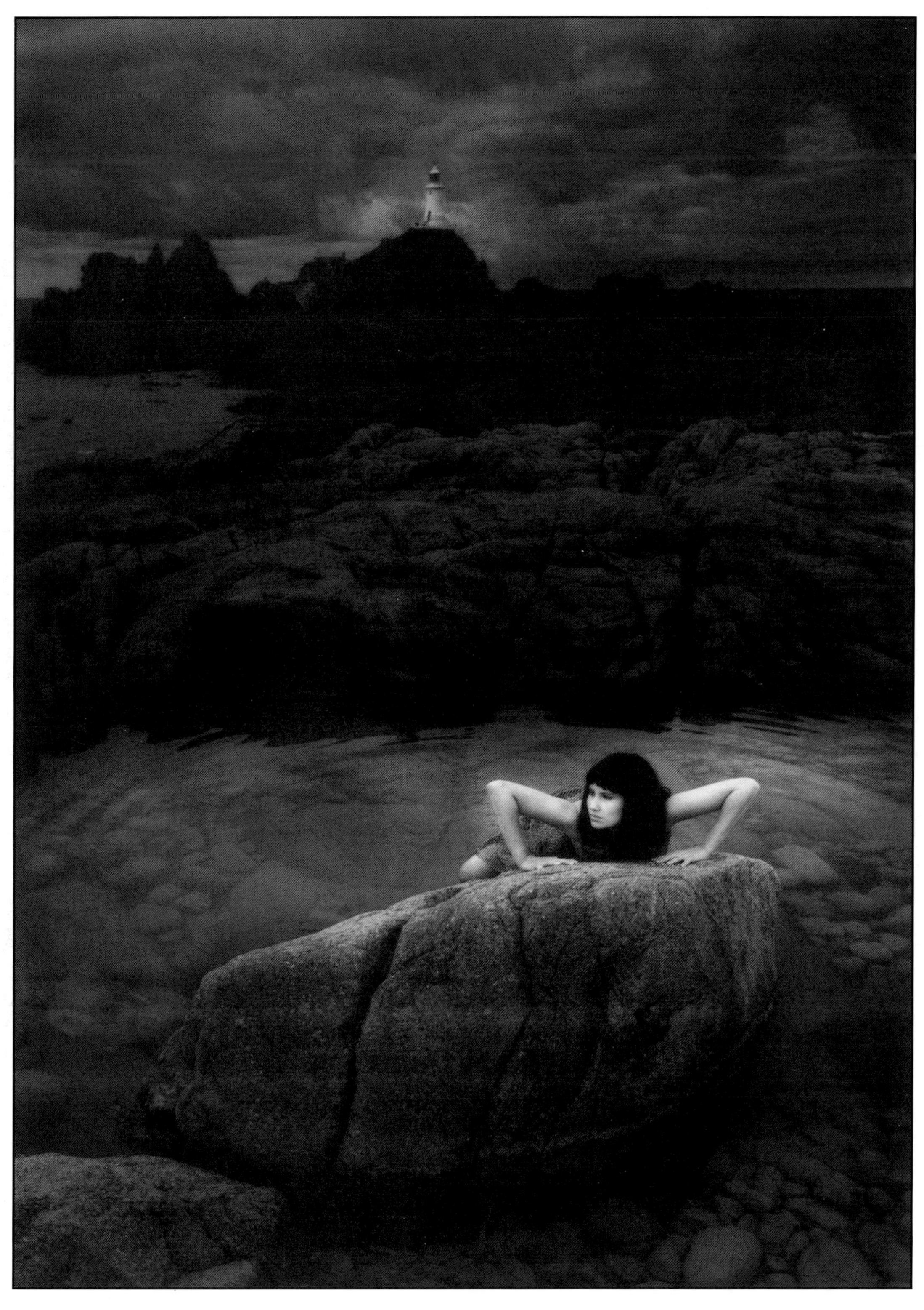

84
Sentinels #11
John Laurens

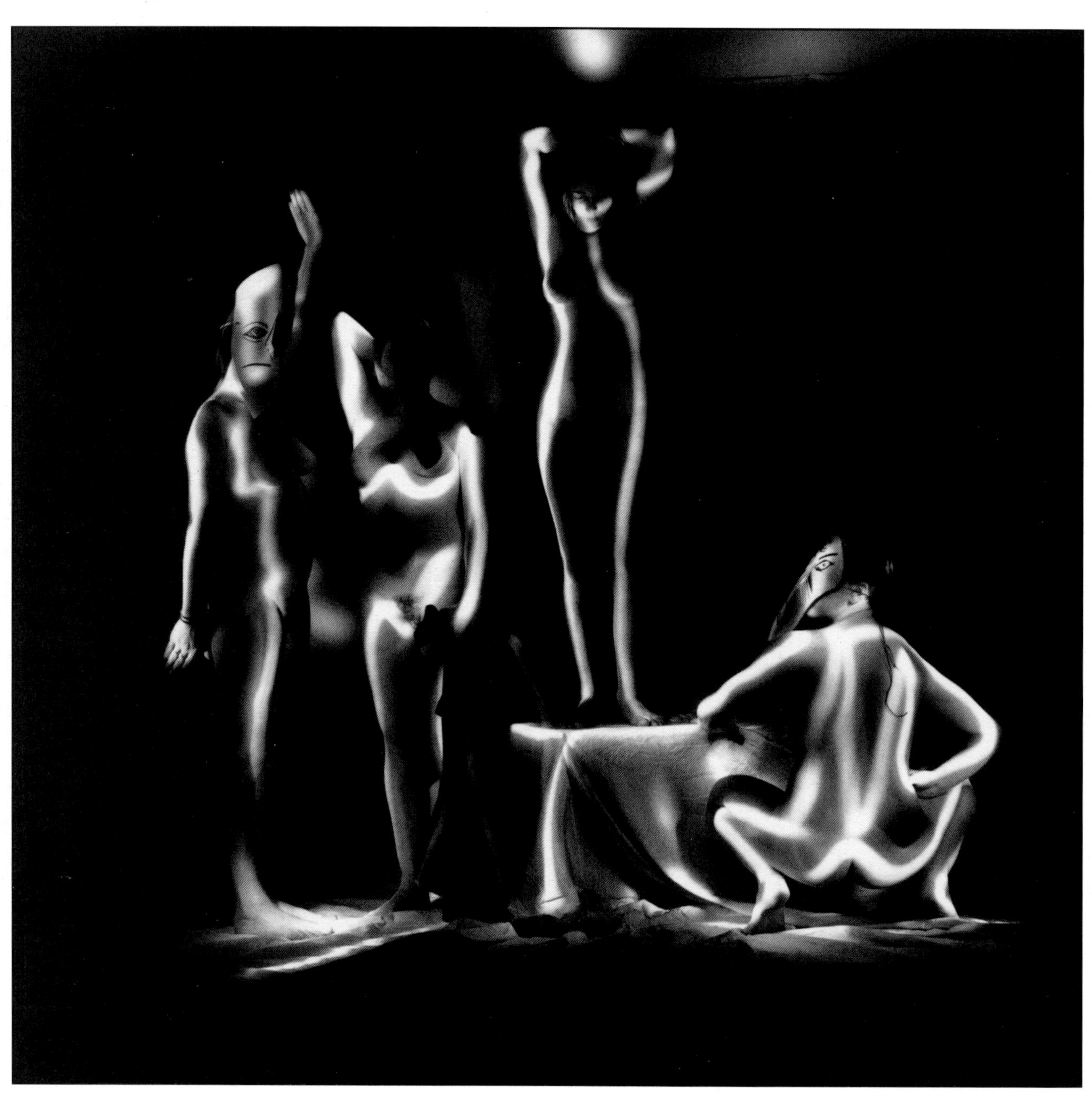

85
One for Pablo
Roger Skinner

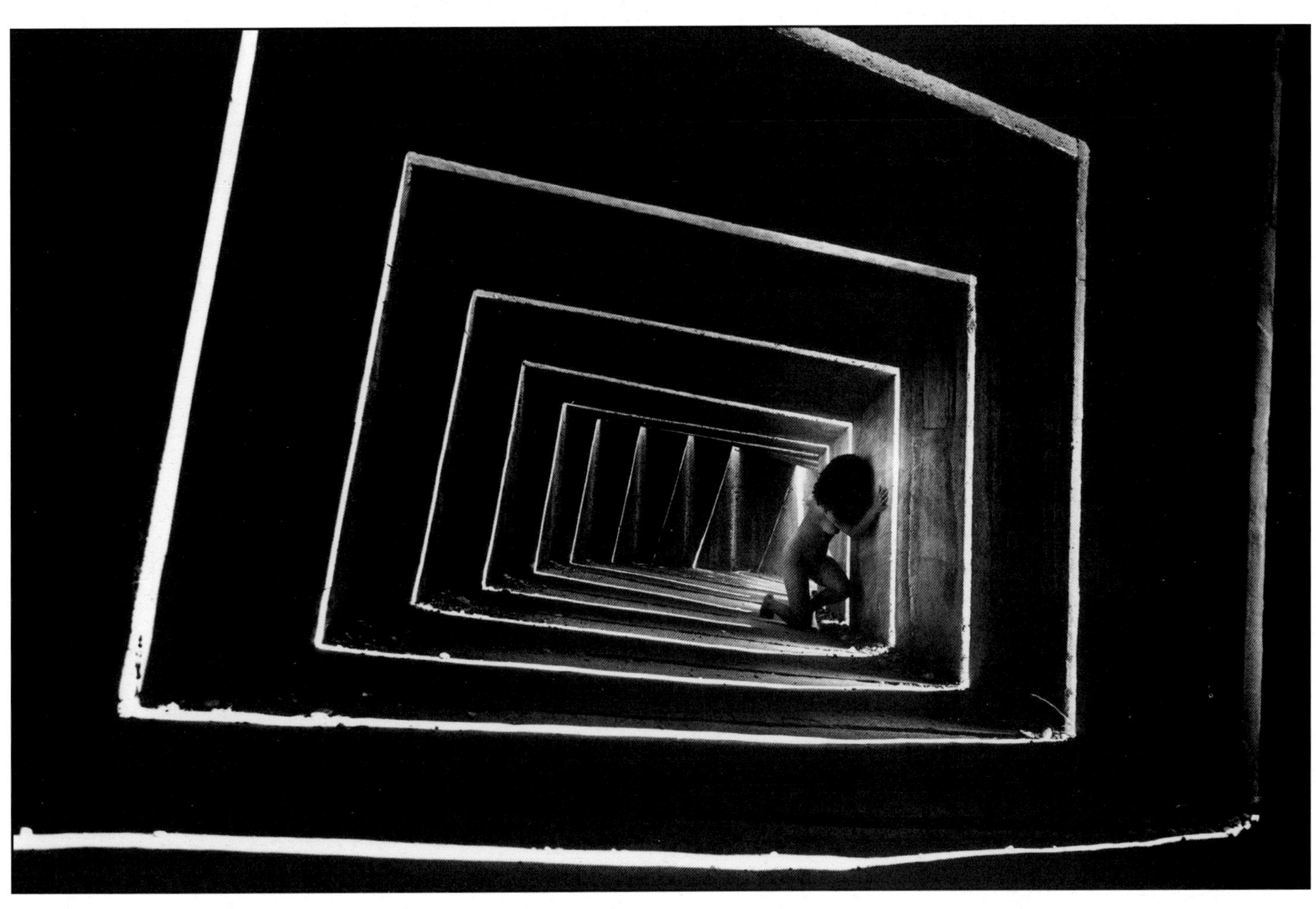

86
The labyrinth
Ron Abrahams

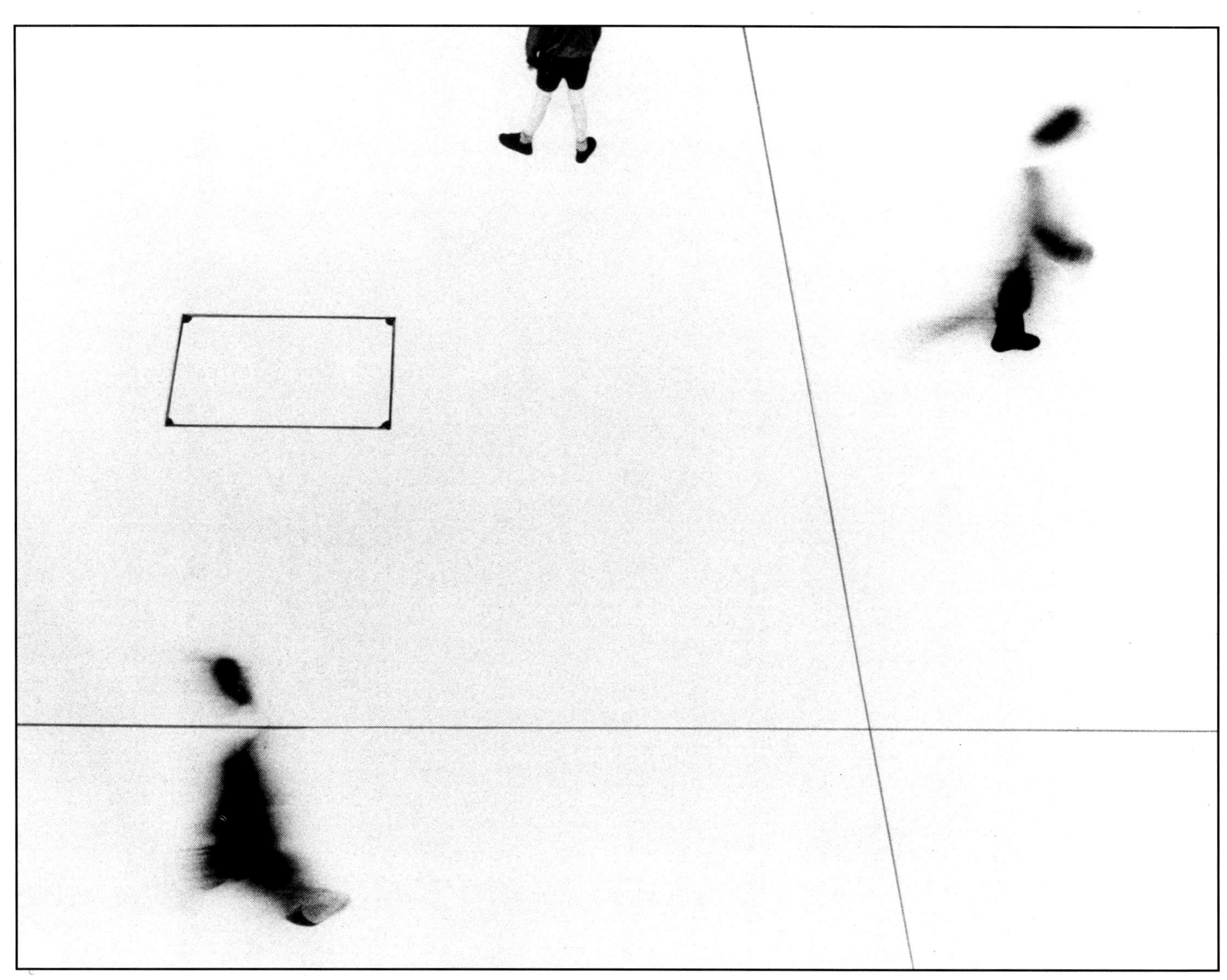

87
Man, woman and child
George Jenkinson

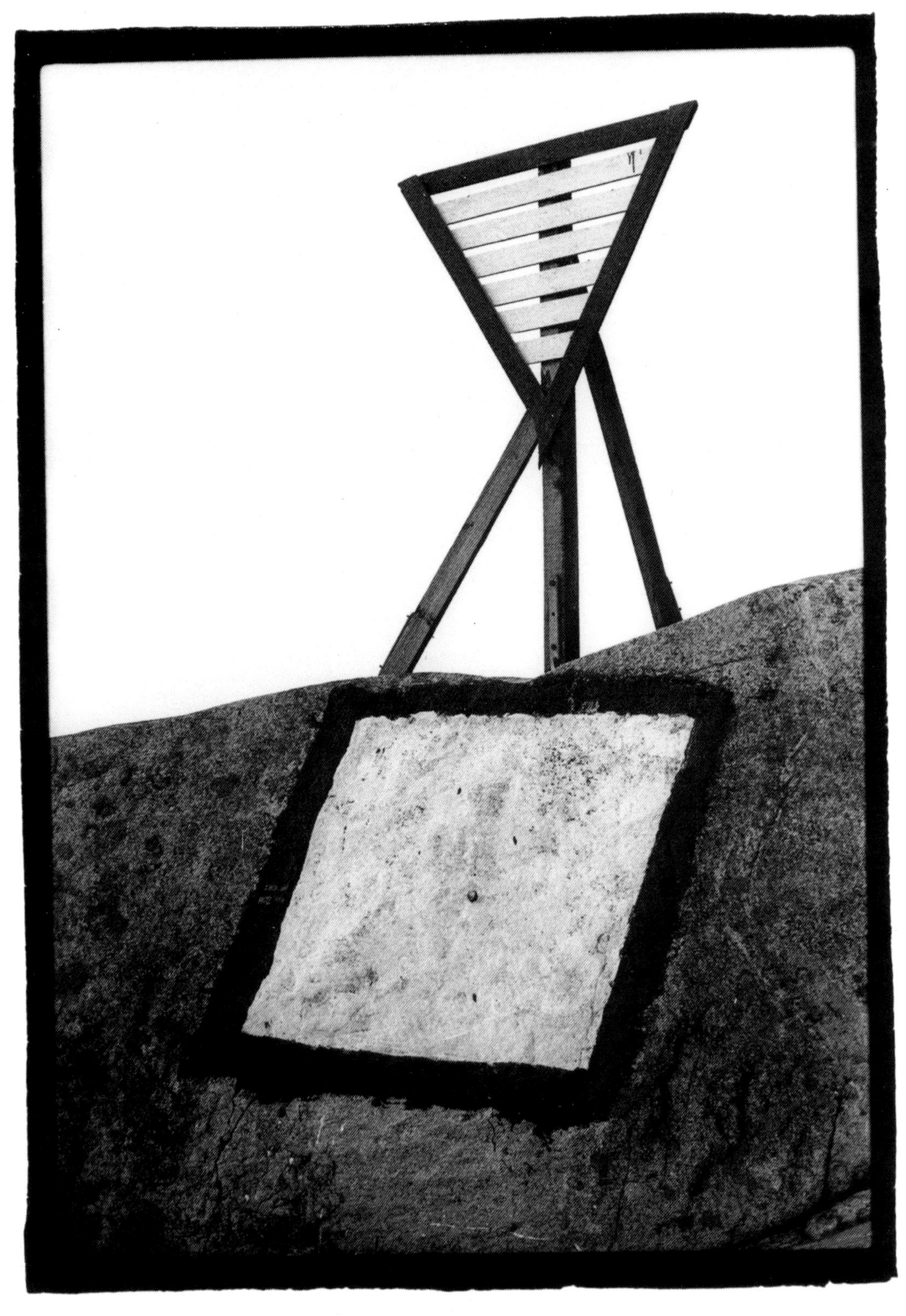

88
At sea
Per-Åke Wärn

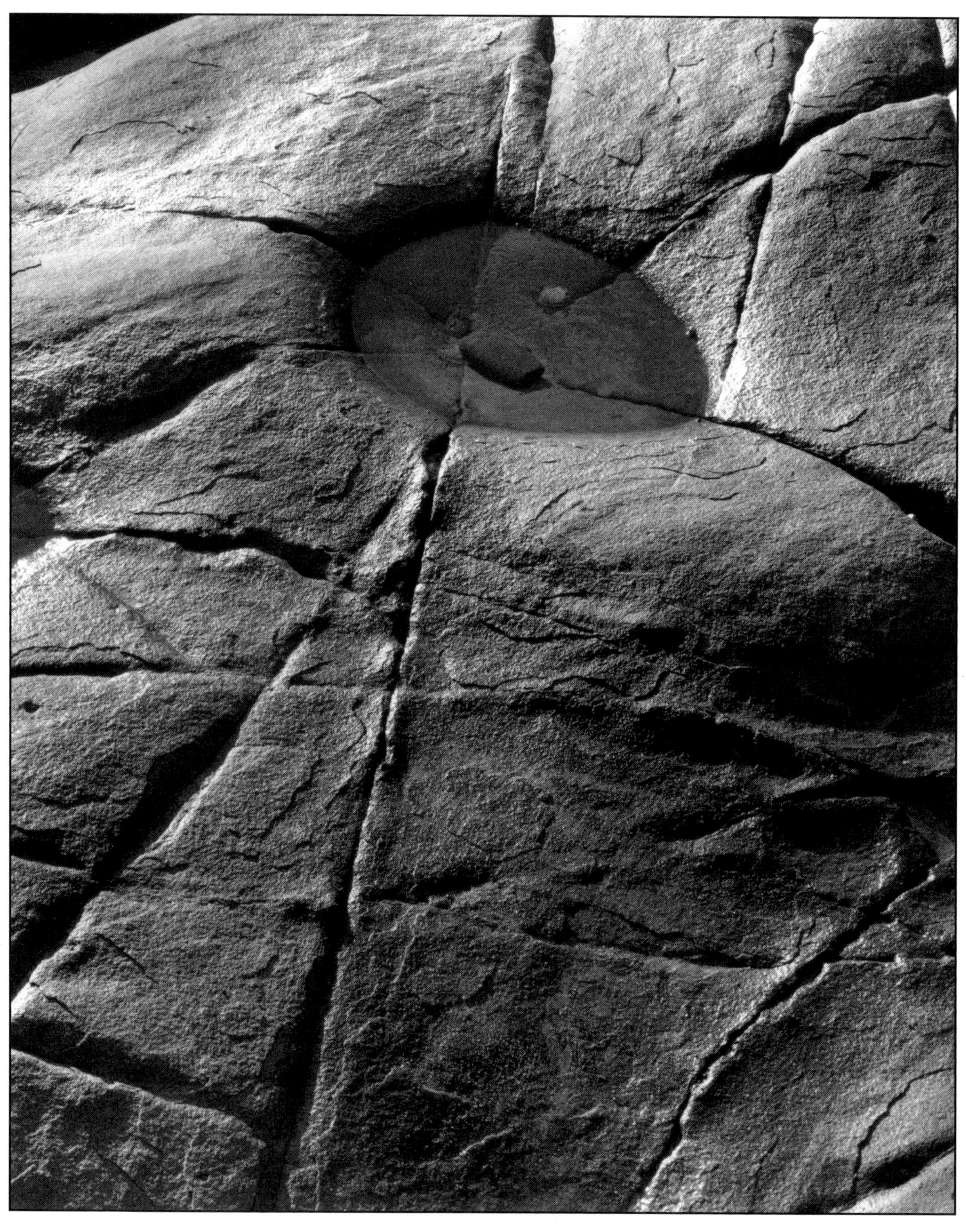

89
Natural geometry
Rob Gray

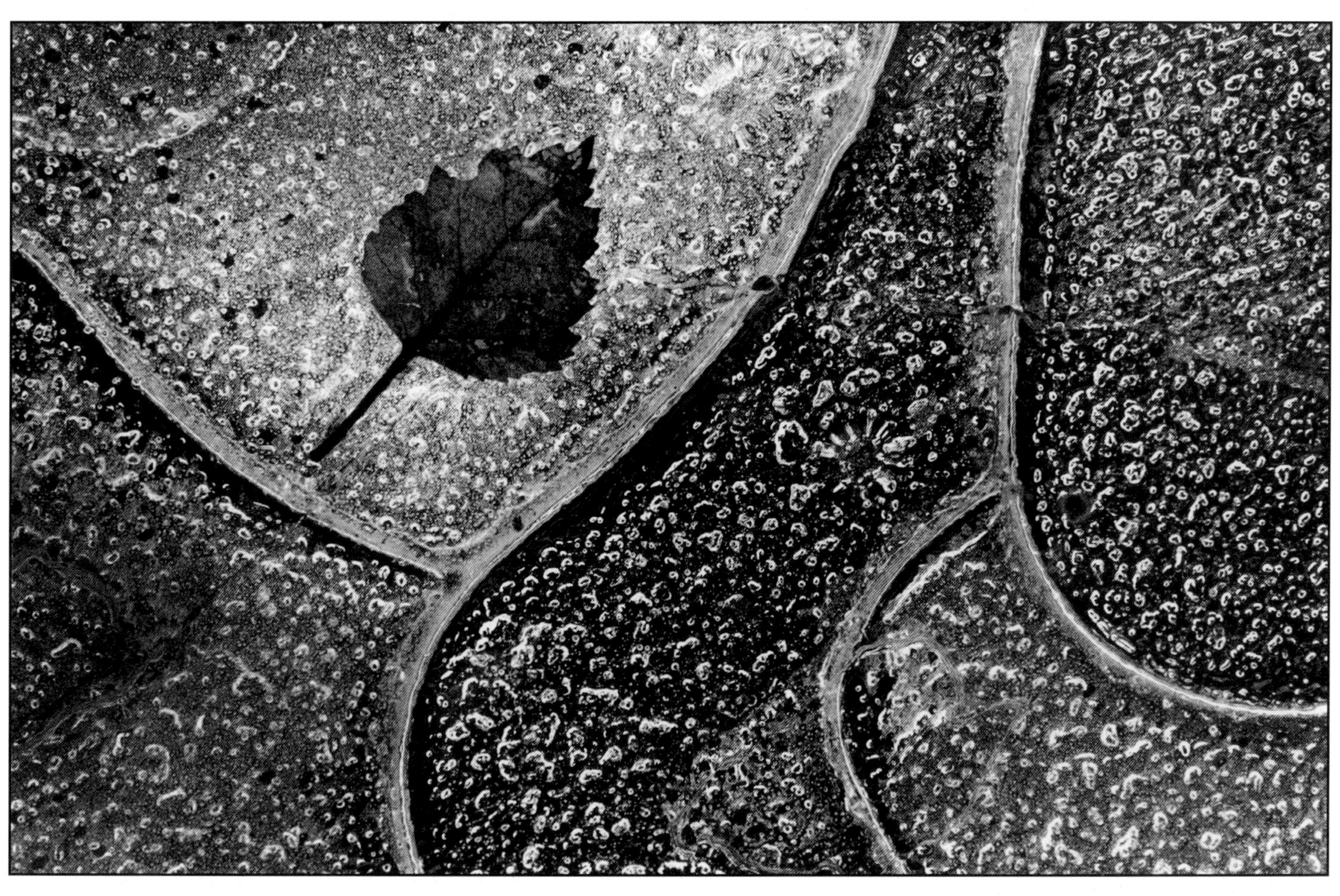

90
Frozen in the ice
John Devenport

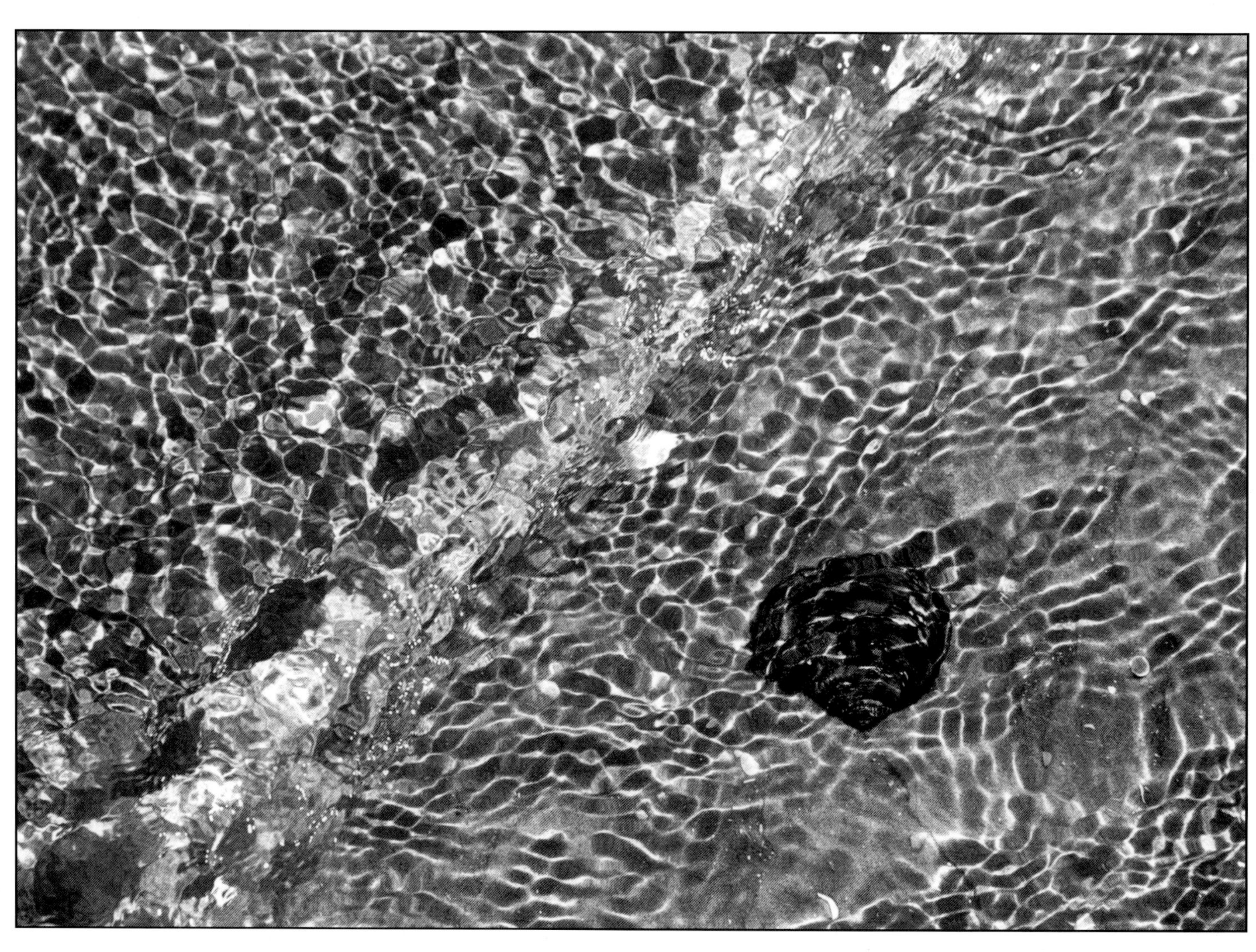

91
Shell and sea patterns
Len Perkis

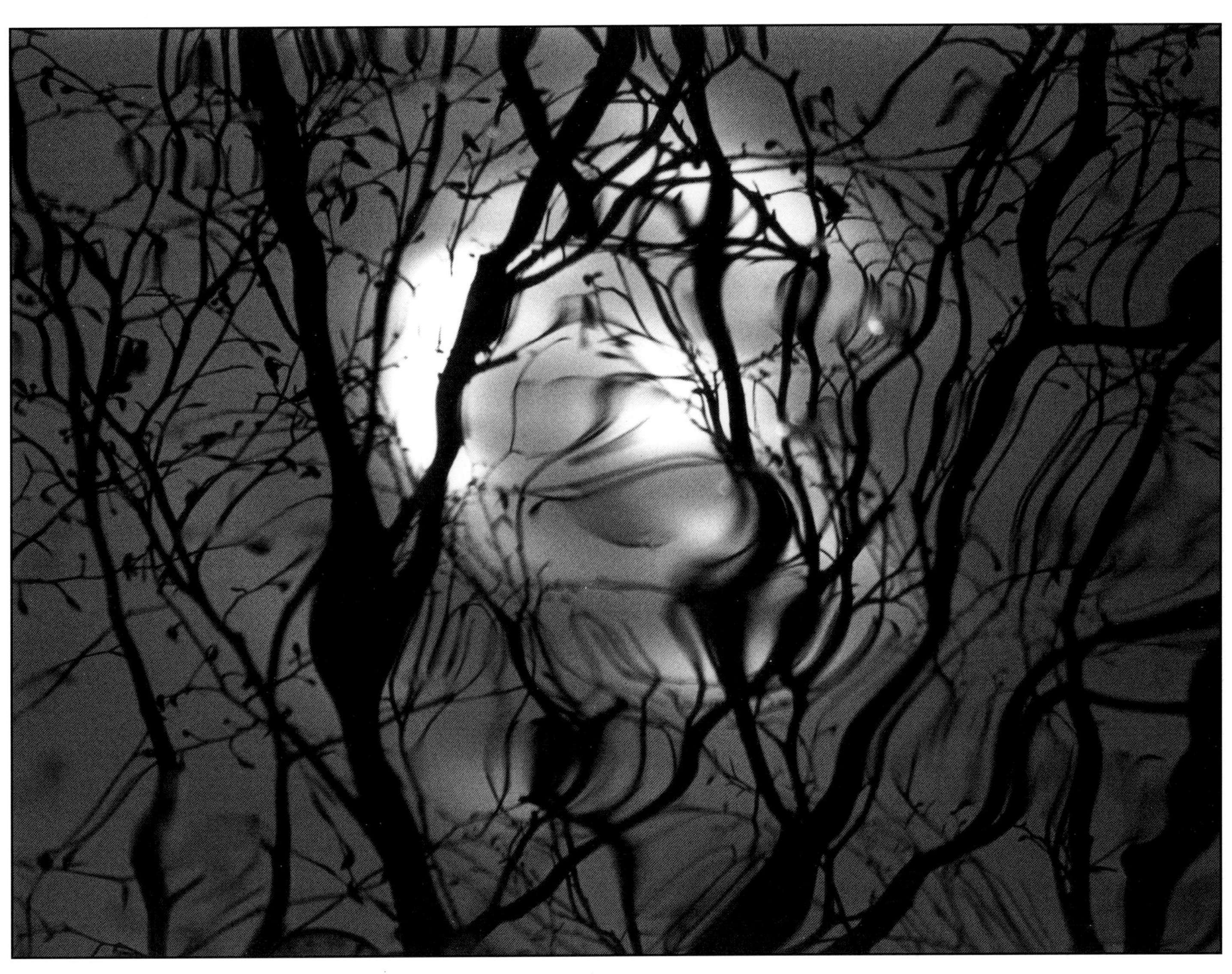

92
The creation
Margaret Rowntree

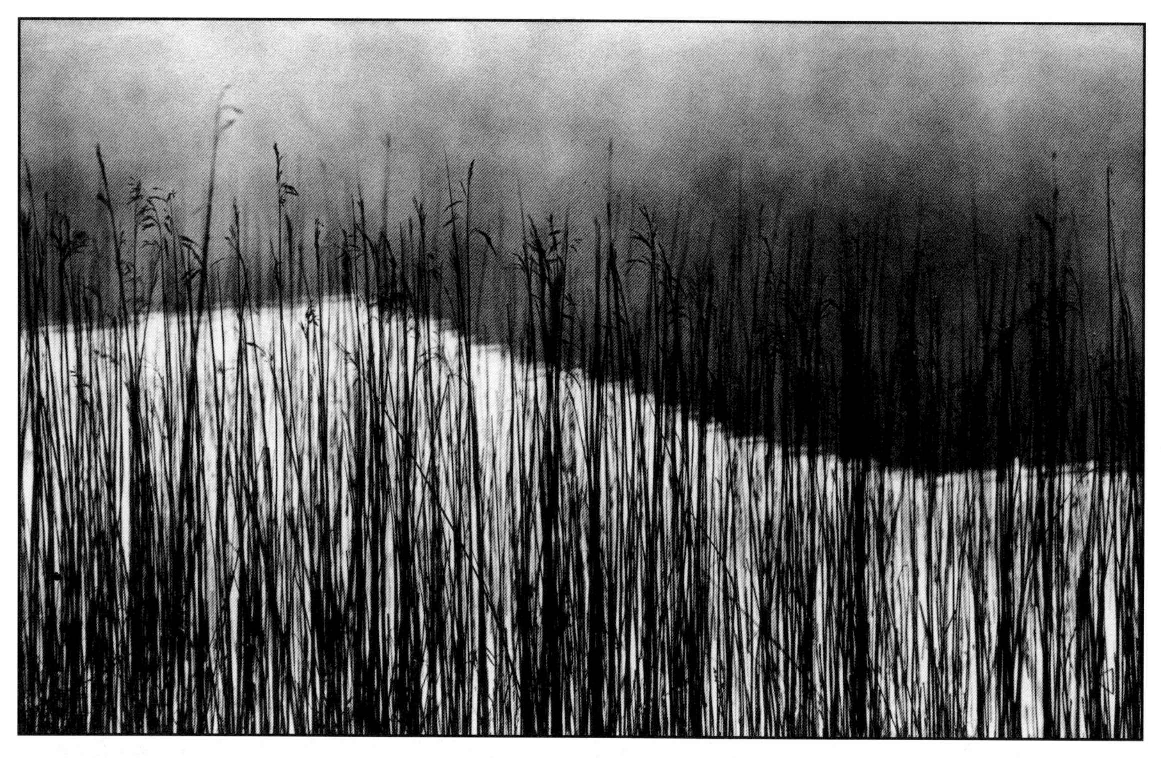

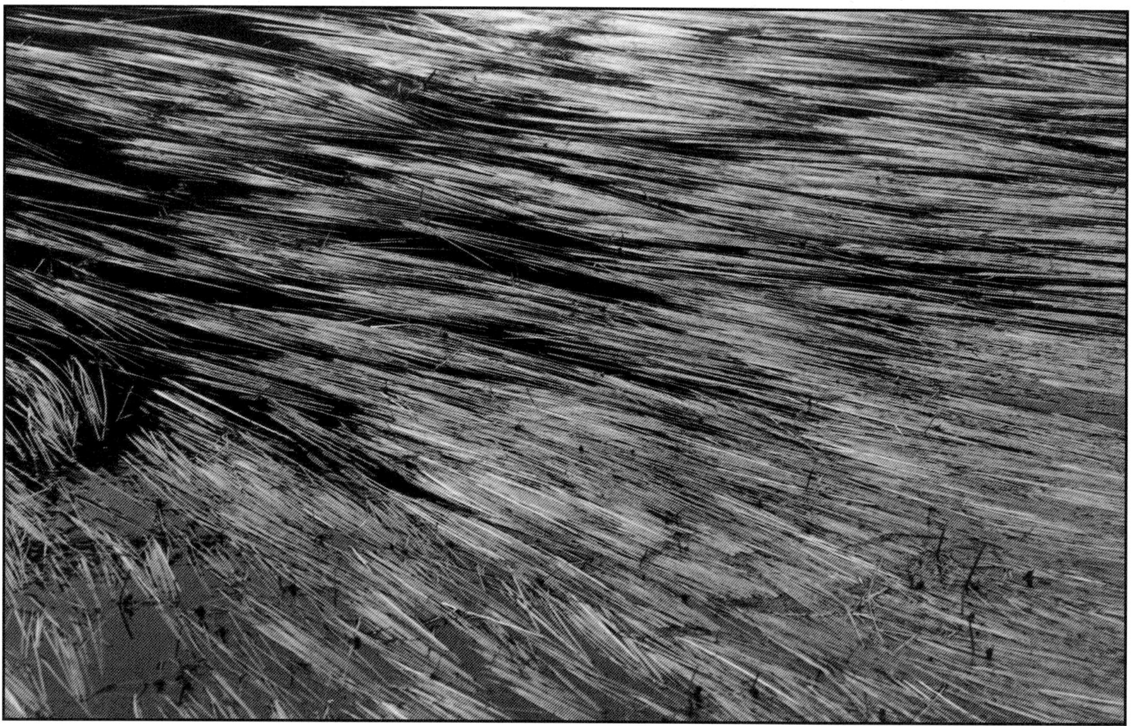

(top) 93, **Grass**; *(below)* 94, **Reeds**
Cliff Threadgold

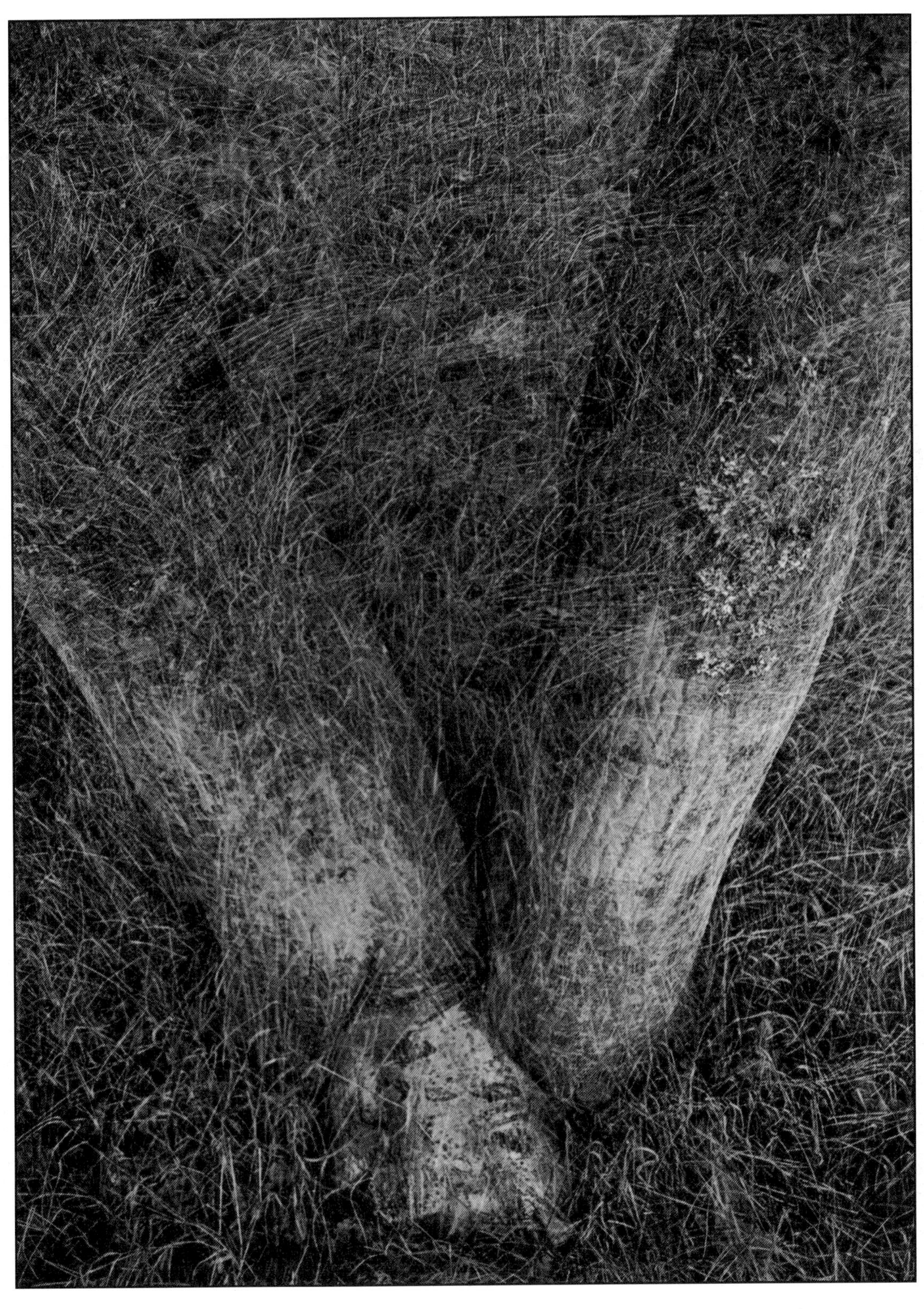

95
Divide
Clive Haynes

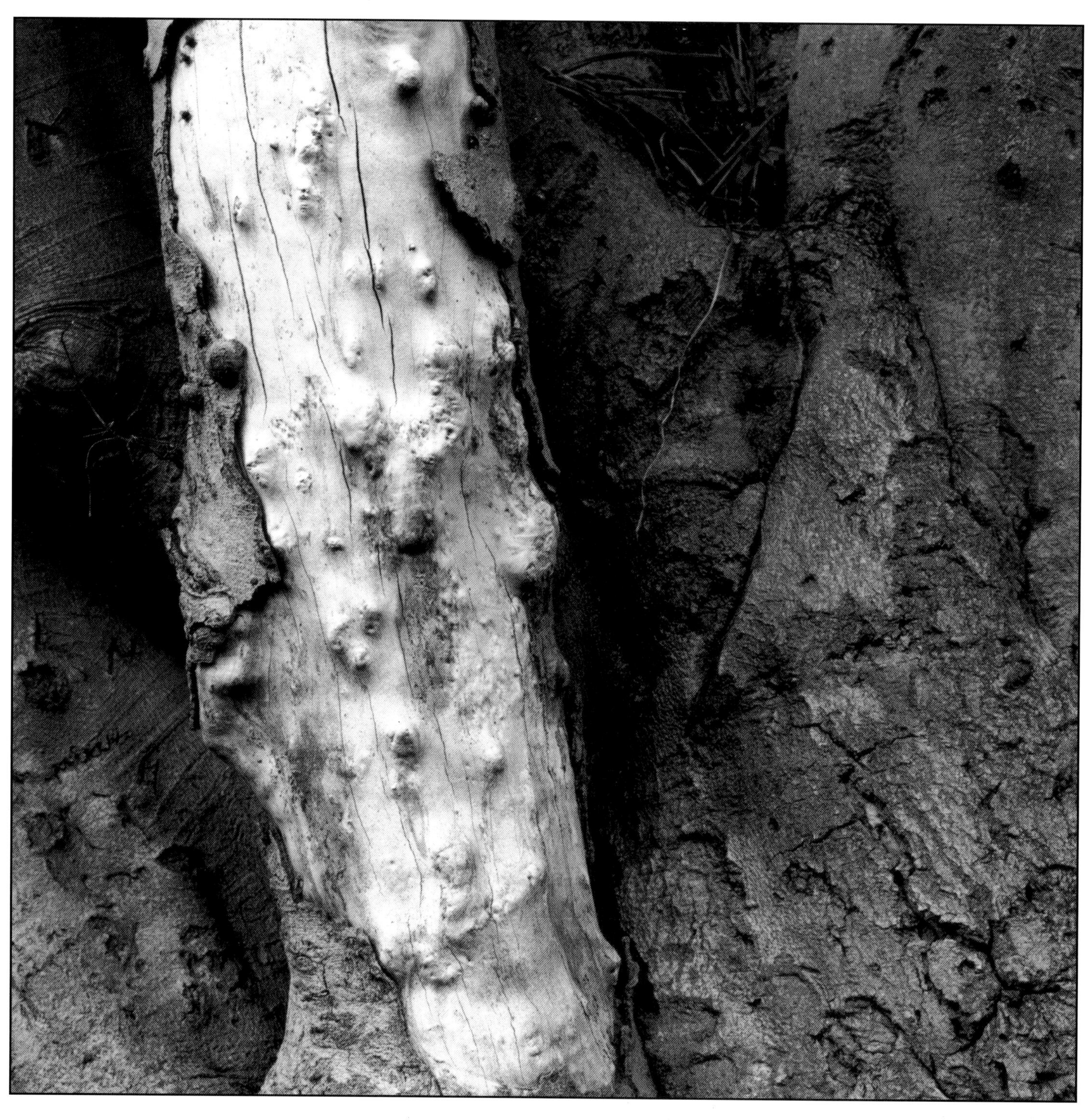

96
Wounded, Cheadle, Staffordshire
Kevin Bridgwood

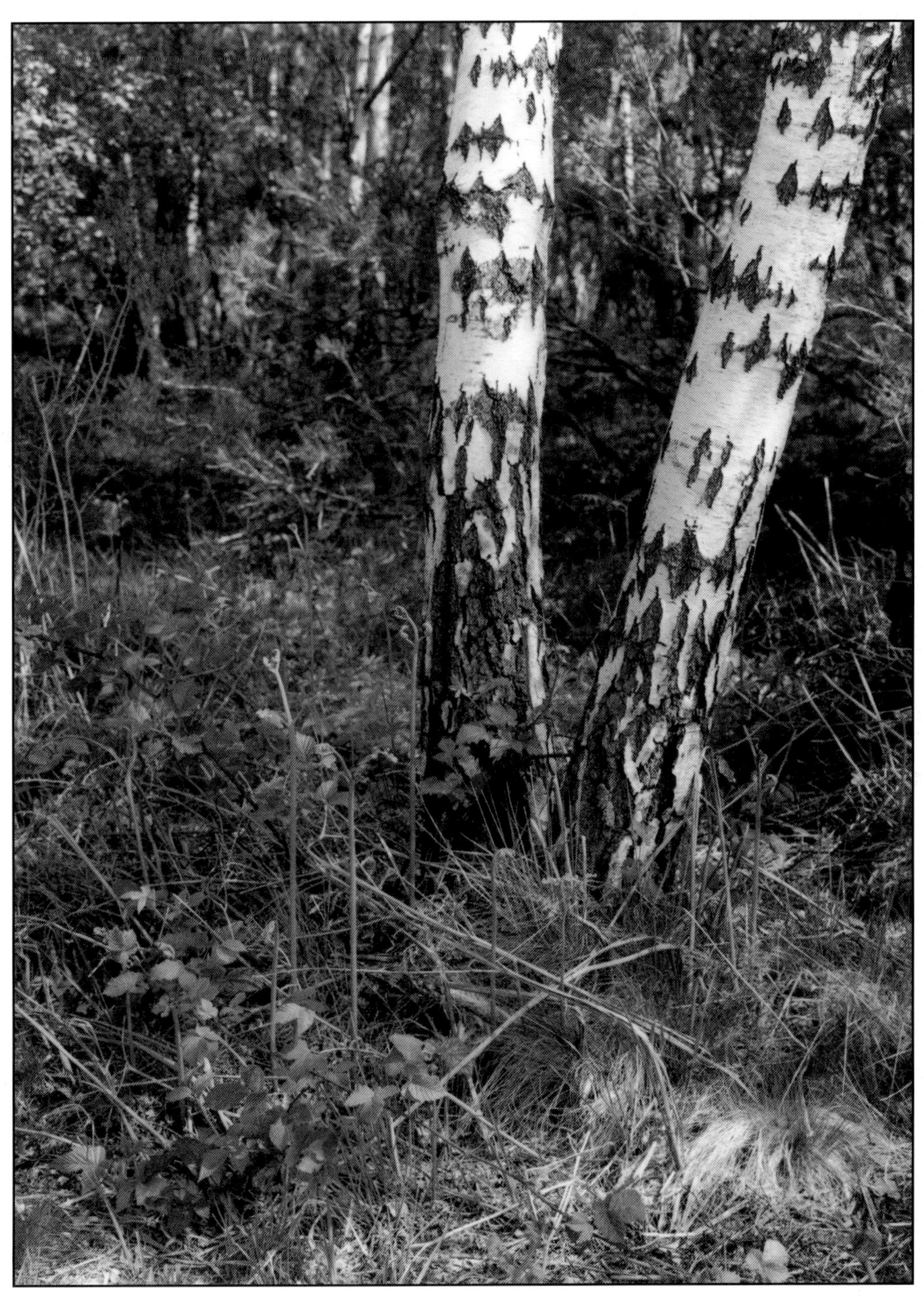

97
Silver birches
Frank Phillips

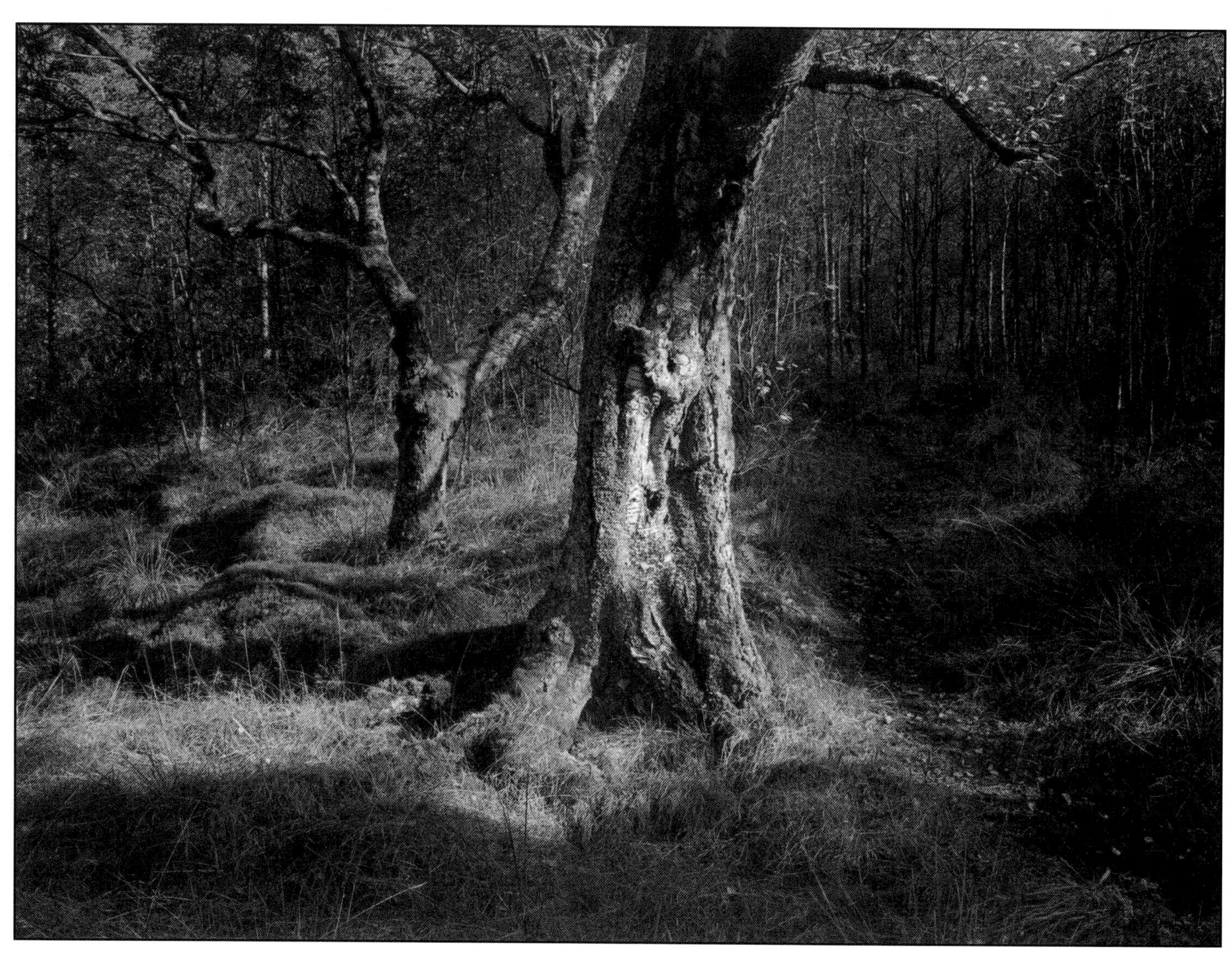

98
The enchanted wood
Ken Huscroft

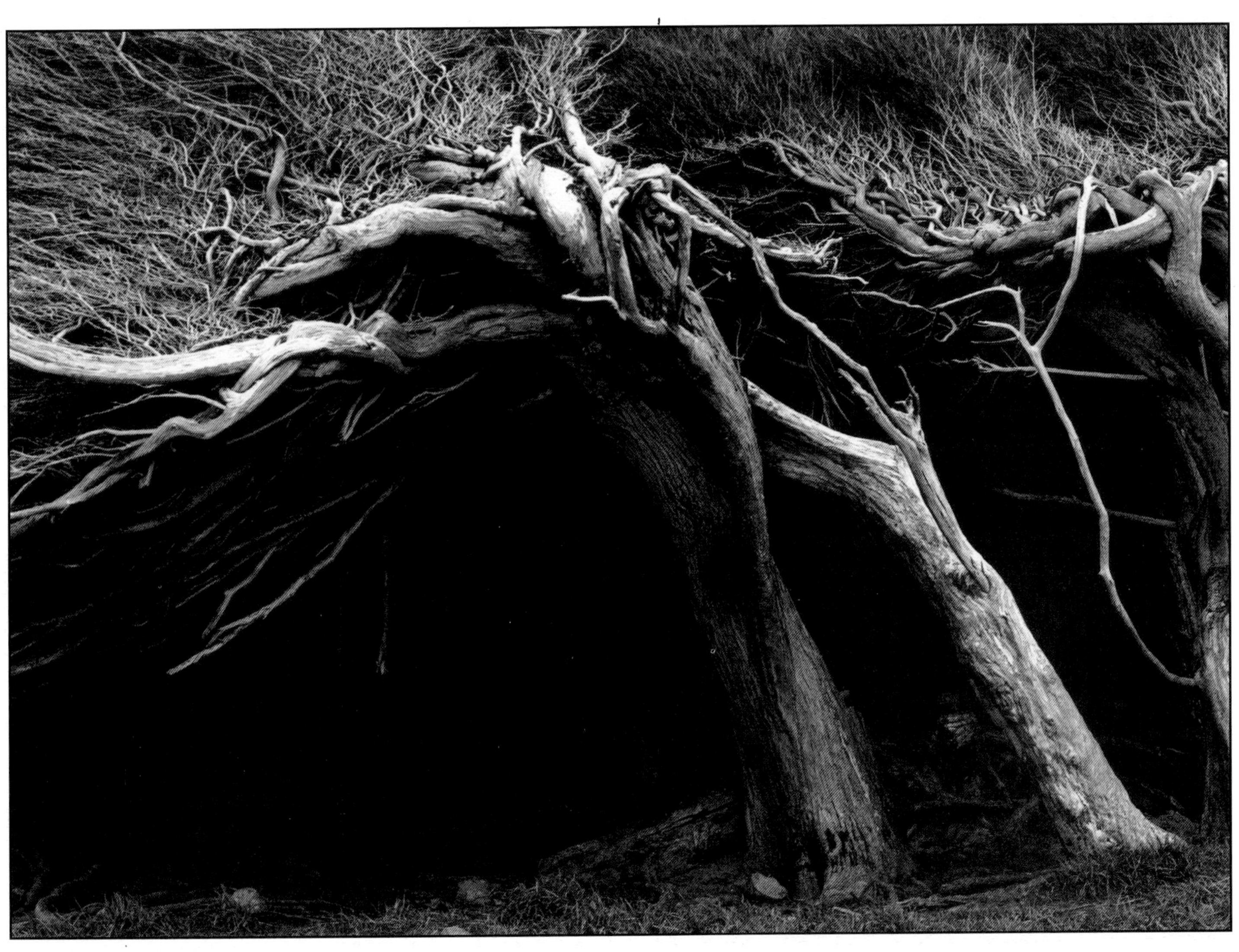

99
Catlin's, New Zealand
Ton van der Laan

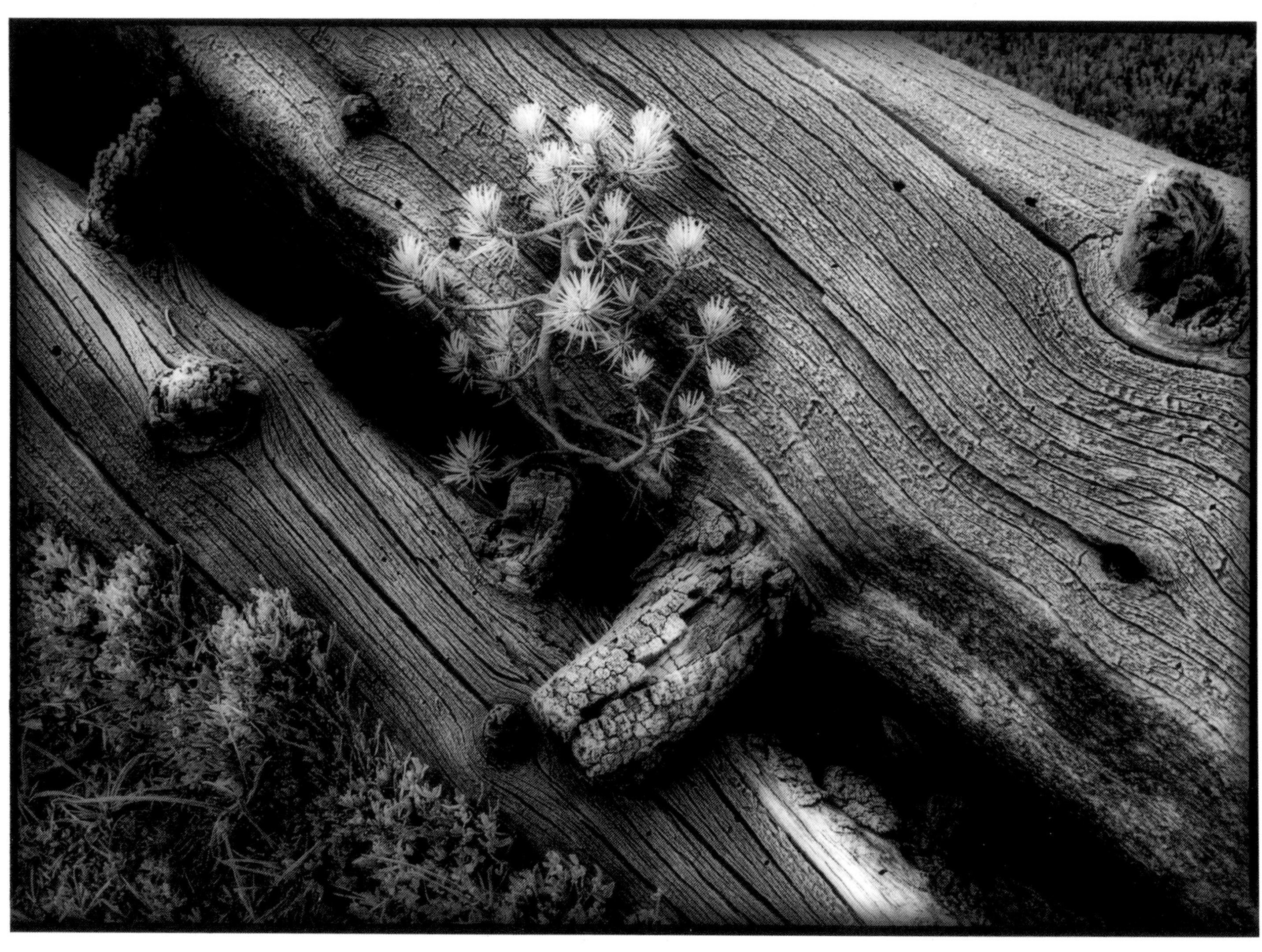

100
Early morning frost
Göran Stenberg

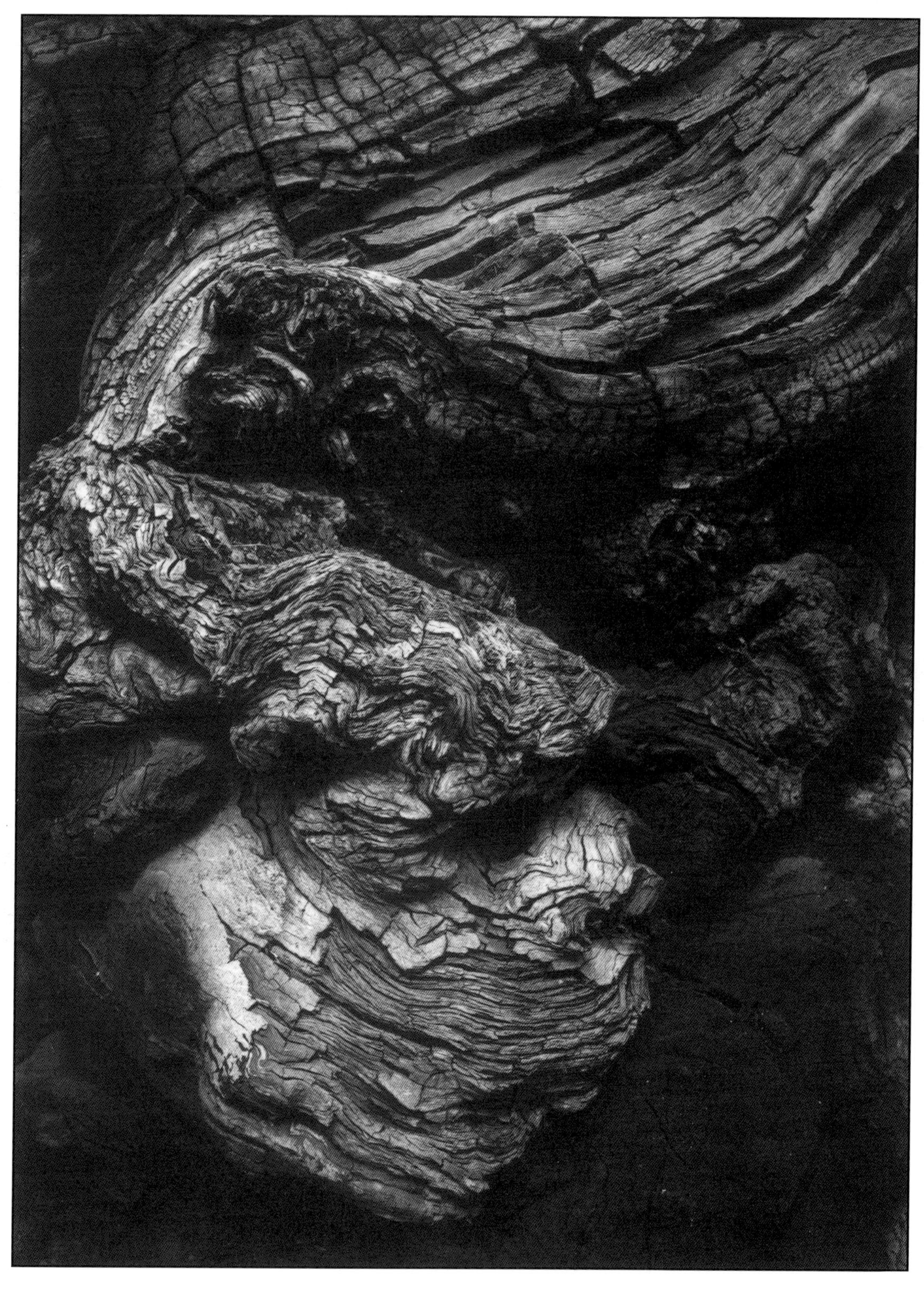

101
Spanish chestnut tree detail
Trevor Crone

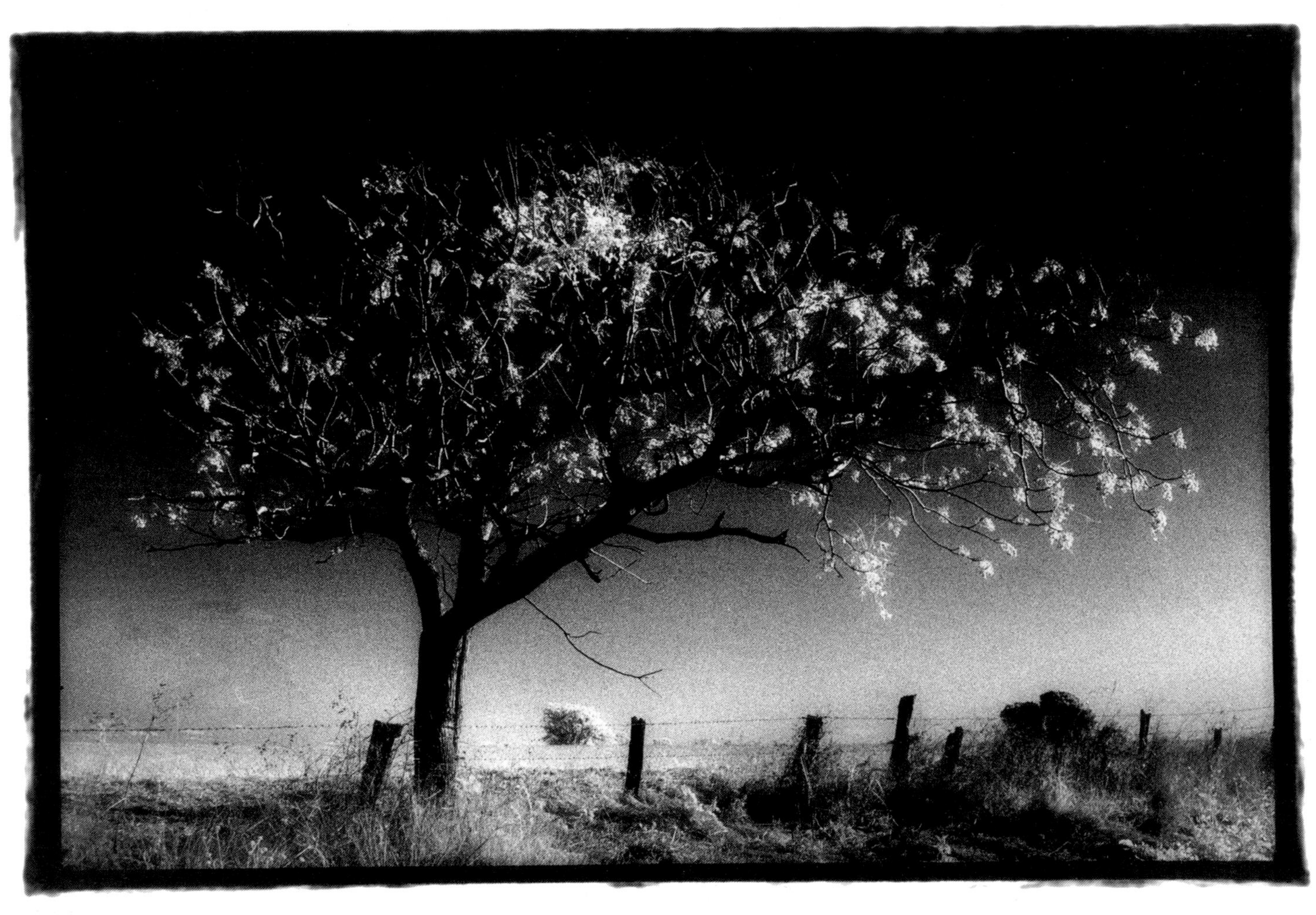

102
Flame tree
Dawn Heath

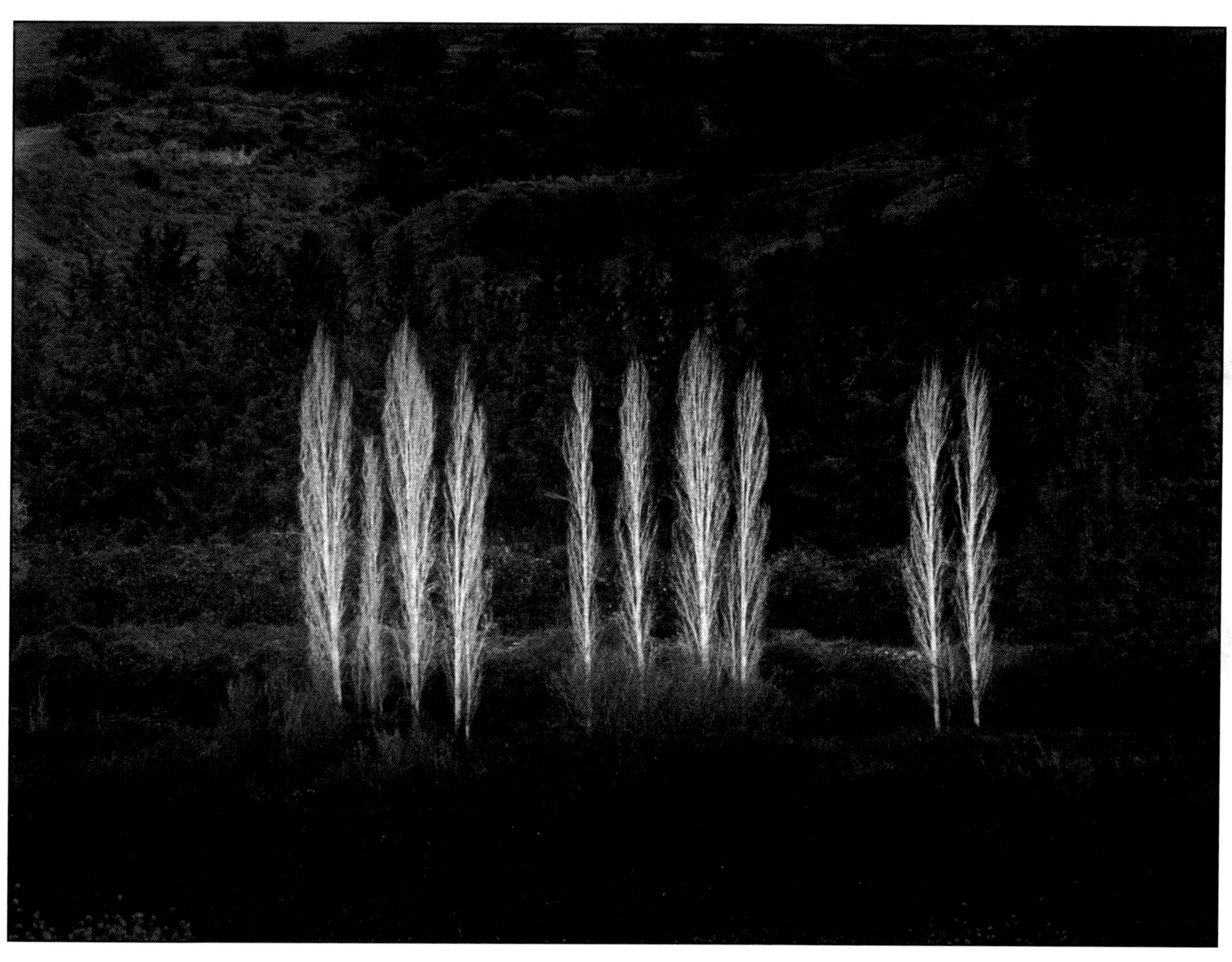

103
Poplars
David Herrod

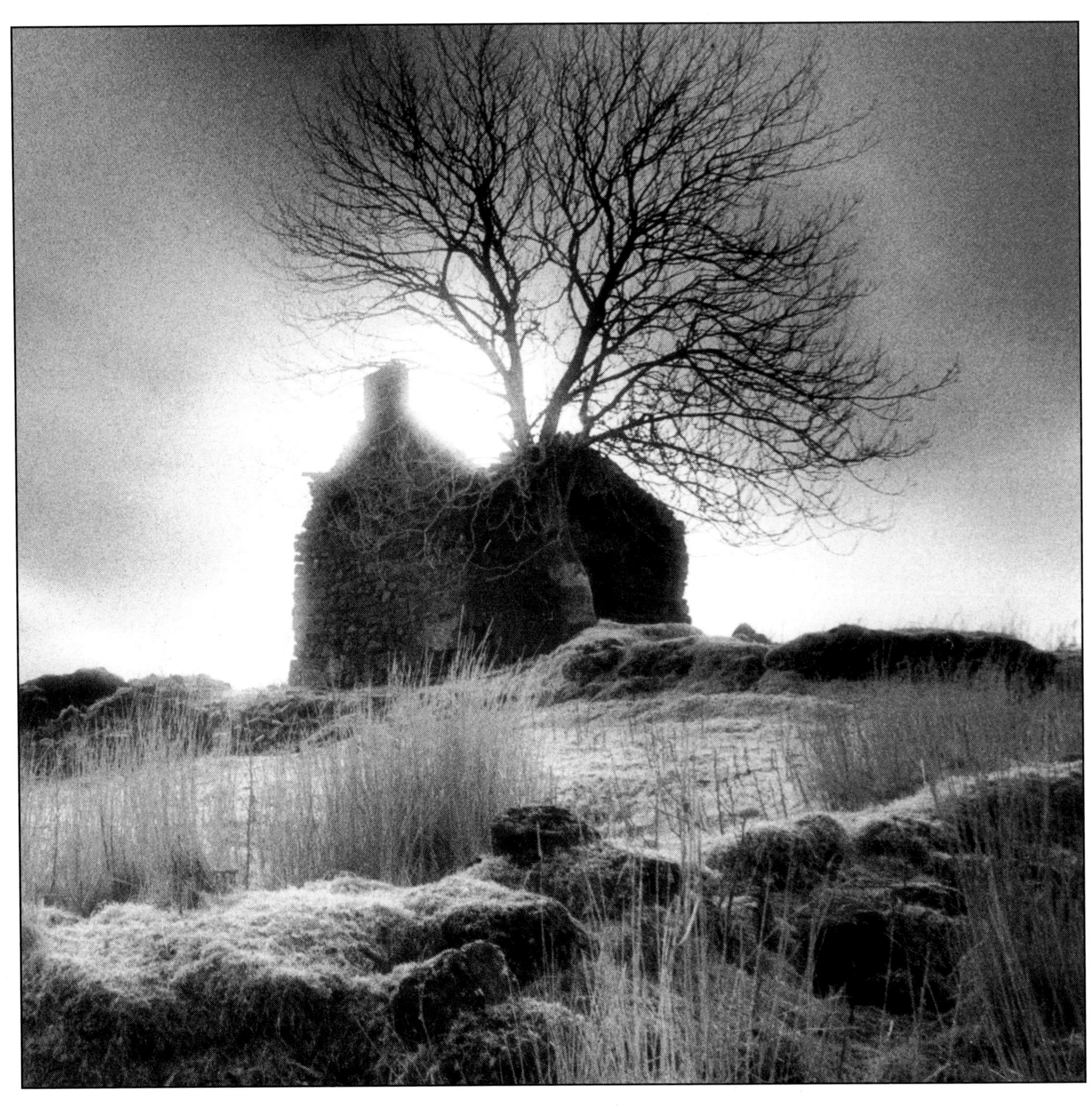

104
Sunrise
Victor Kelly

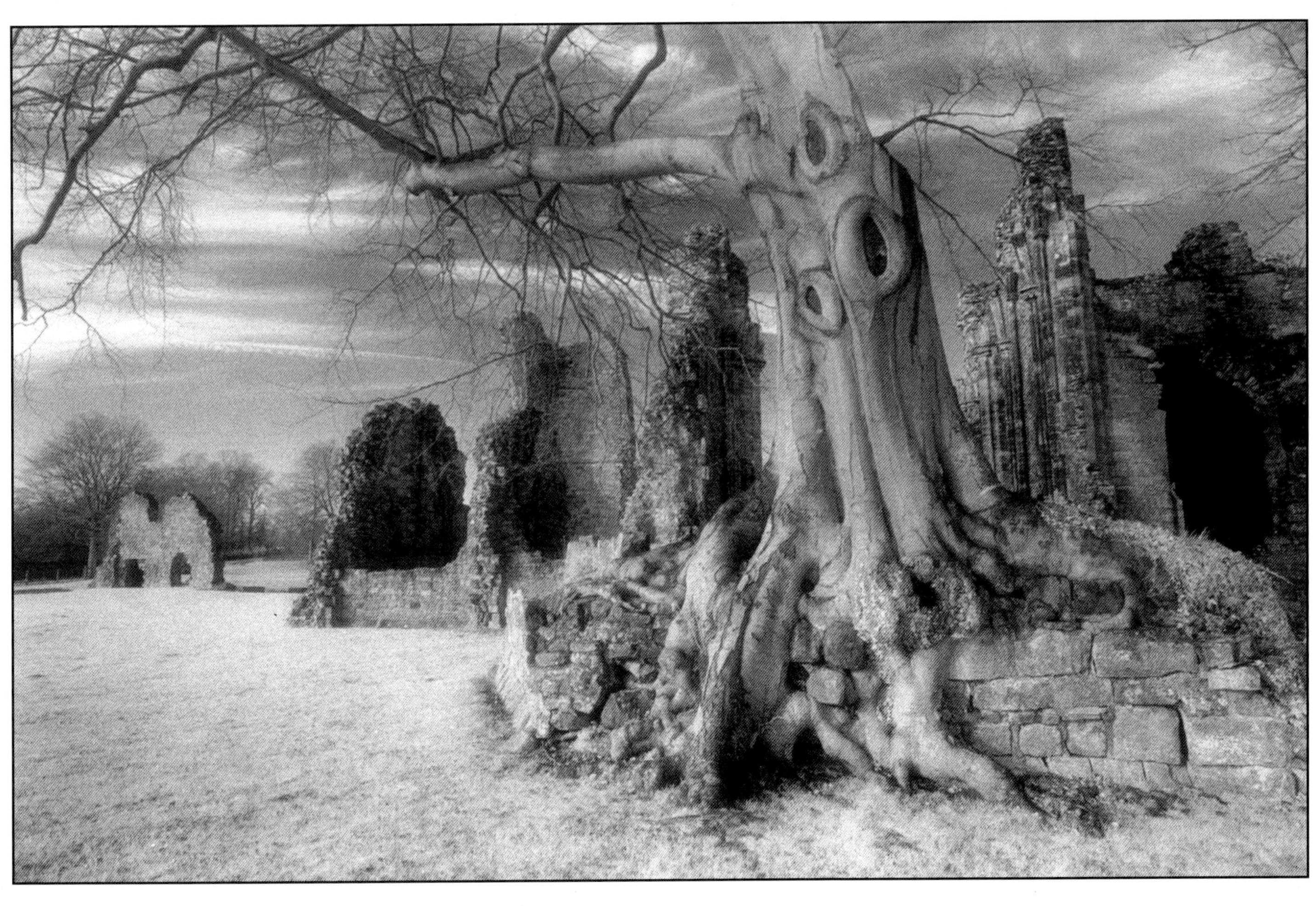

105
The tree at Bayham Abbey
David Dixon

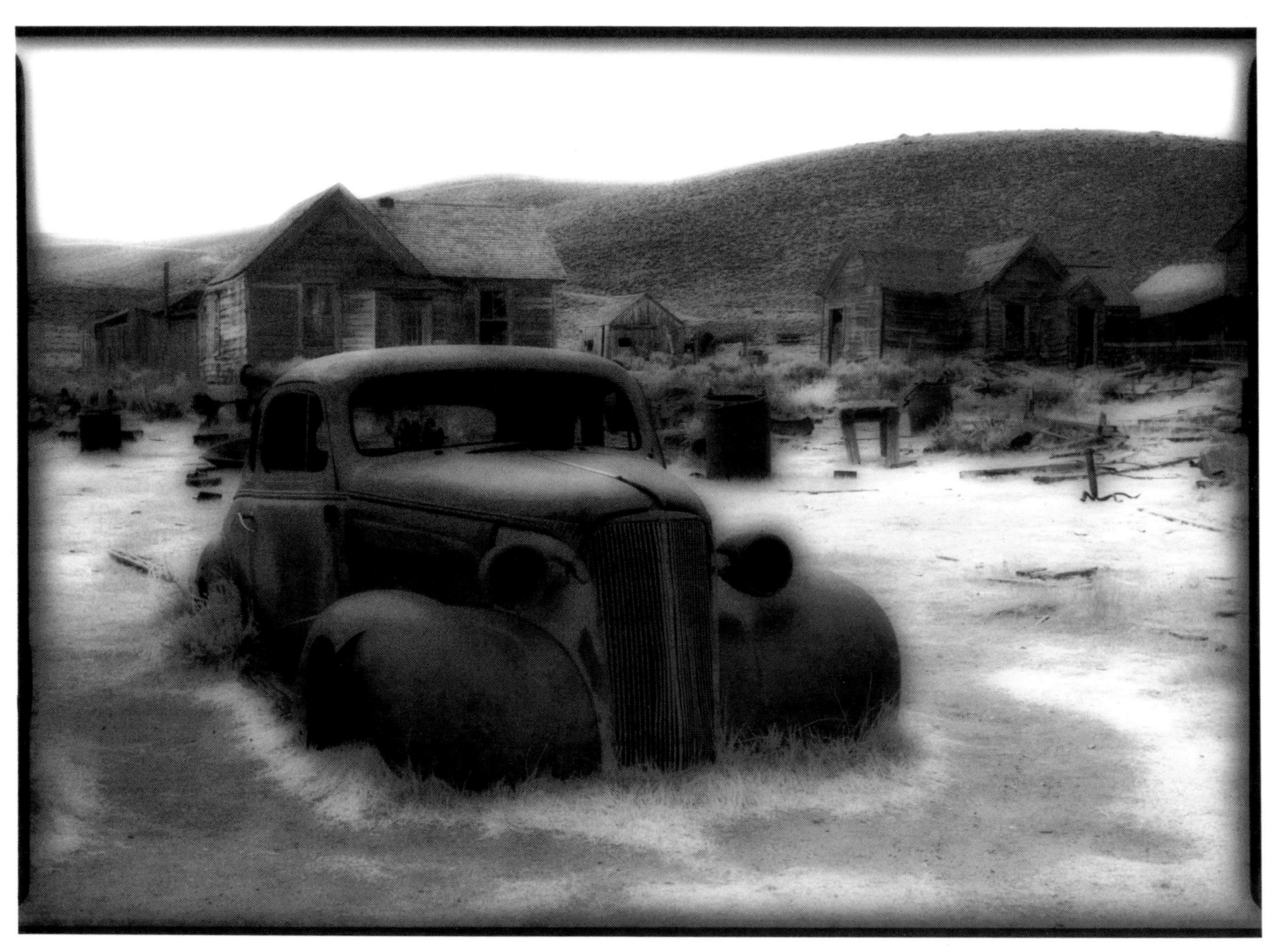

106
Ghost town, Bodie, California
Göran Stenberg

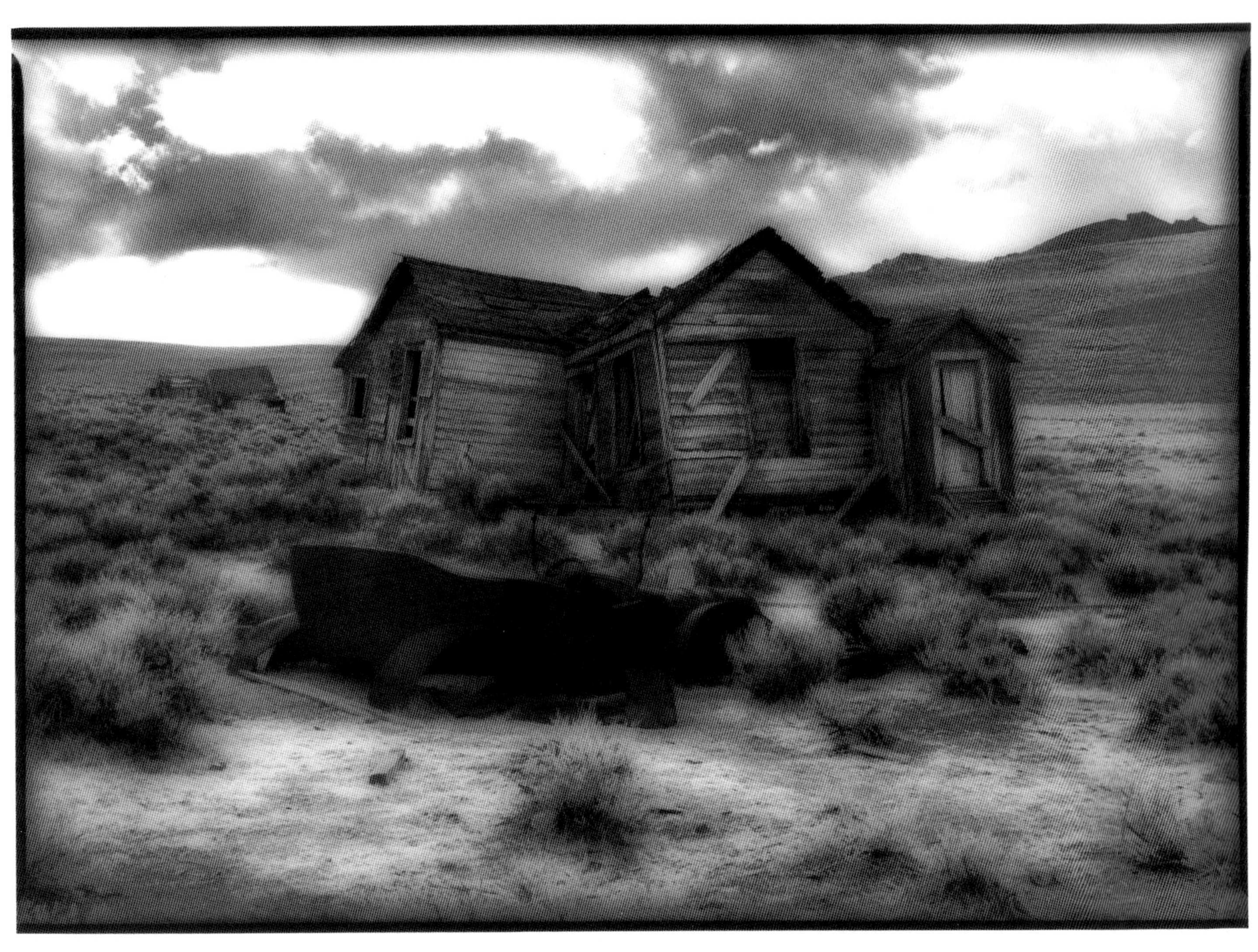

107
Ghost town, Bodie, California
Göran Stenberg

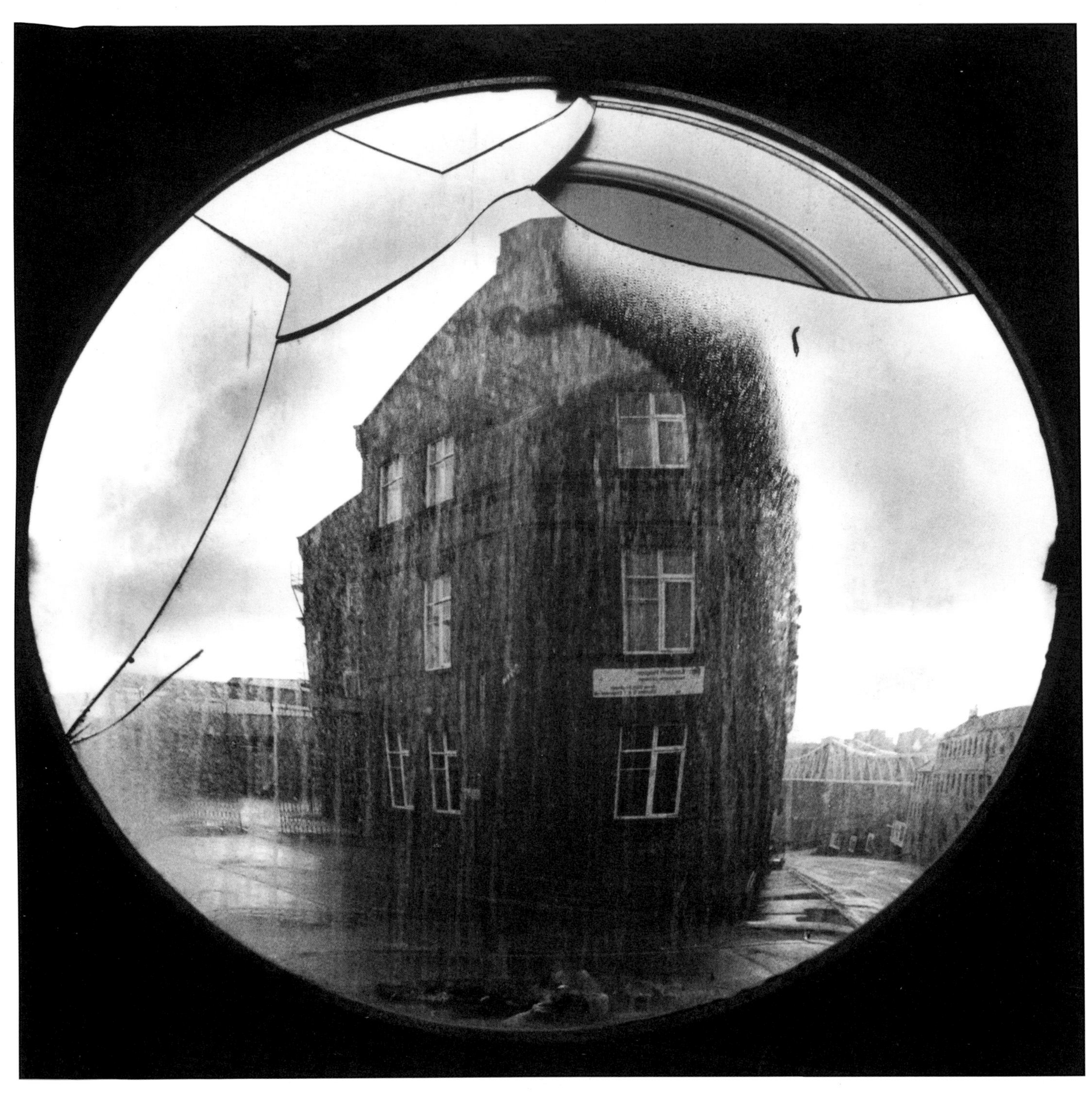

108
Image of industrial decay
Arnold Hubbard

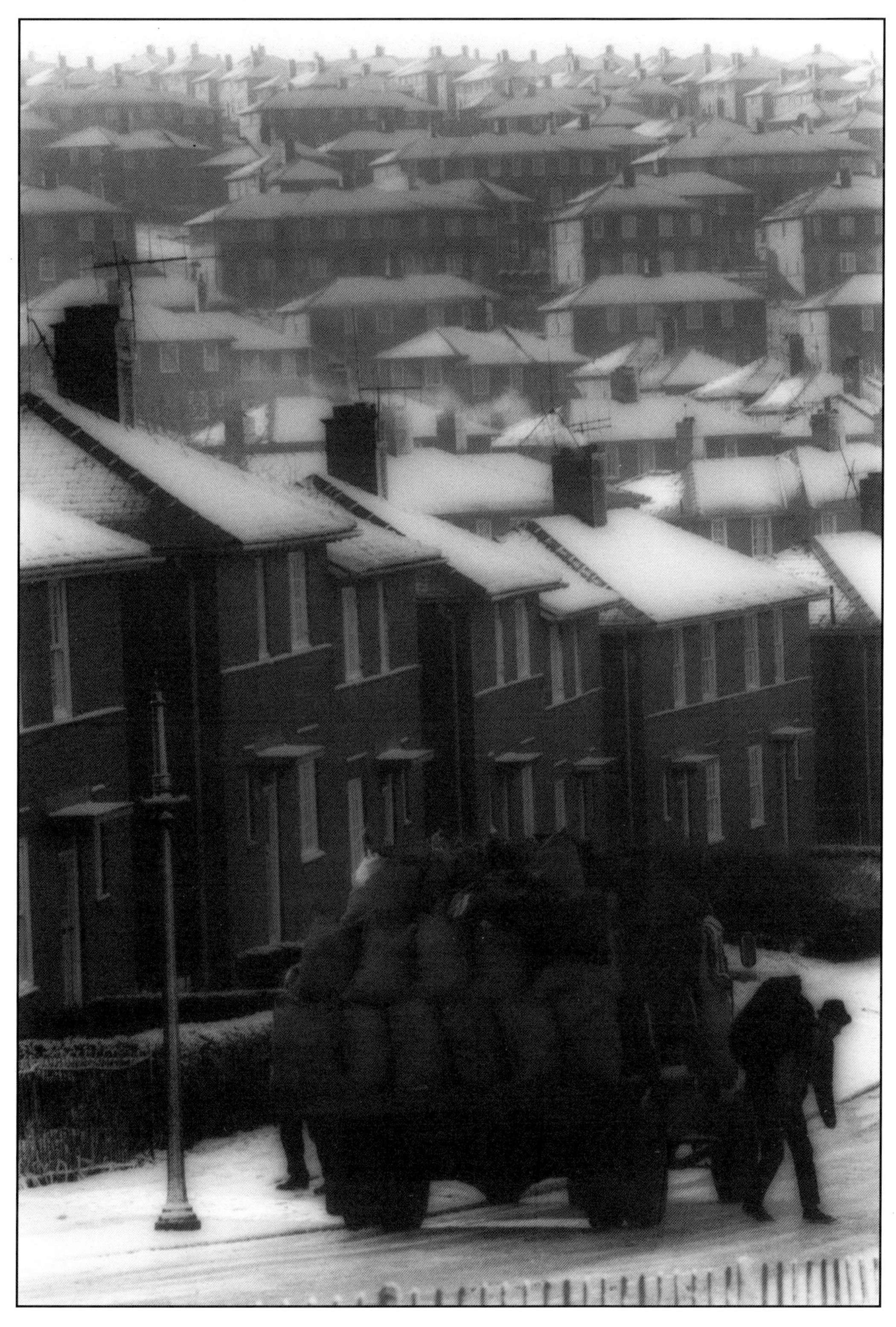

109
Coal delivery, Sheffield
Mike Coles (London)

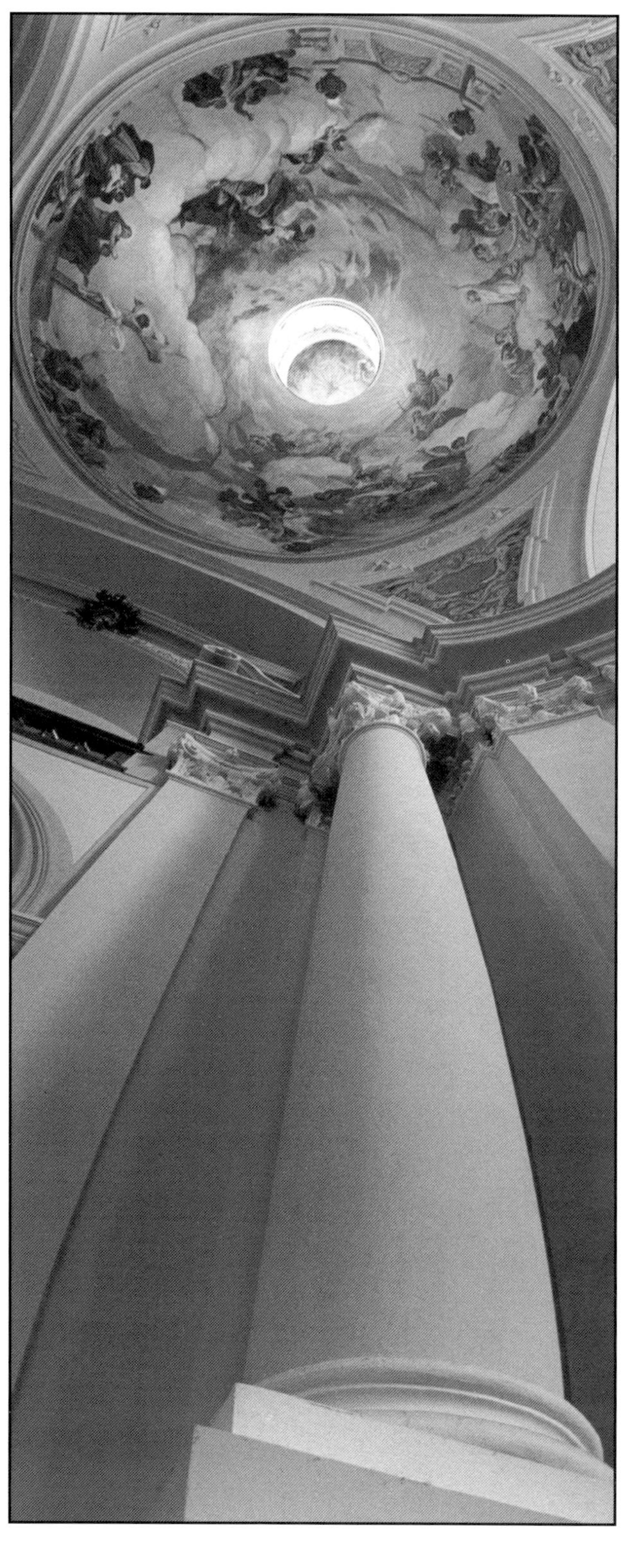

110
Architecture I
Jiri Bartos

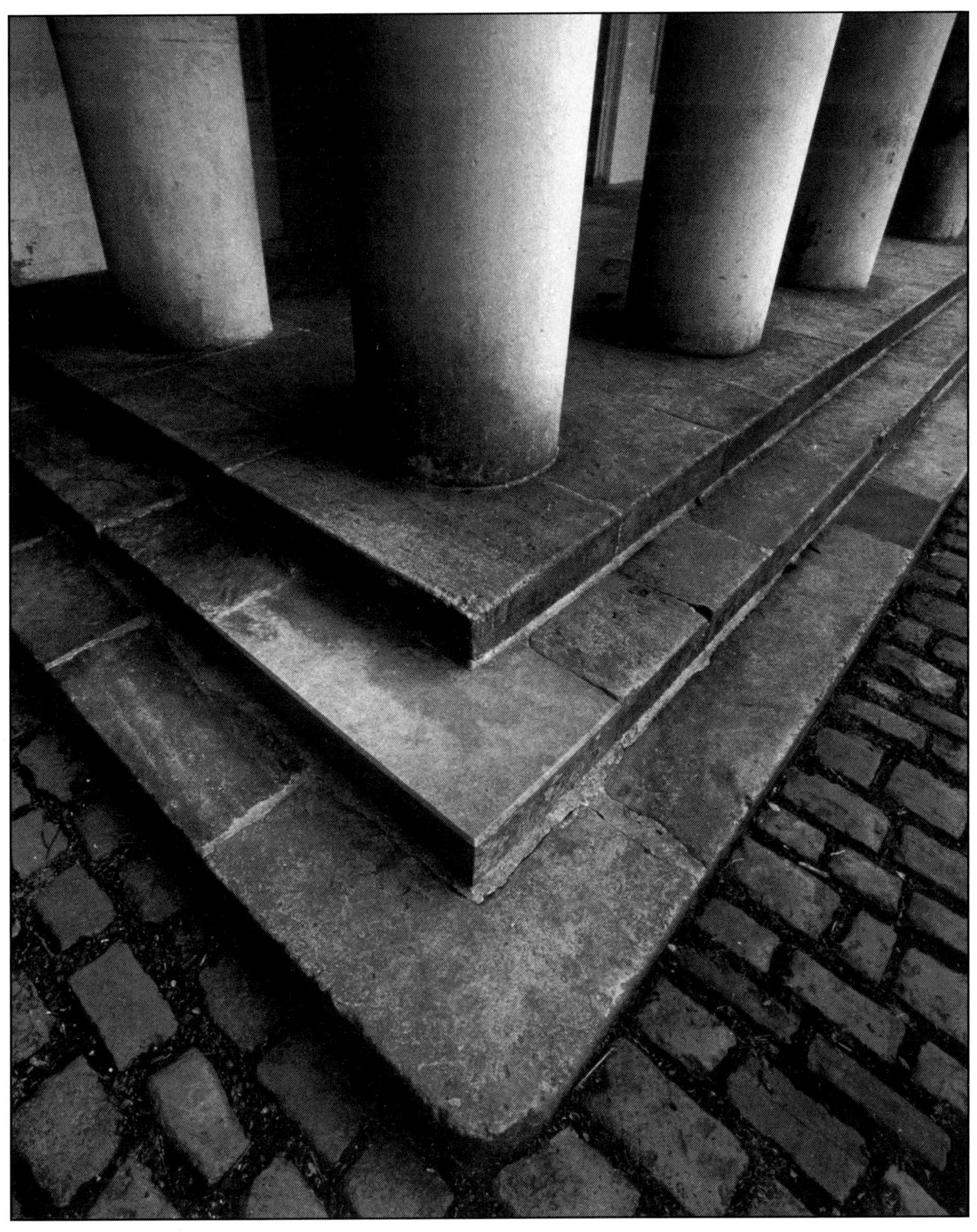

111
Steps and columns
Laurie Scott

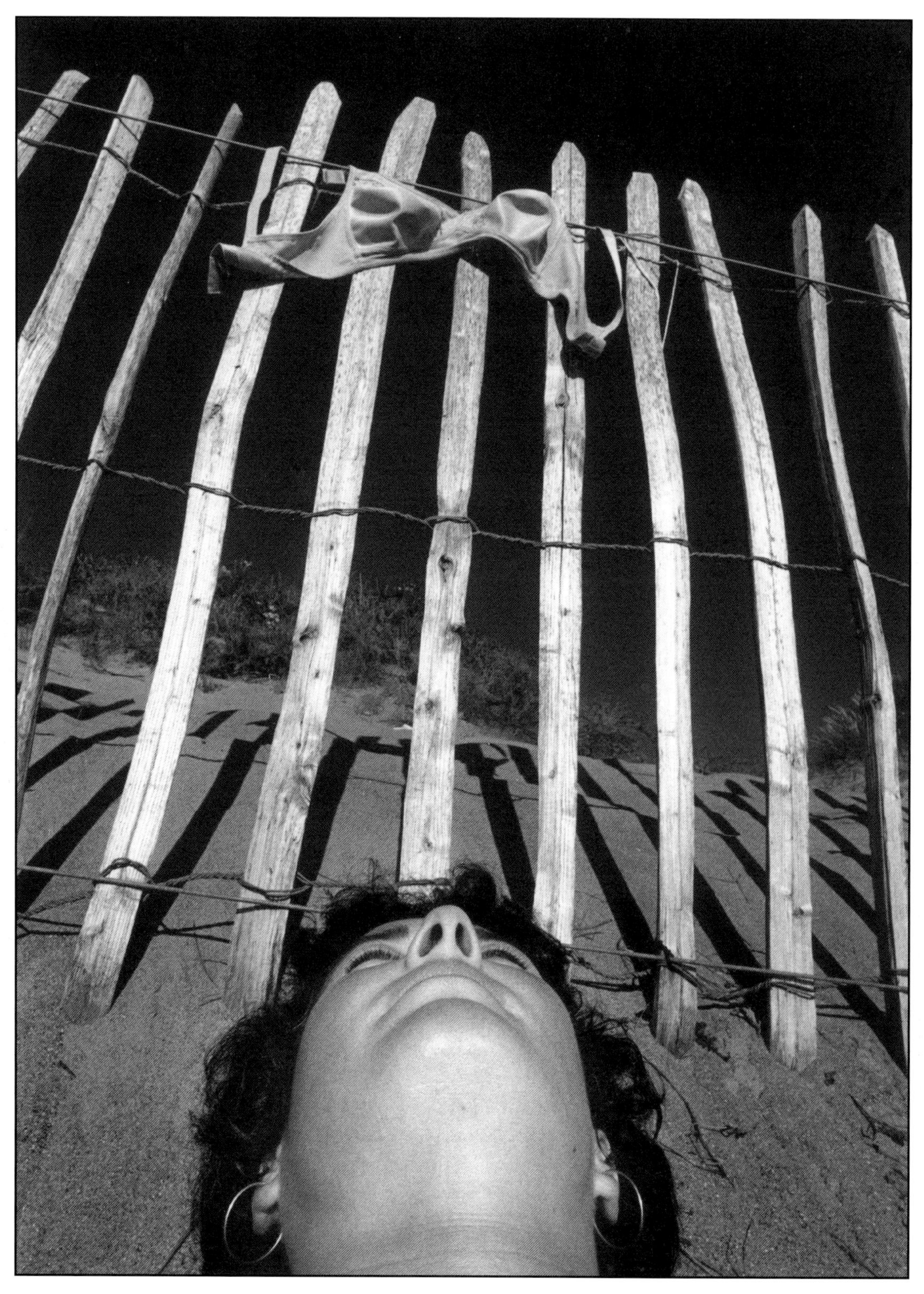

112
On the beach
Tom Dodd

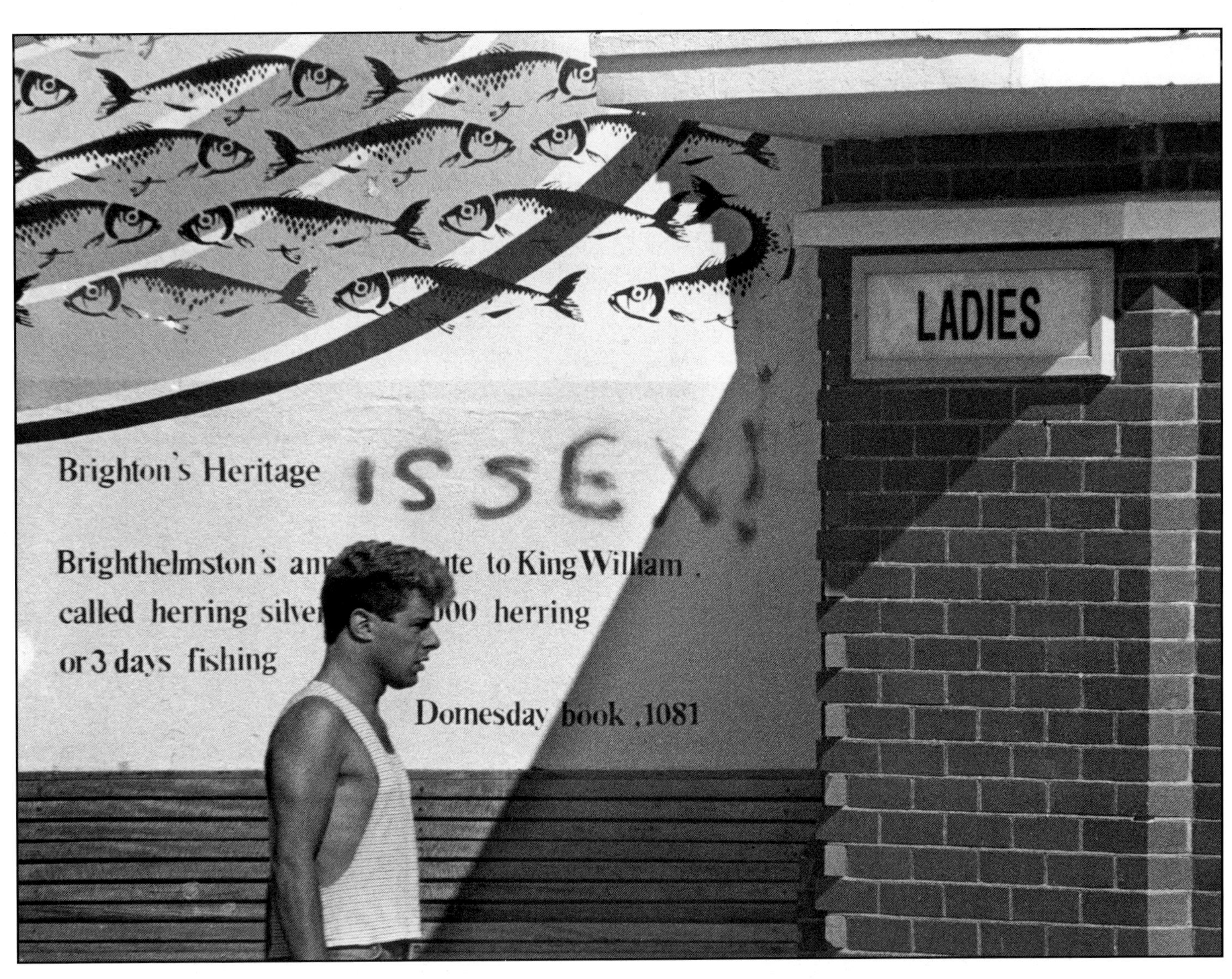

113
Brighton
David Valdes

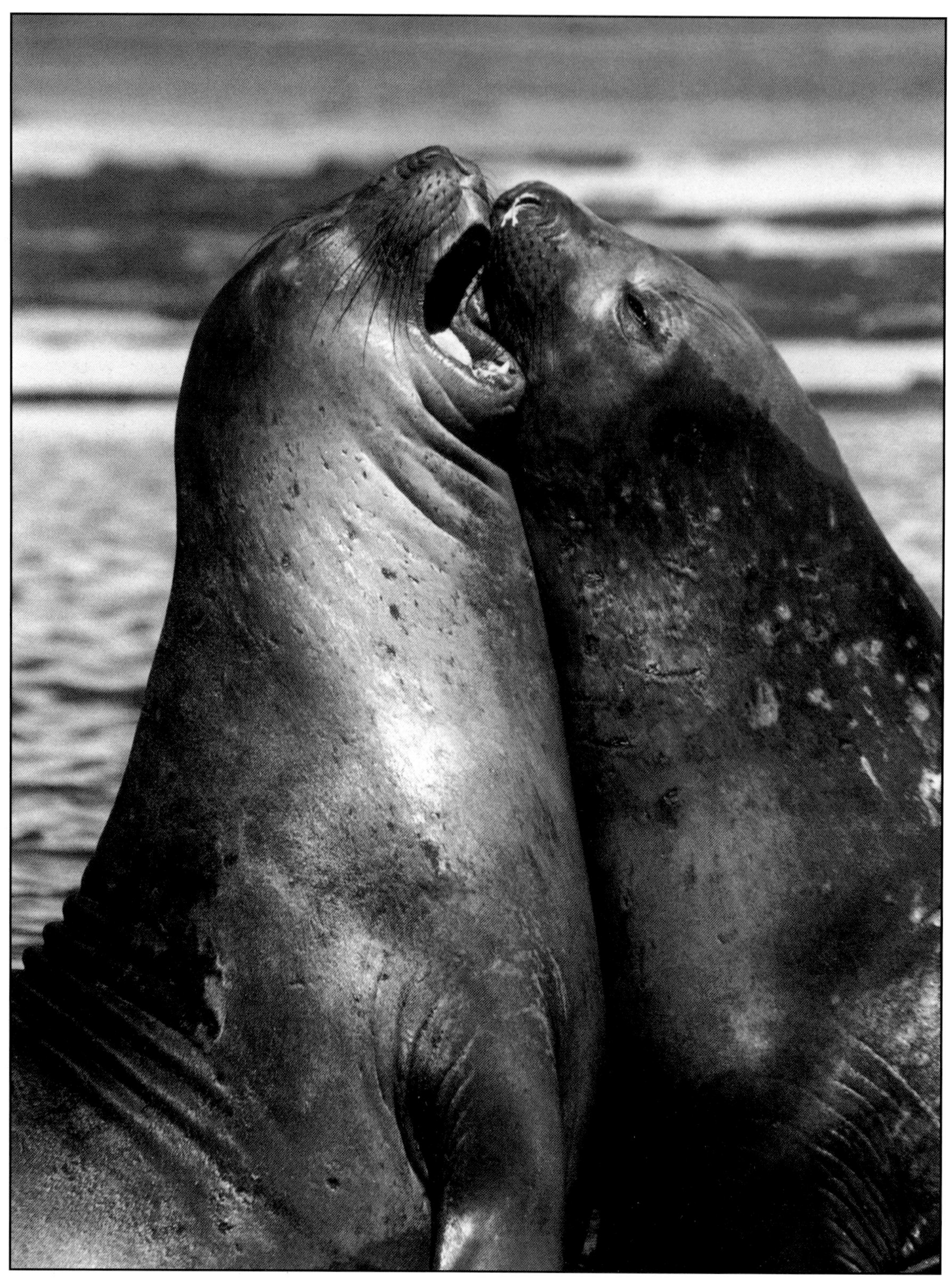

114
Battle scarred
David Conway

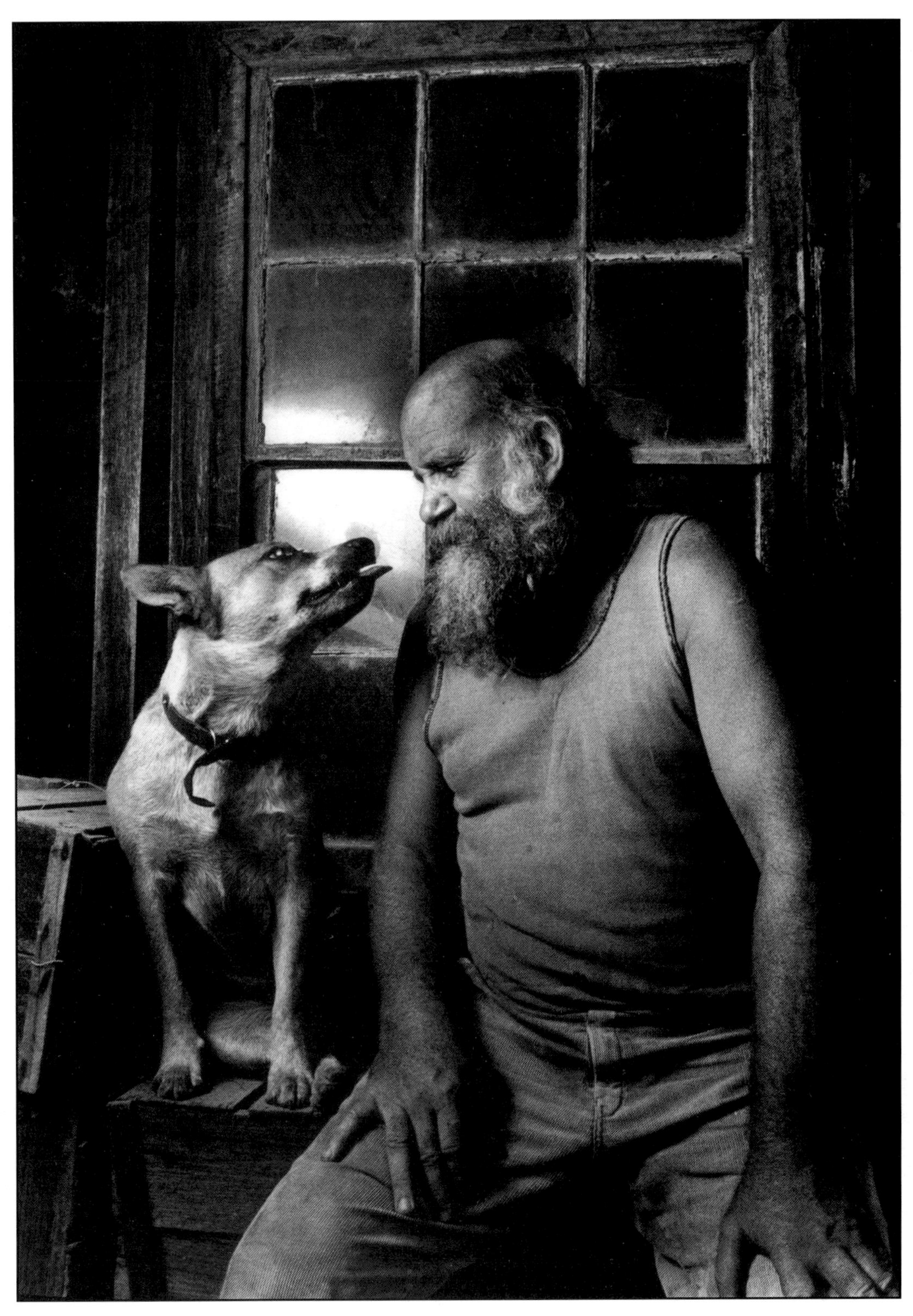

115
Cheeky boy
David Mahony

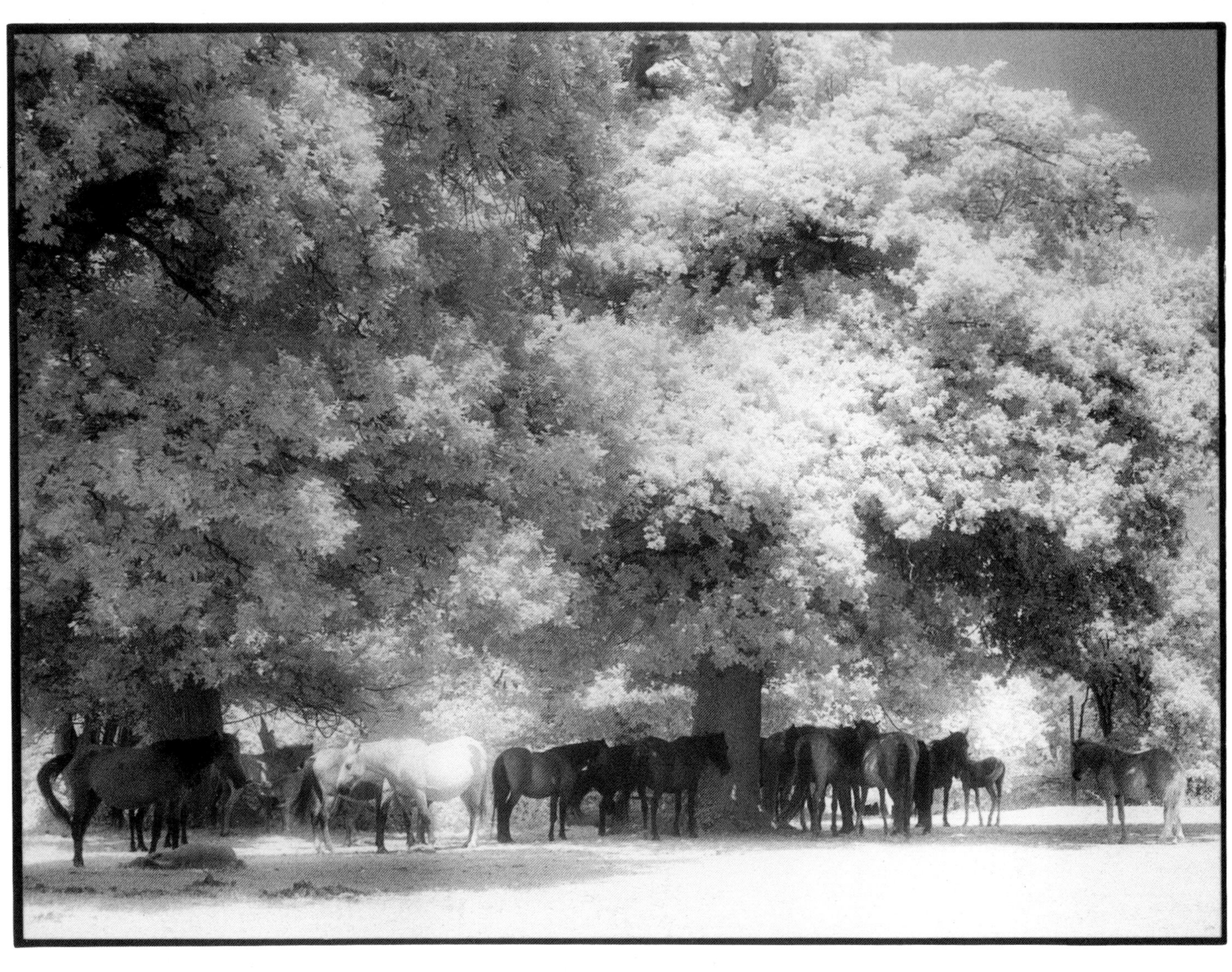

116
The gathering
Kathleen Harcom

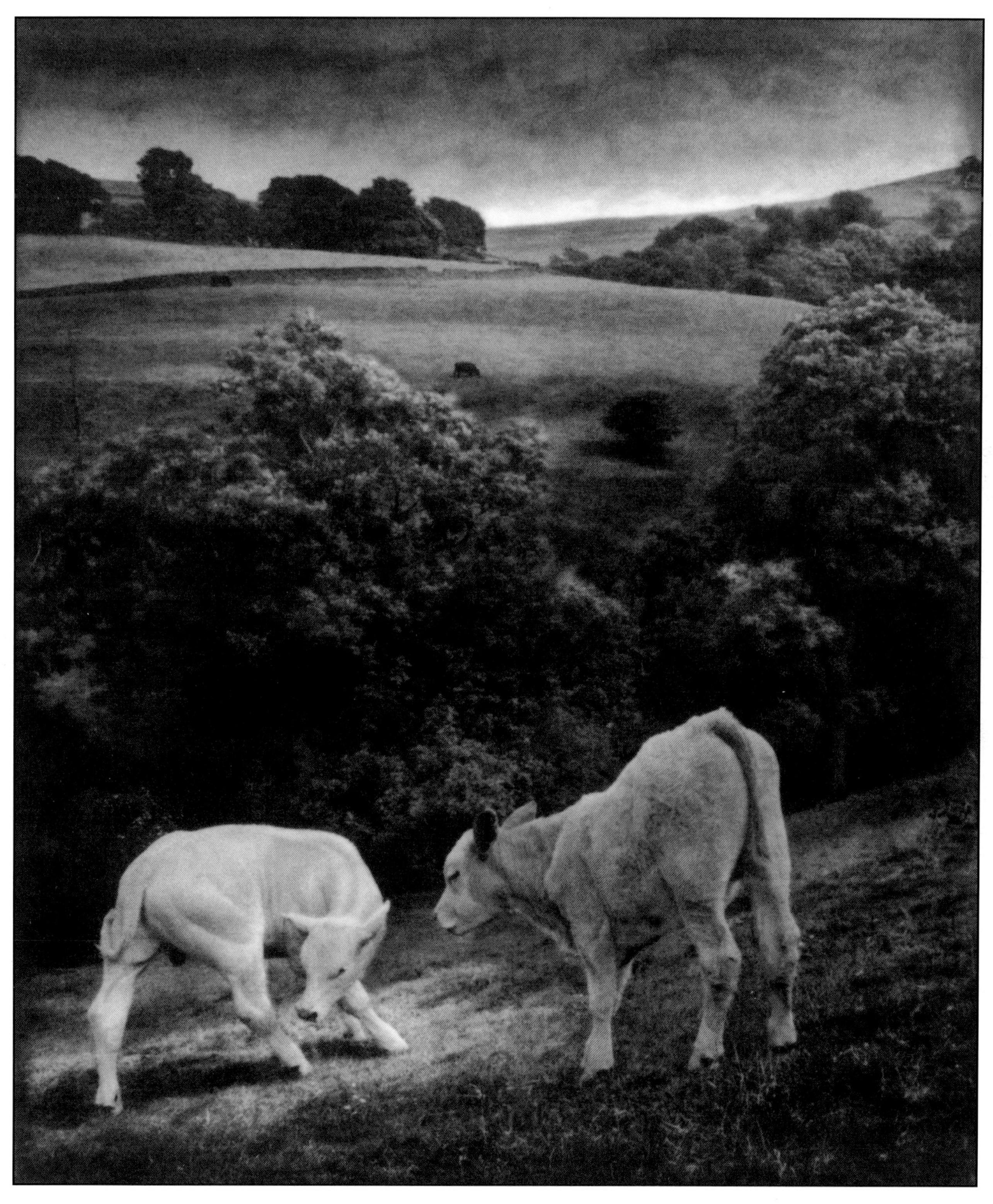

117
Two cows
Andrew Sanderson

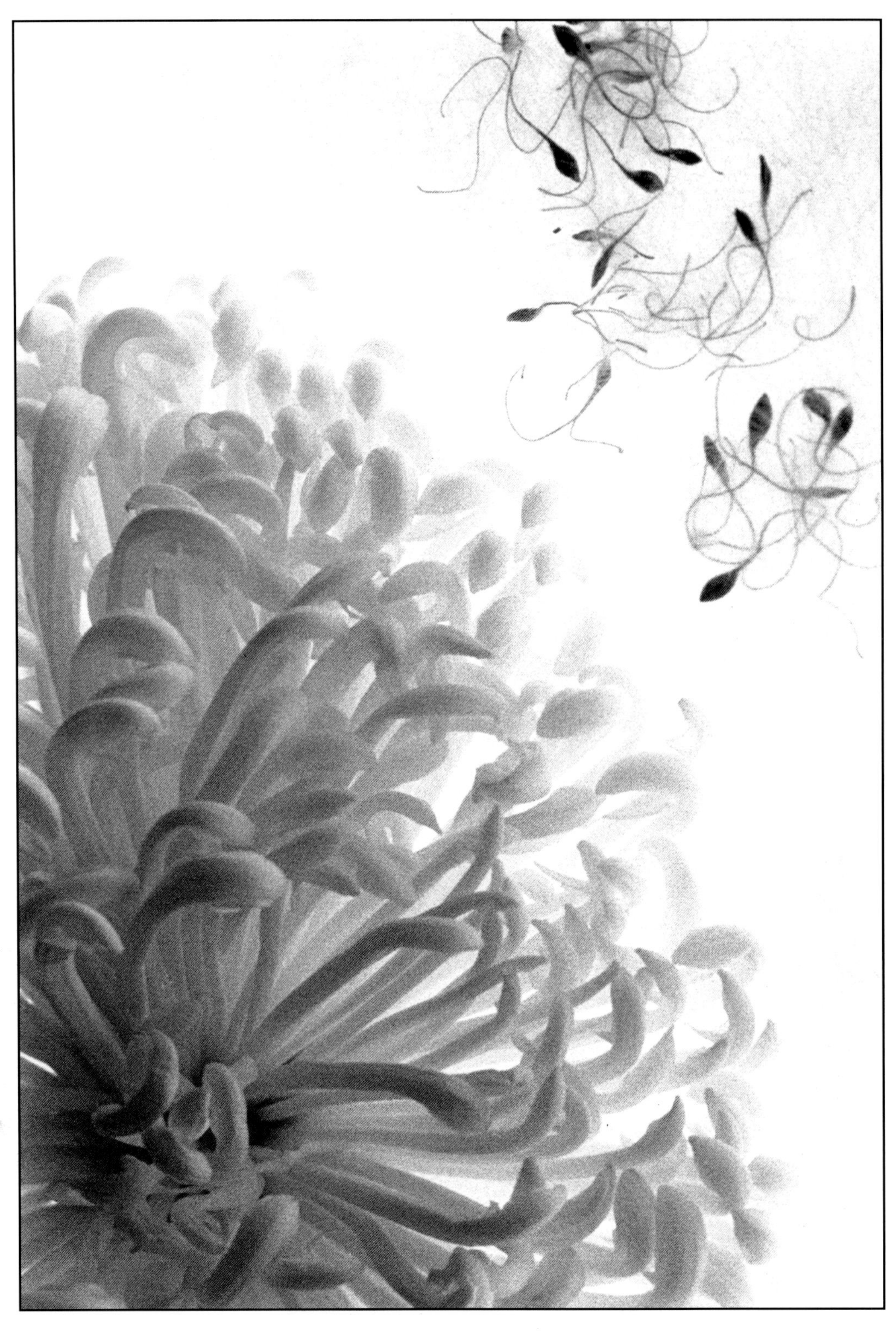

118
Untitled
Priscilla Thomas

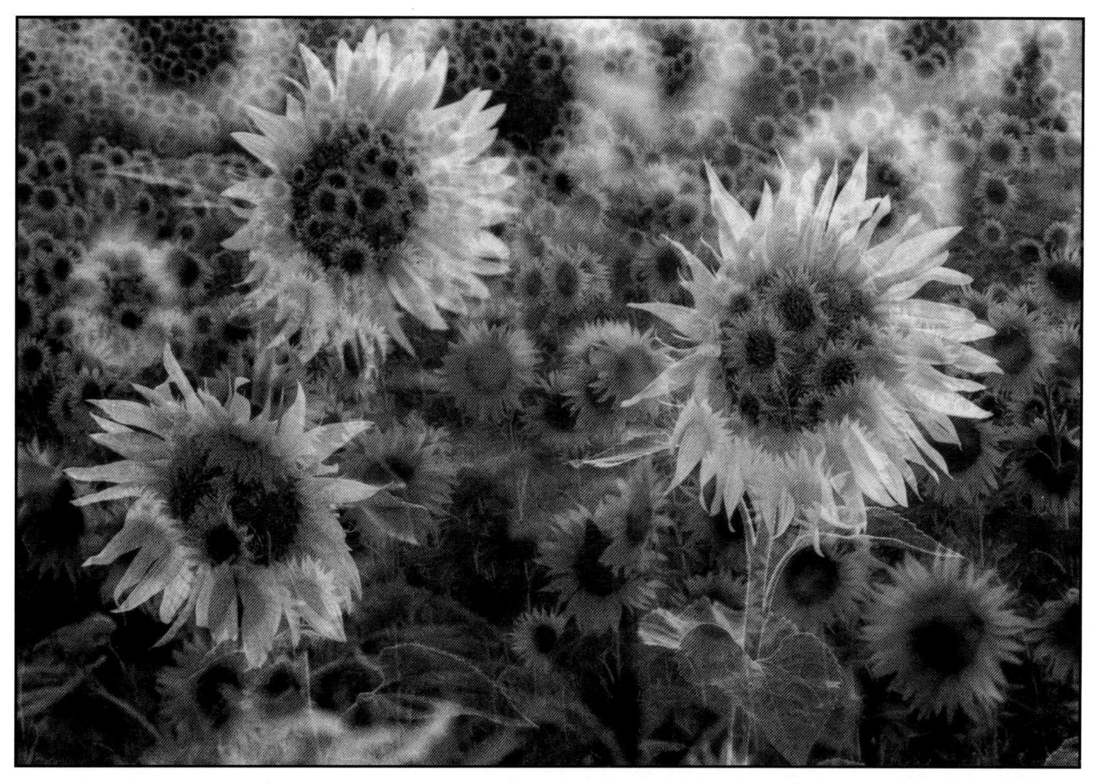

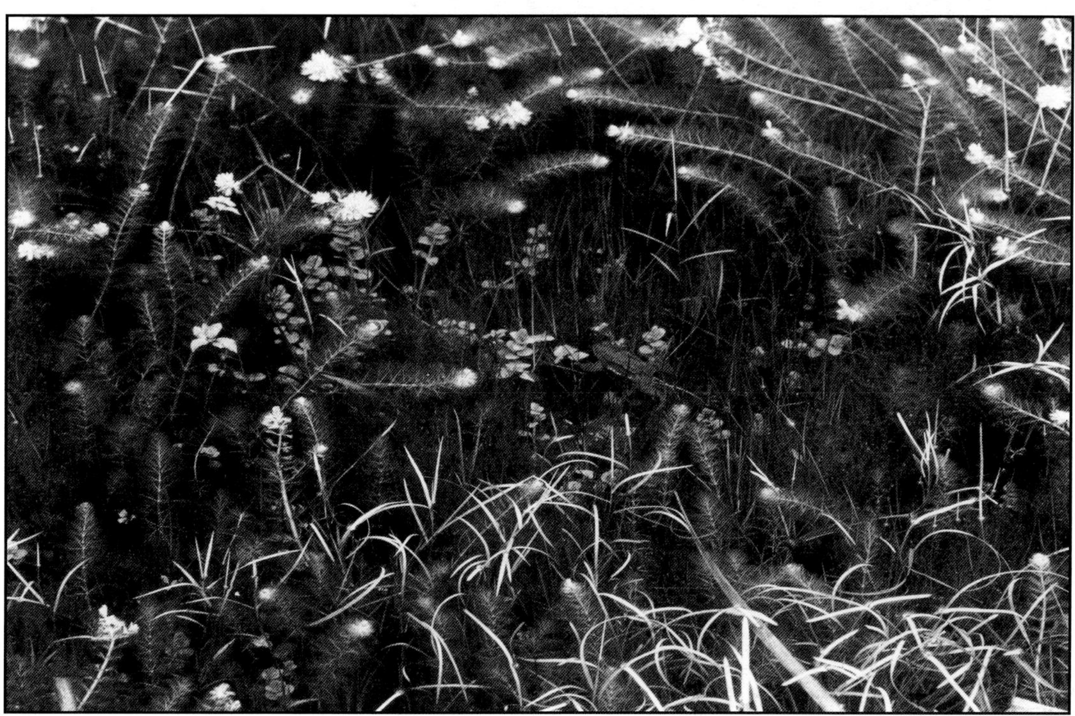

(top) 119, **Helios**, *Clive Haynes*
(below) 120, **Pond-life**, *Steve Cull*

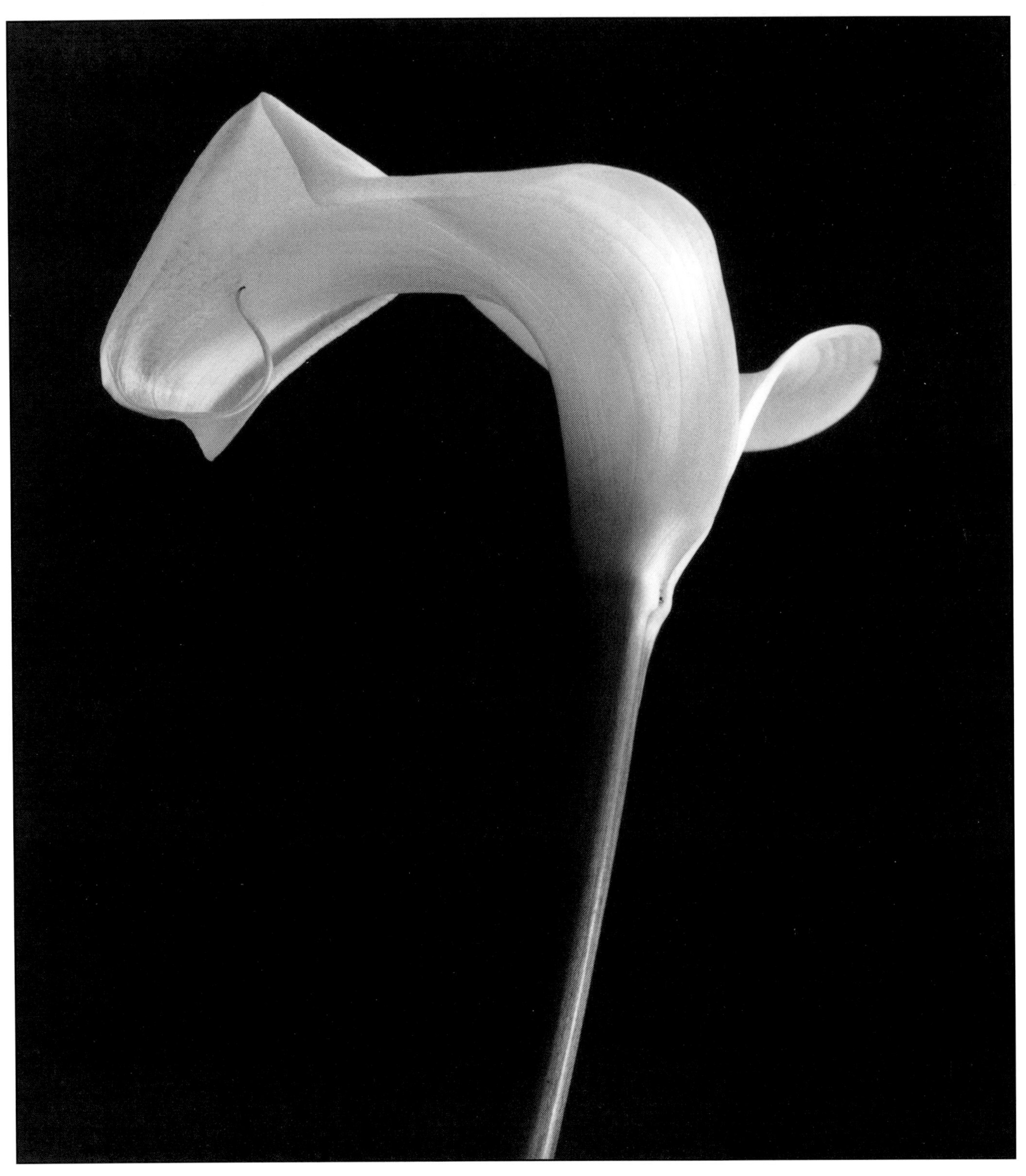

121
Arum #1
Mike Tinsley

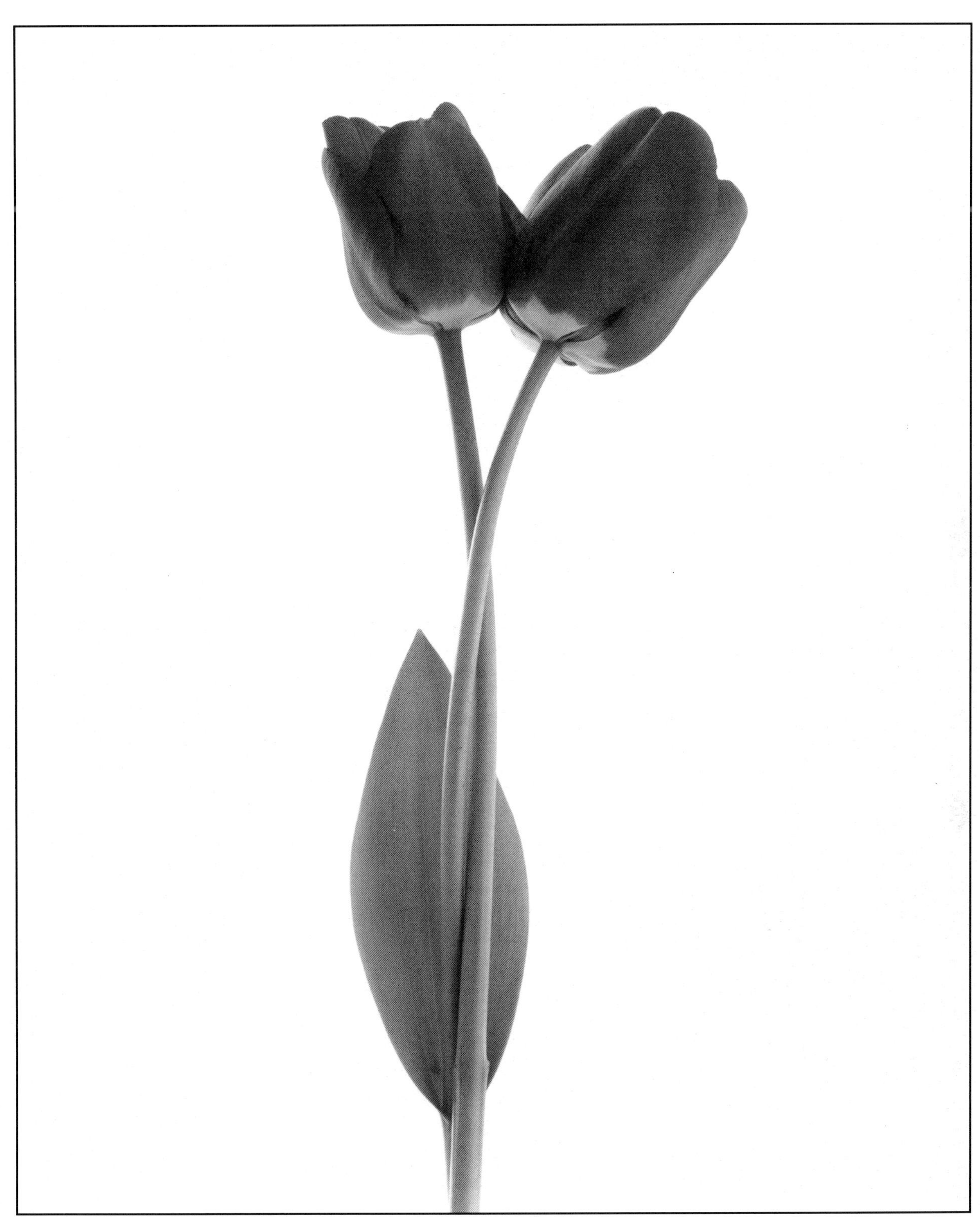

122
Tulips
Andrew Foley

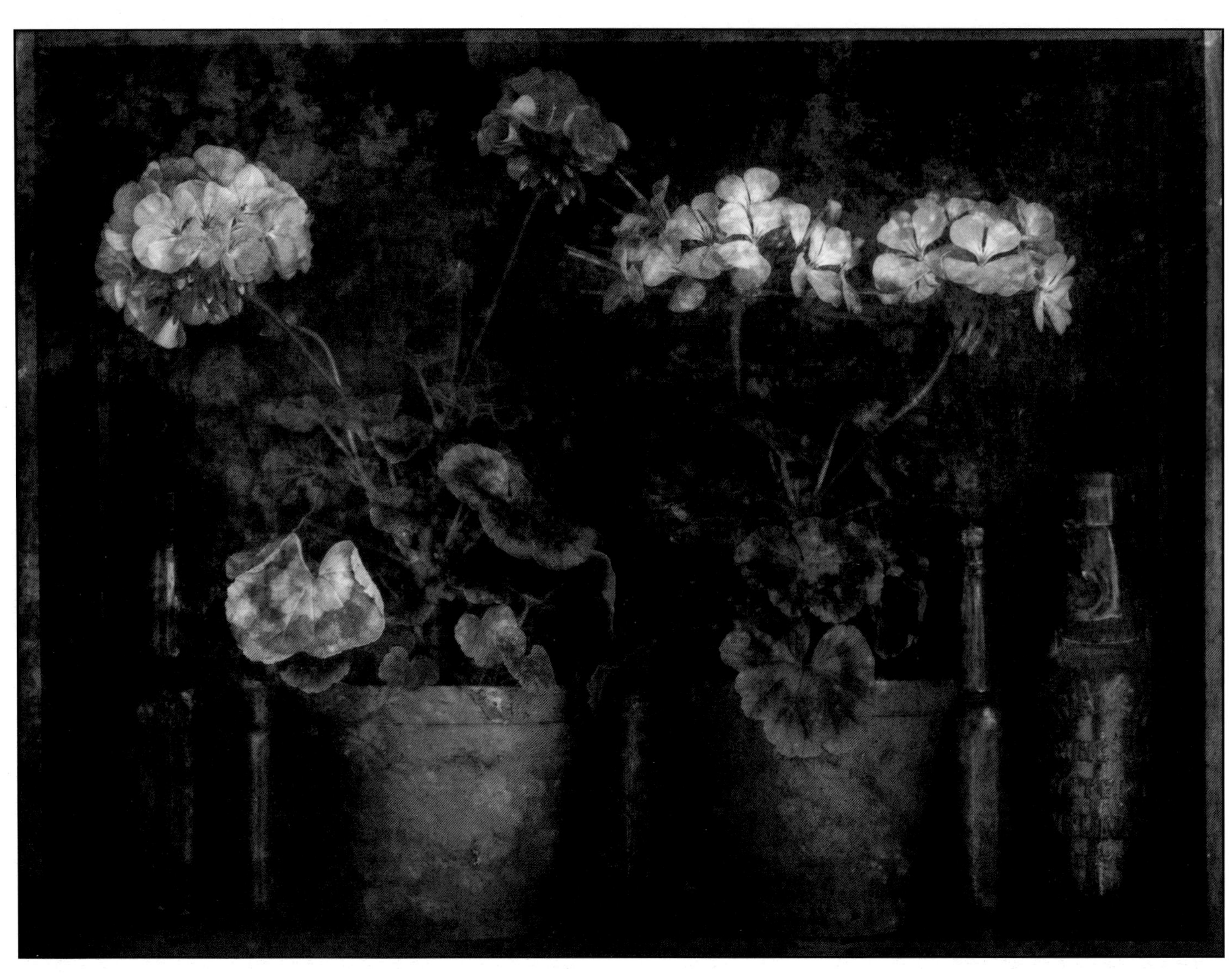

123
Potted Geraniums
Sue Davies

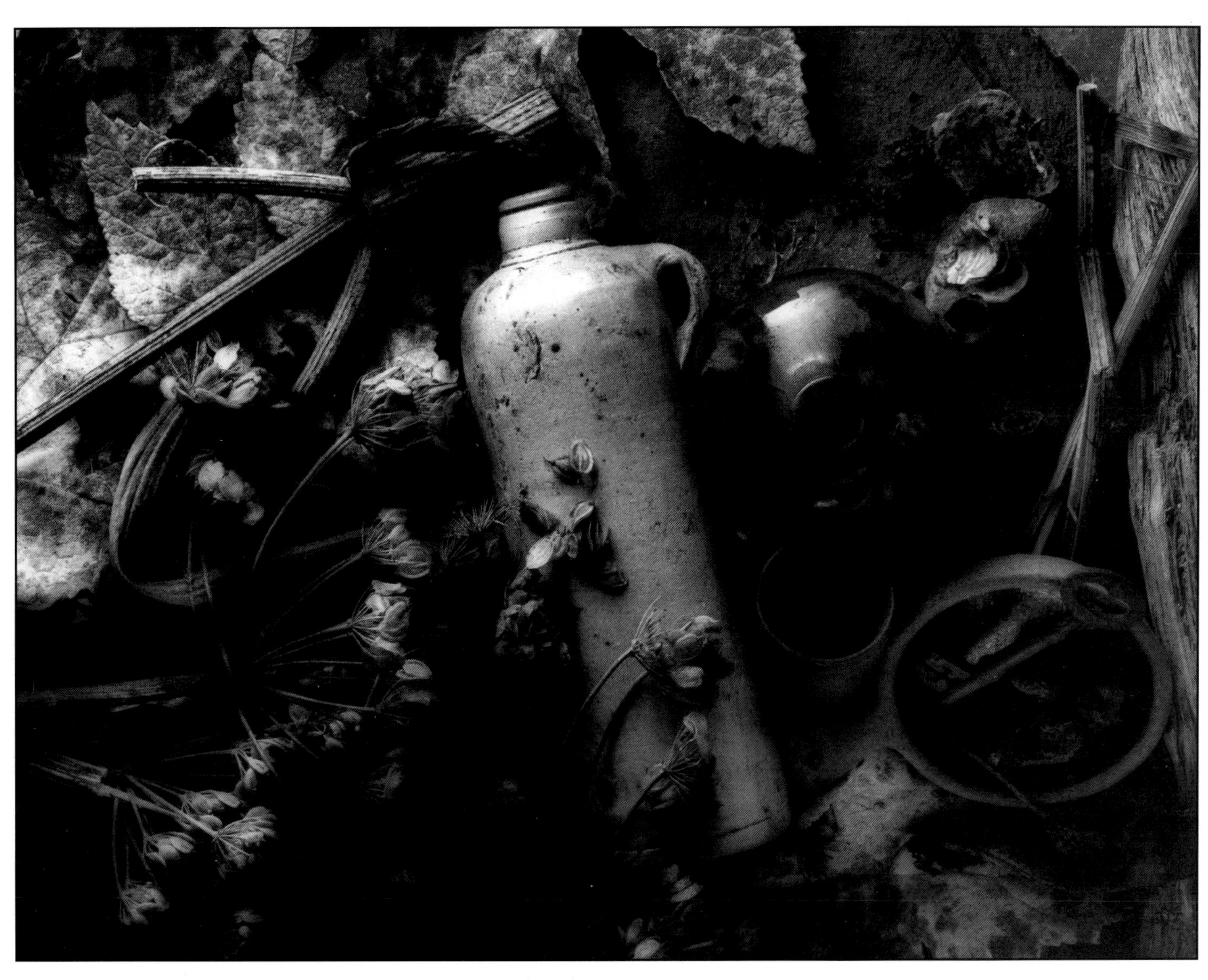

124
Gardener's corner
Rex Bamber

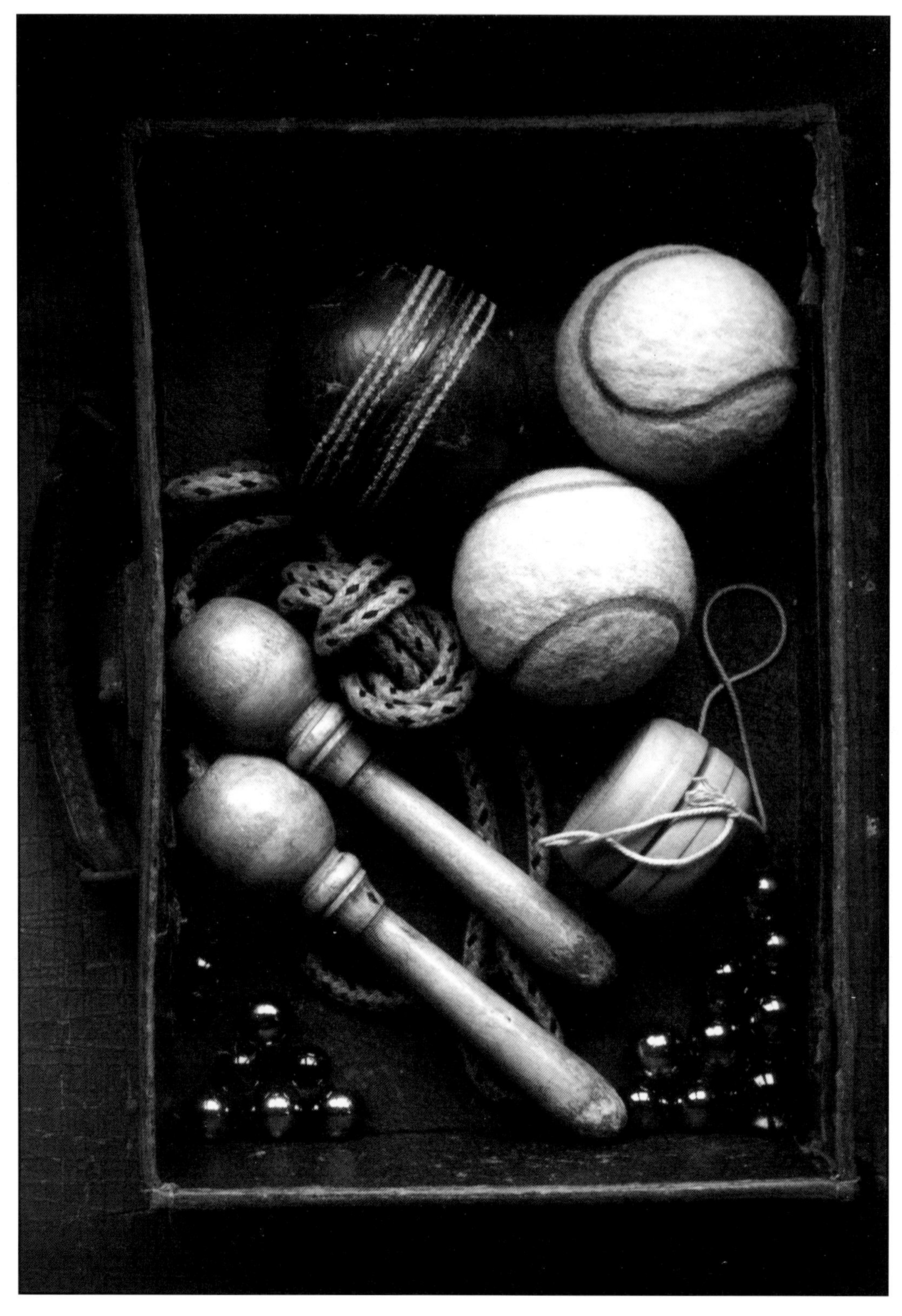

125
Skipping rope and balls
Den Reader

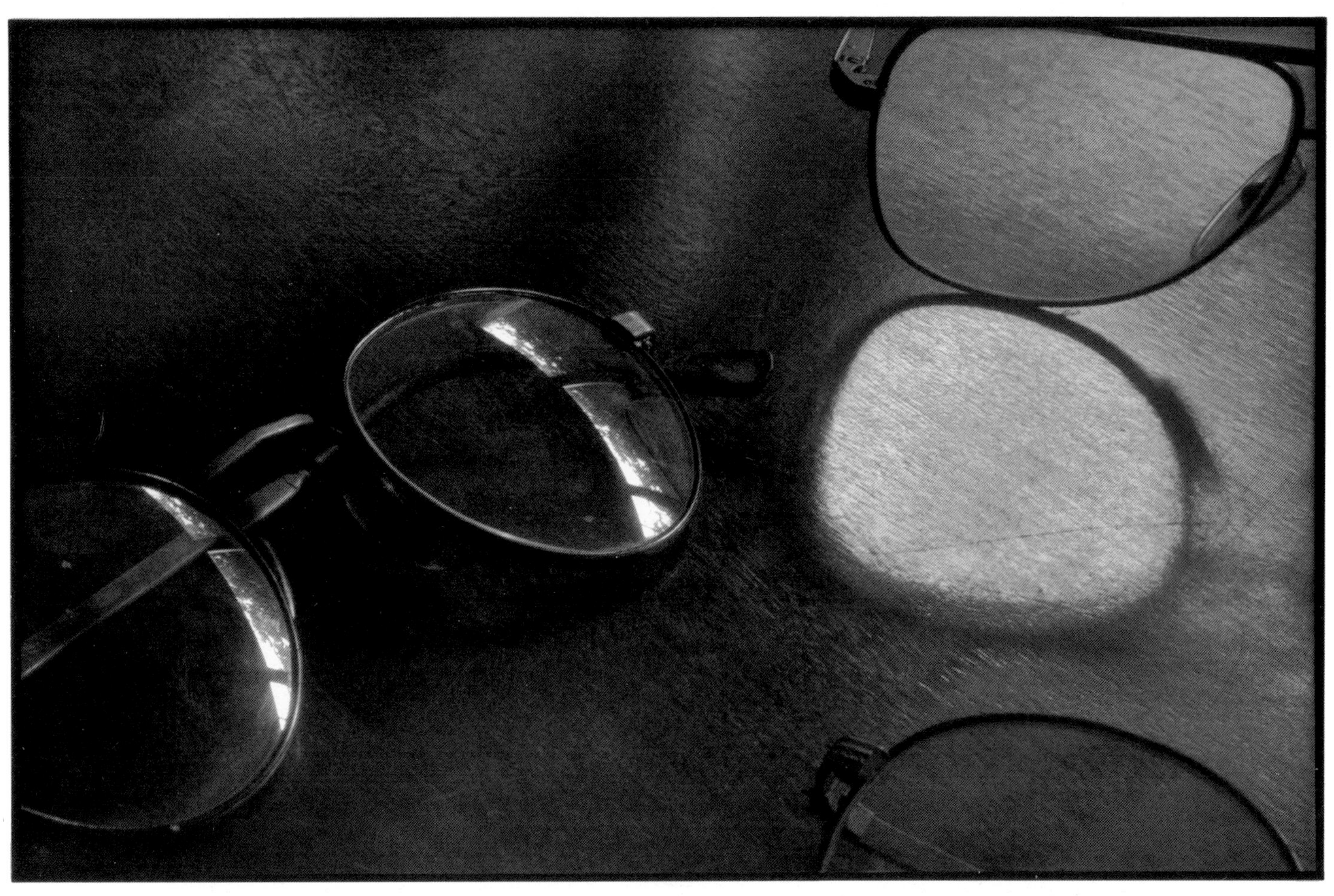

126
Oculos
Ernesto Tarnoczy Jr

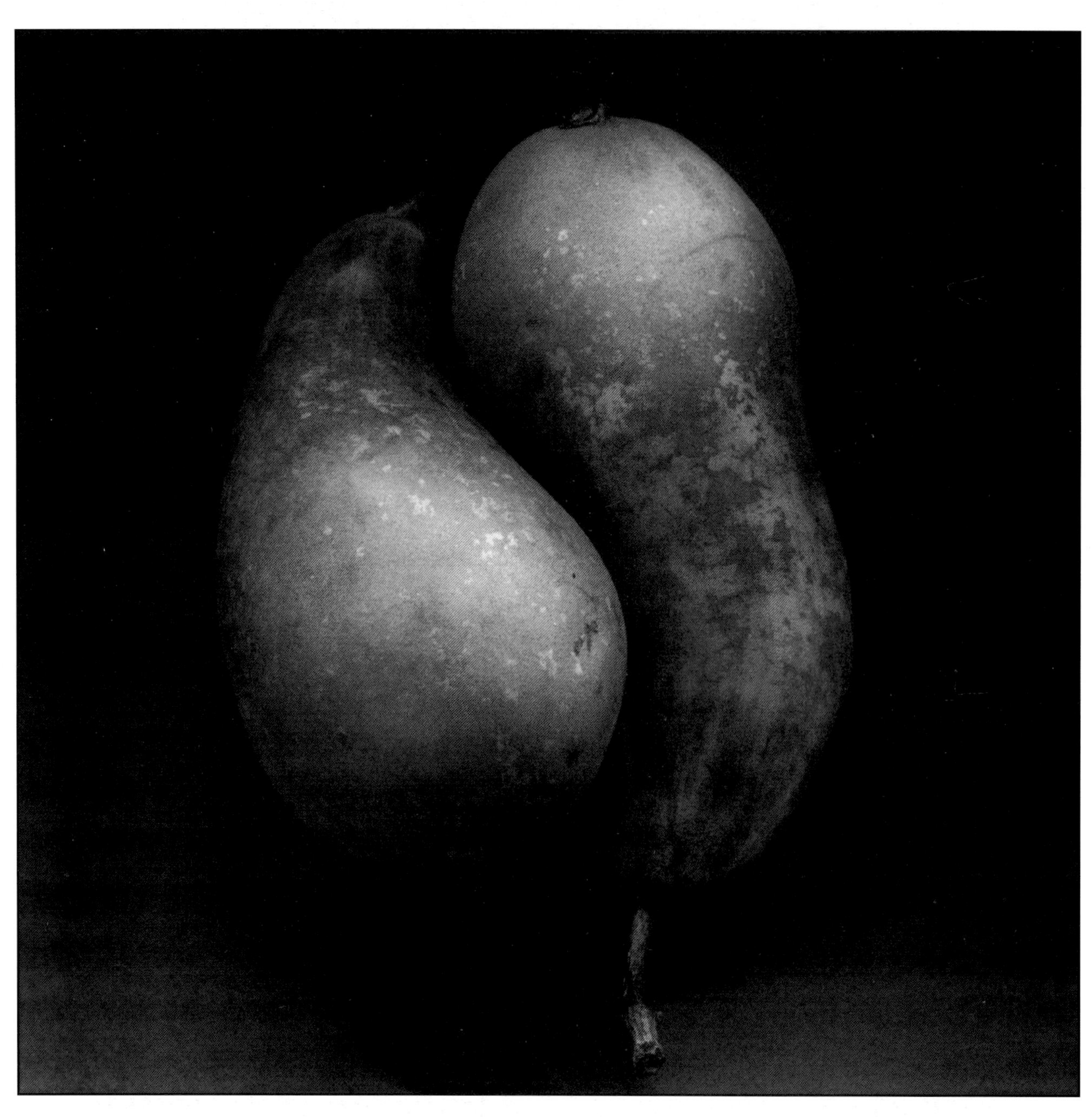

127
Togetherness
David Herrod

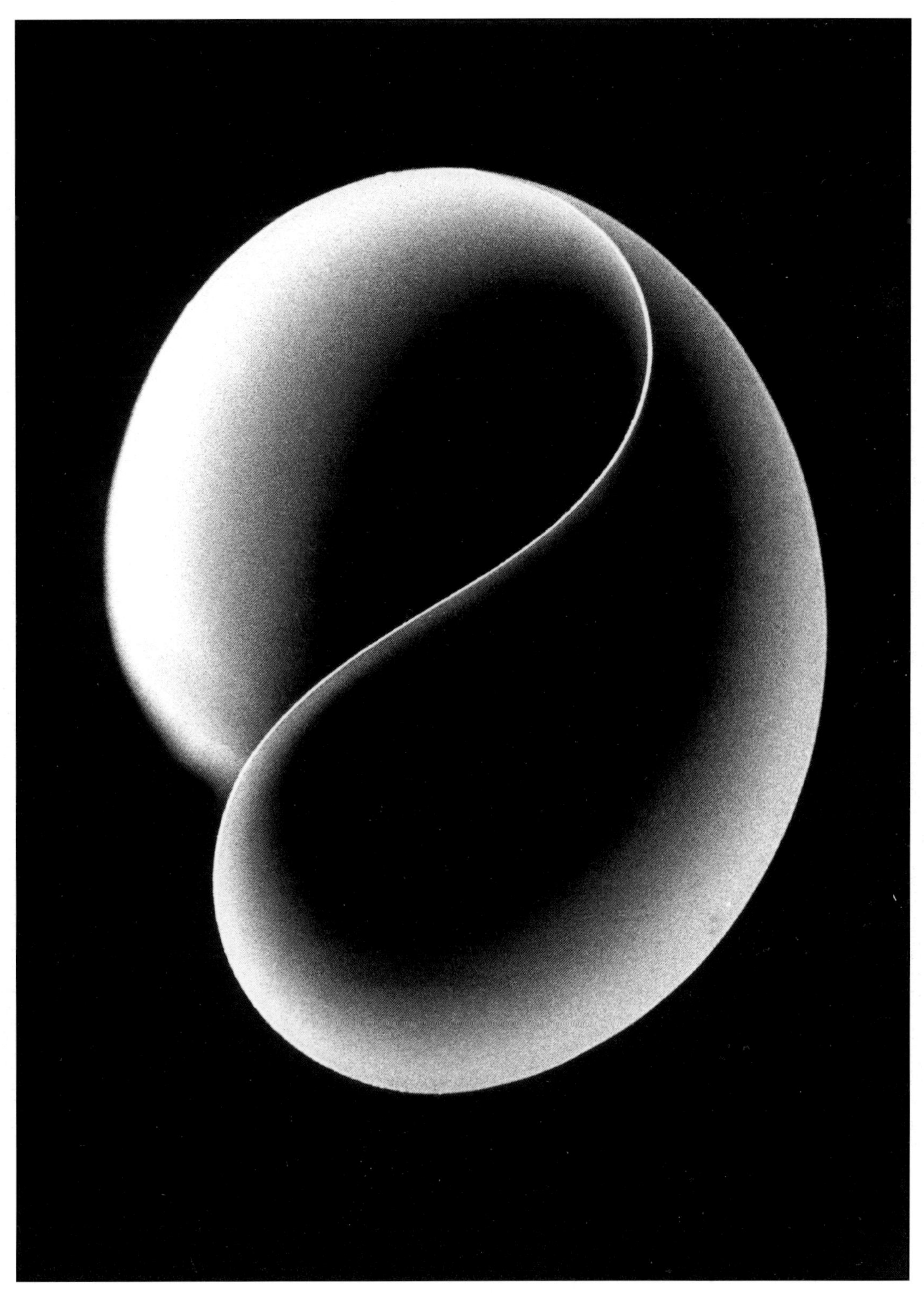

128
Embryo (experimental)
Peter Motton

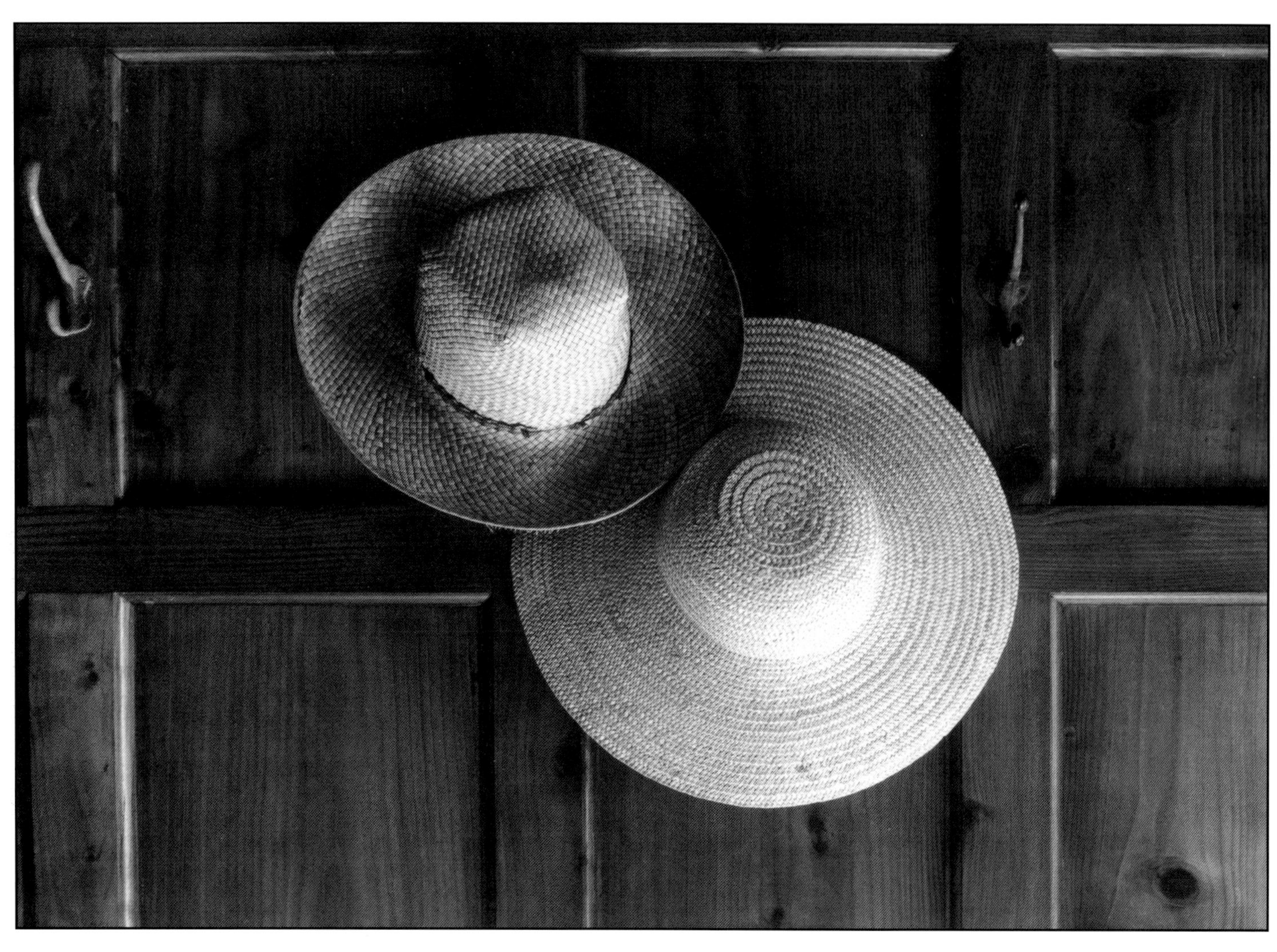

129
Two hats
Malcolm Thomson

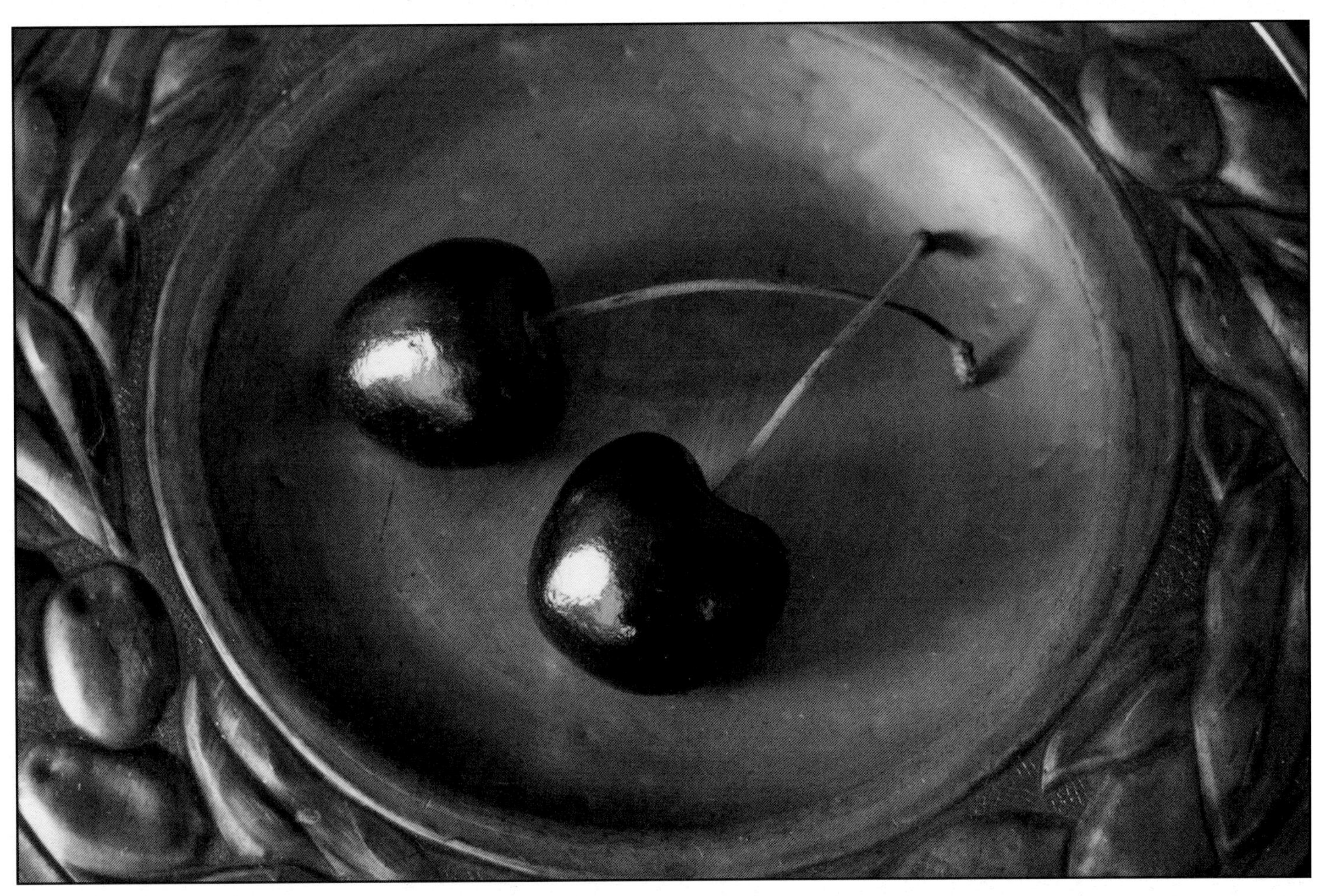

130
Two cherries
Den Reader

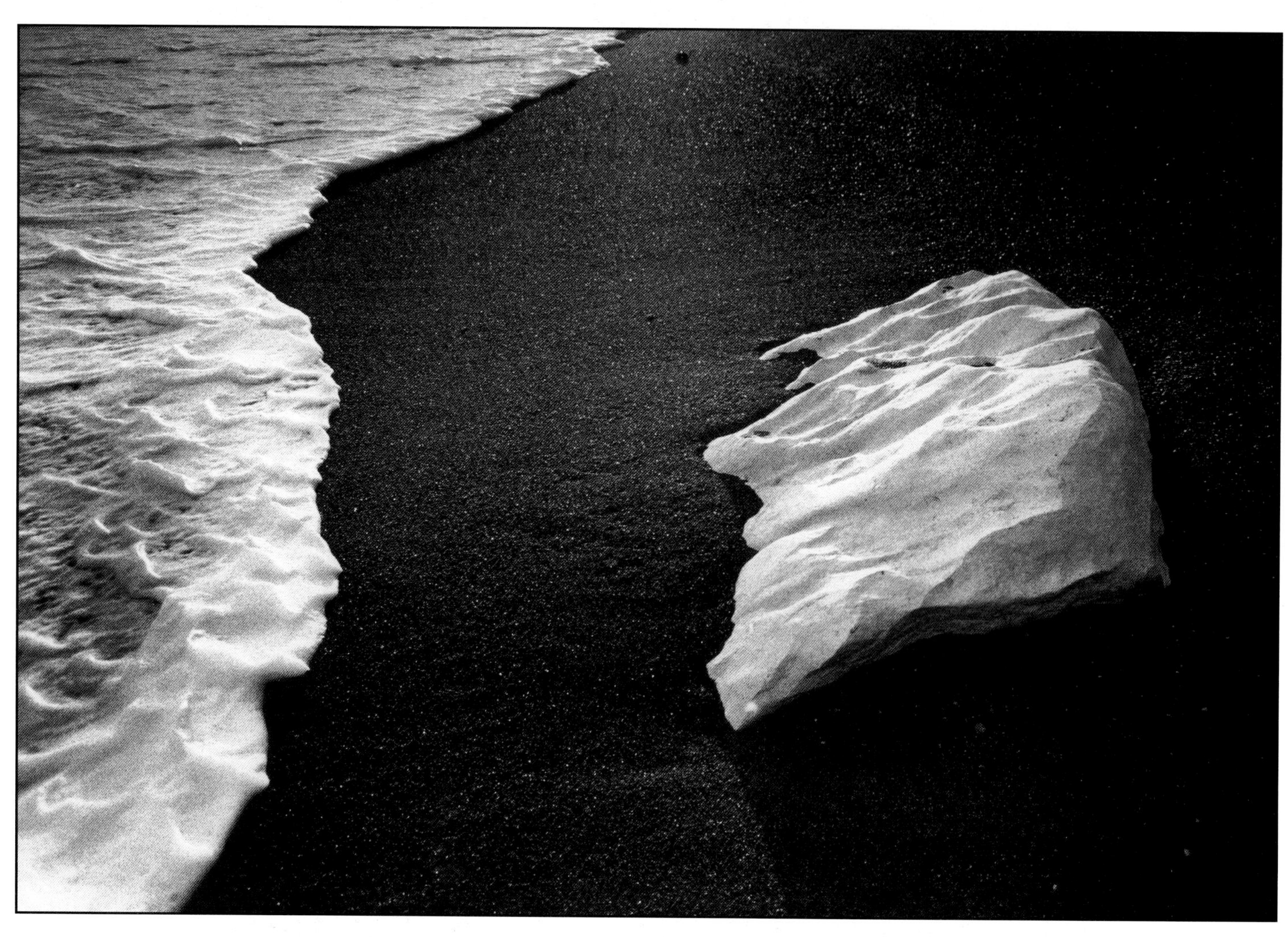

131
Wave and rock, Dorset
Ian Shorrock

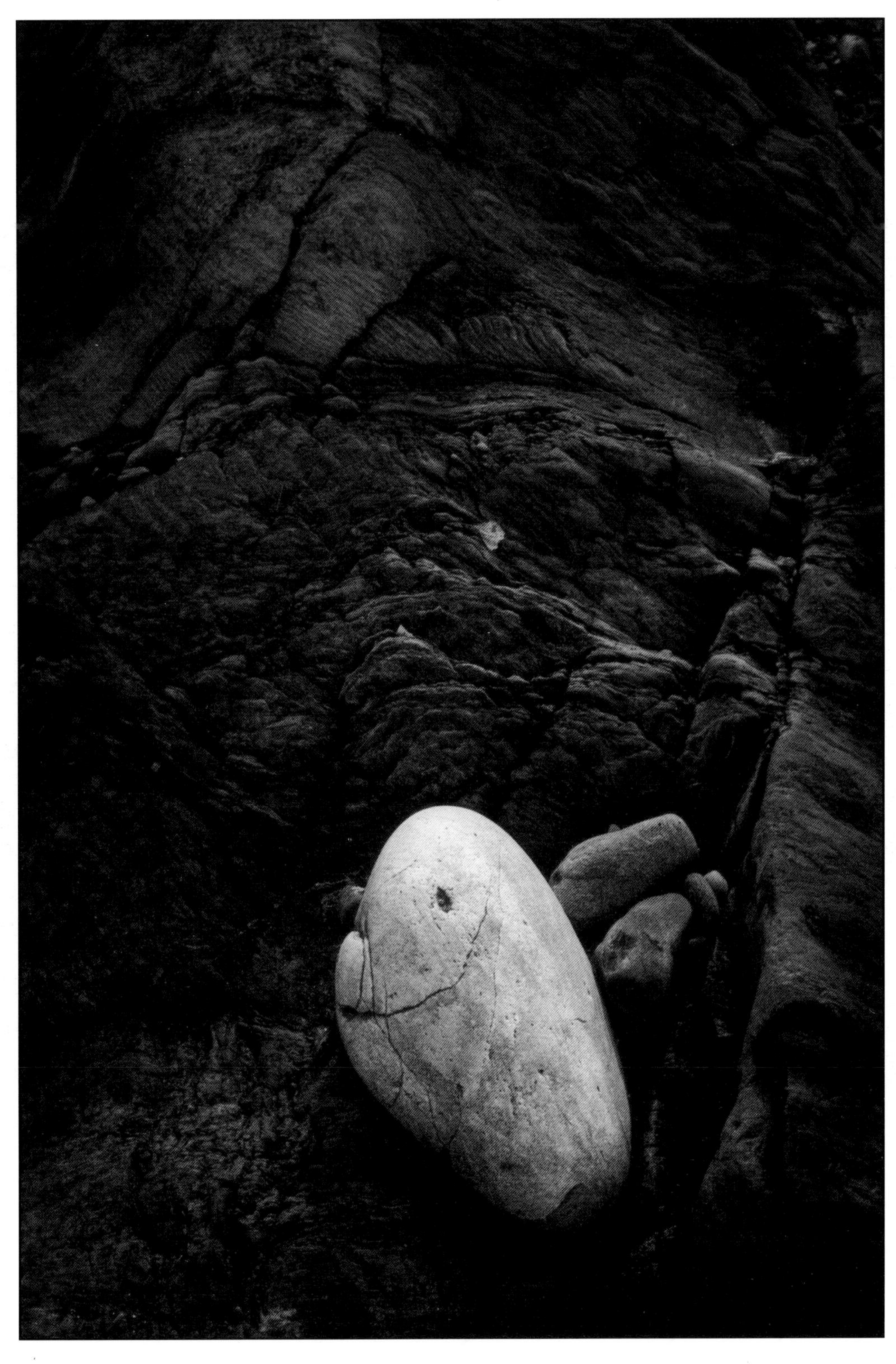

132
Rock study
Andrew Sanderson

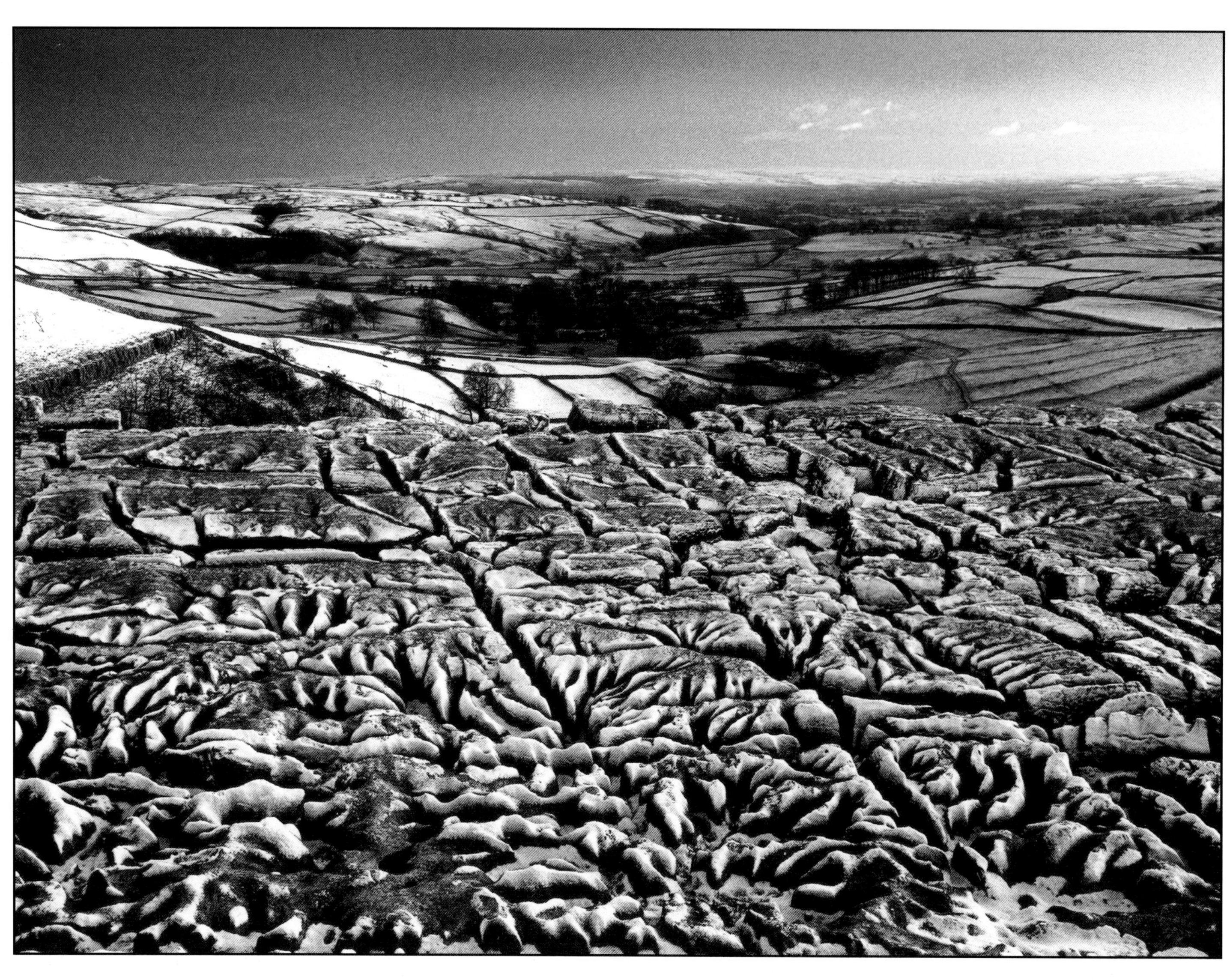

133
Frosted limestone pavement, Malham
Tom Chatterley

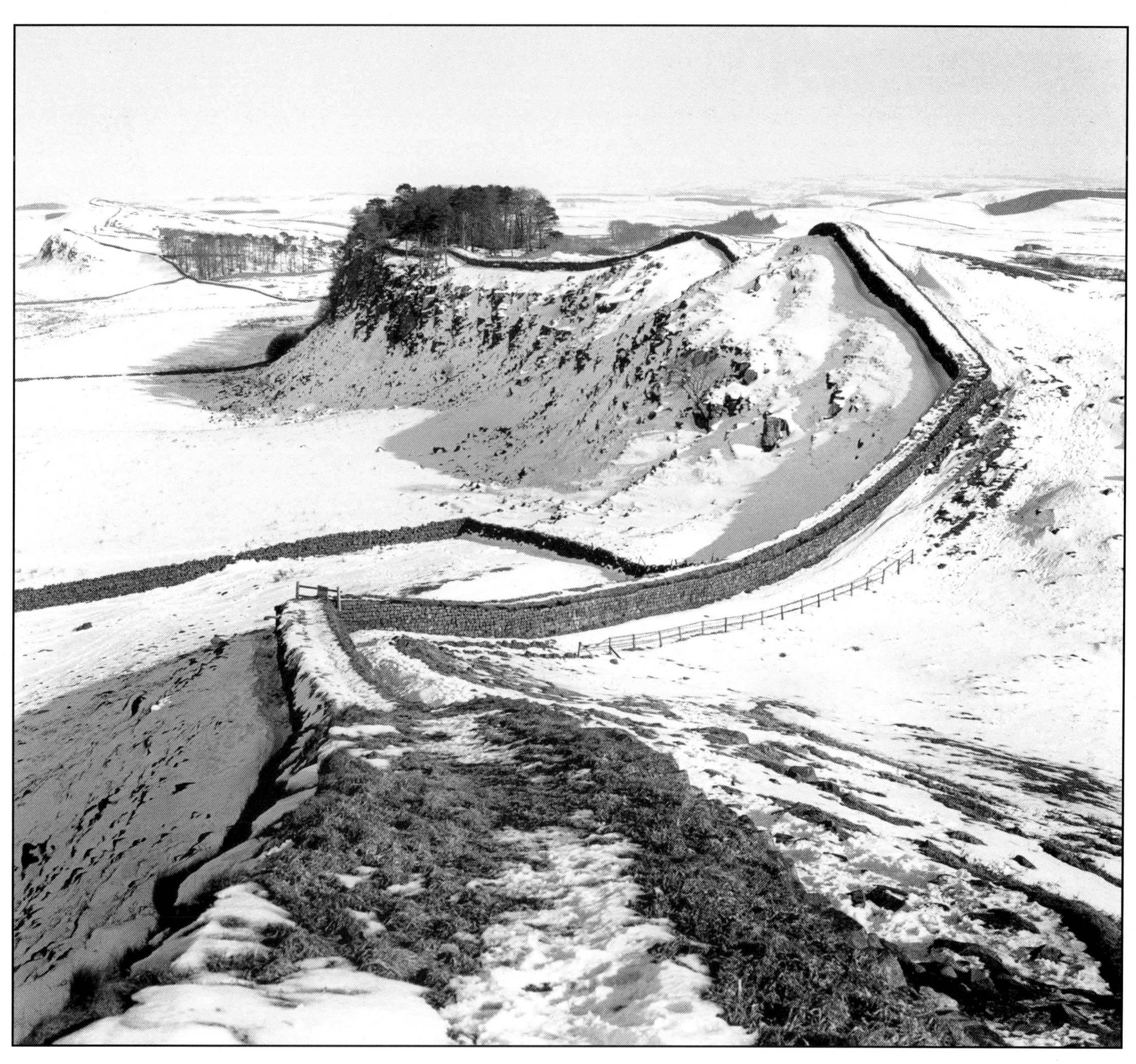

134
Winter on the wall
Trevor Ermel

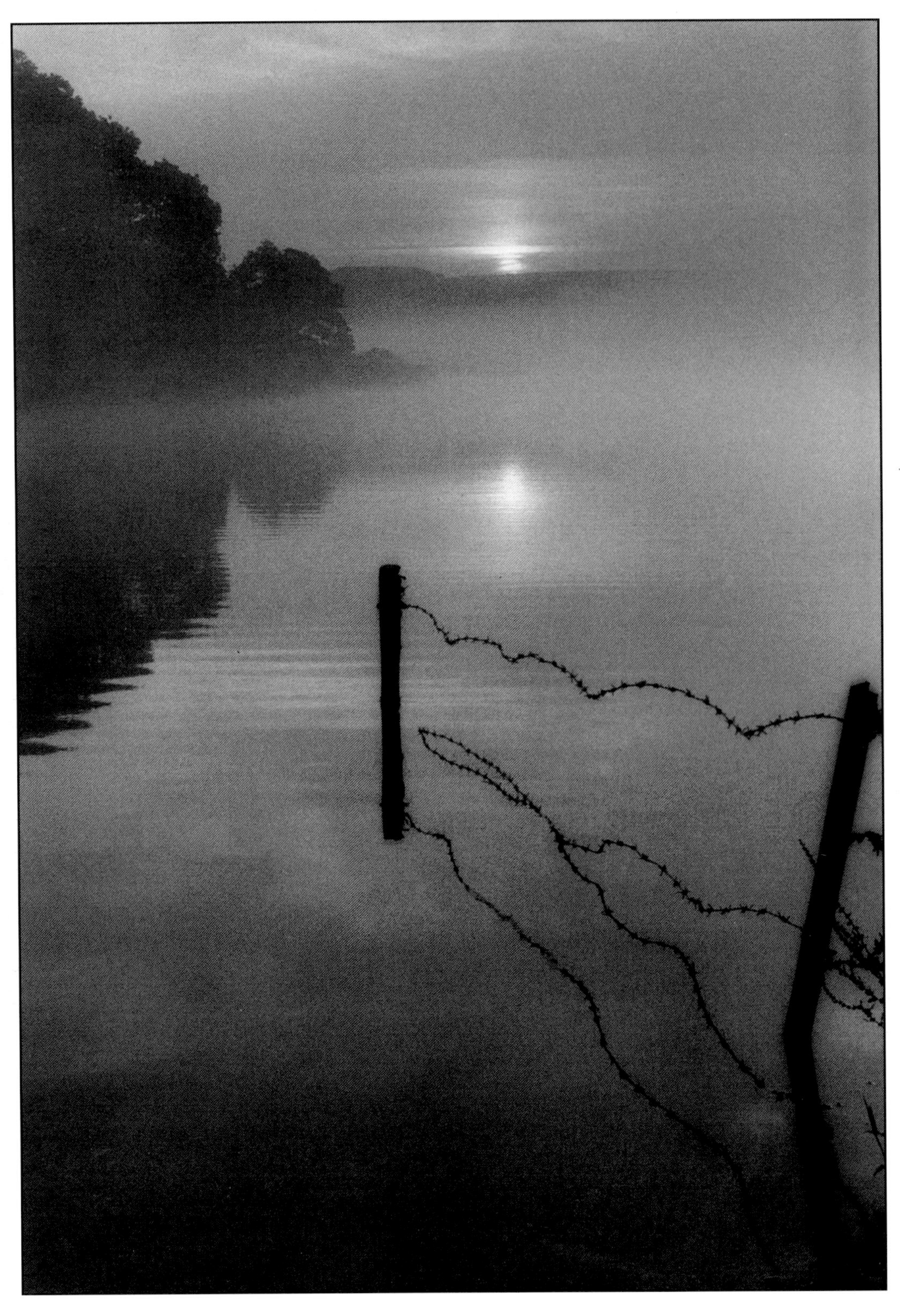

135
Pemrose dawn
Clive Vincent

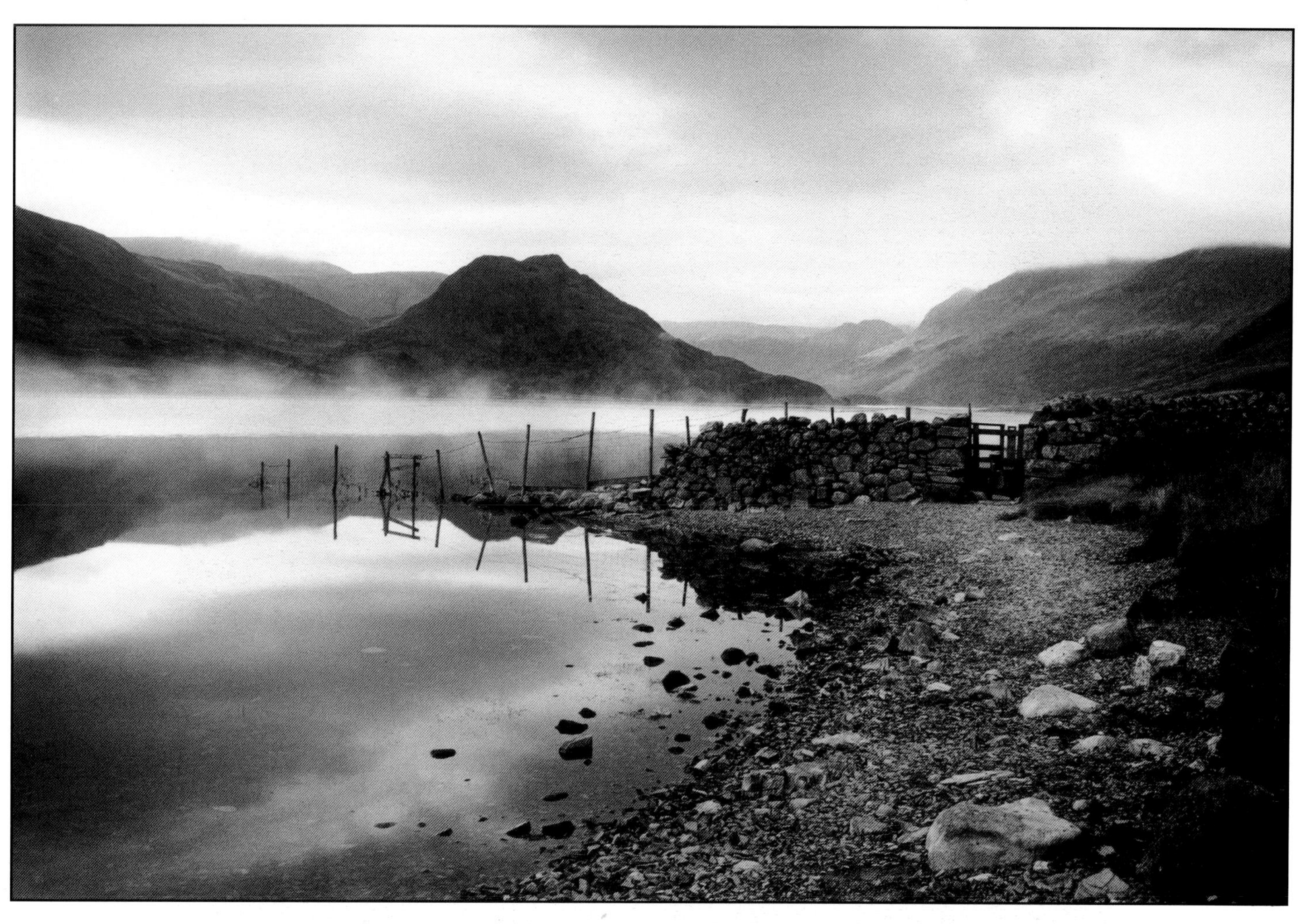

136
Dawn mists amidst the stillness of Crummock Water
Keith Launchbury

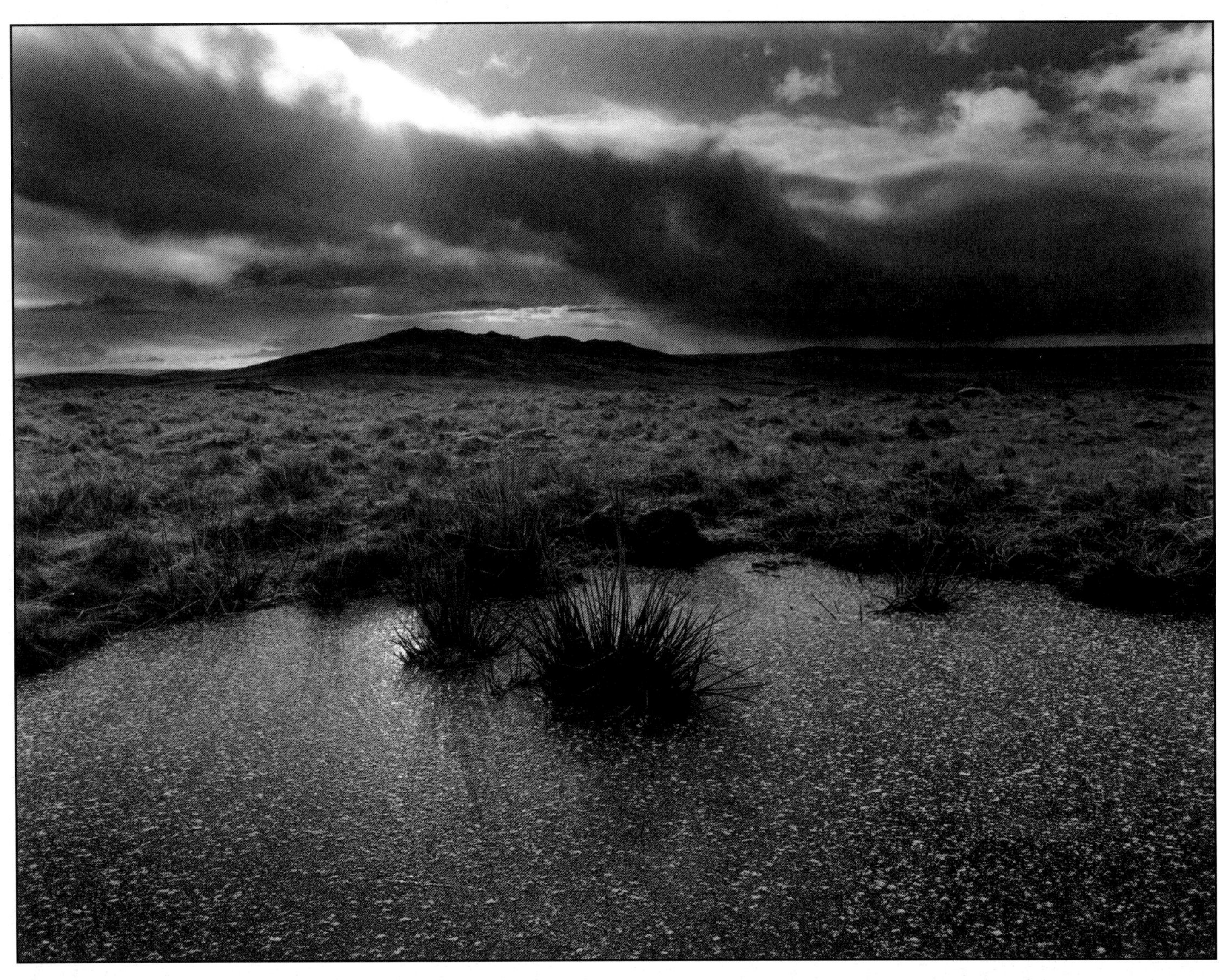

137
Fire and ice
Clive Vincent

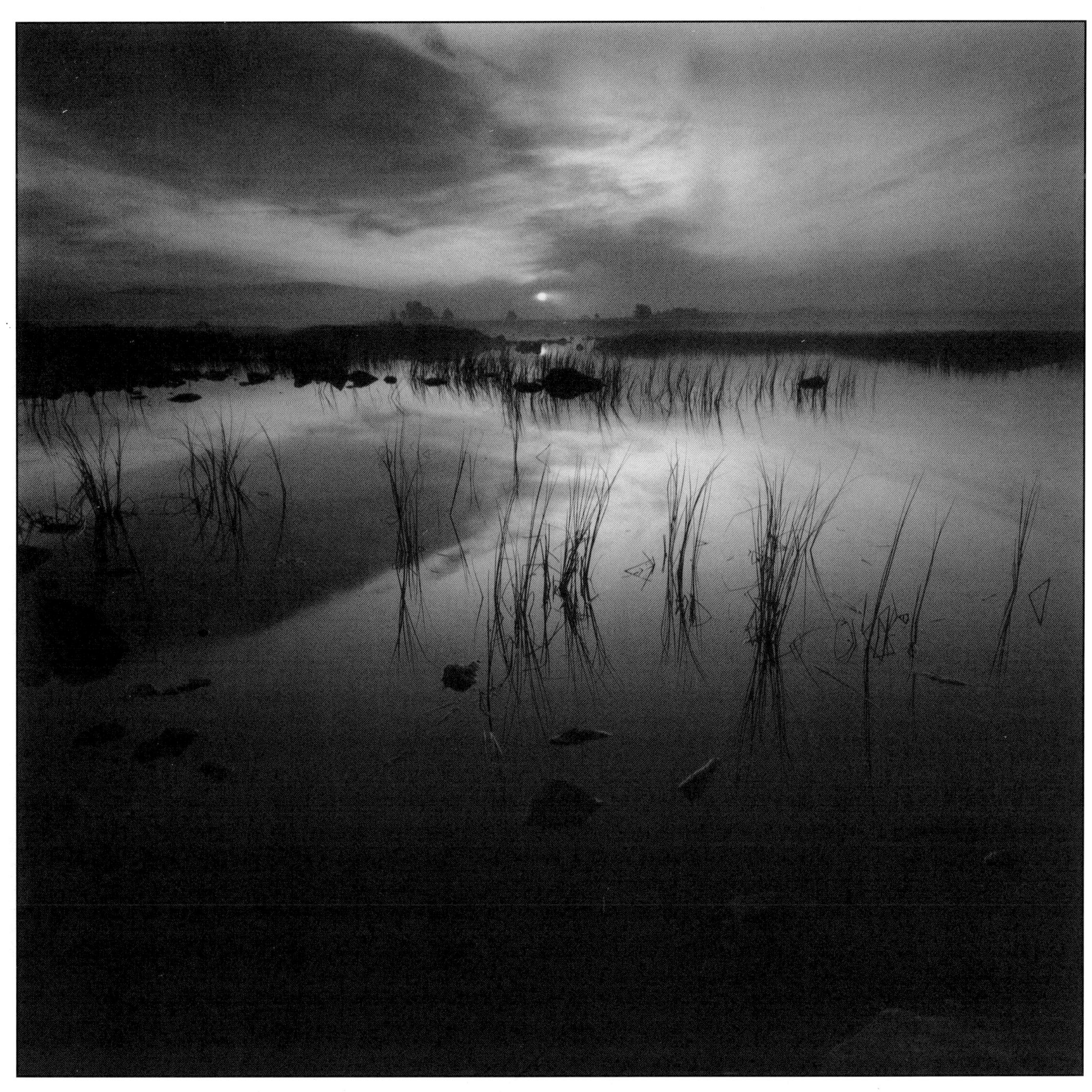

138
Rannoch Moor
Mark Snowdon

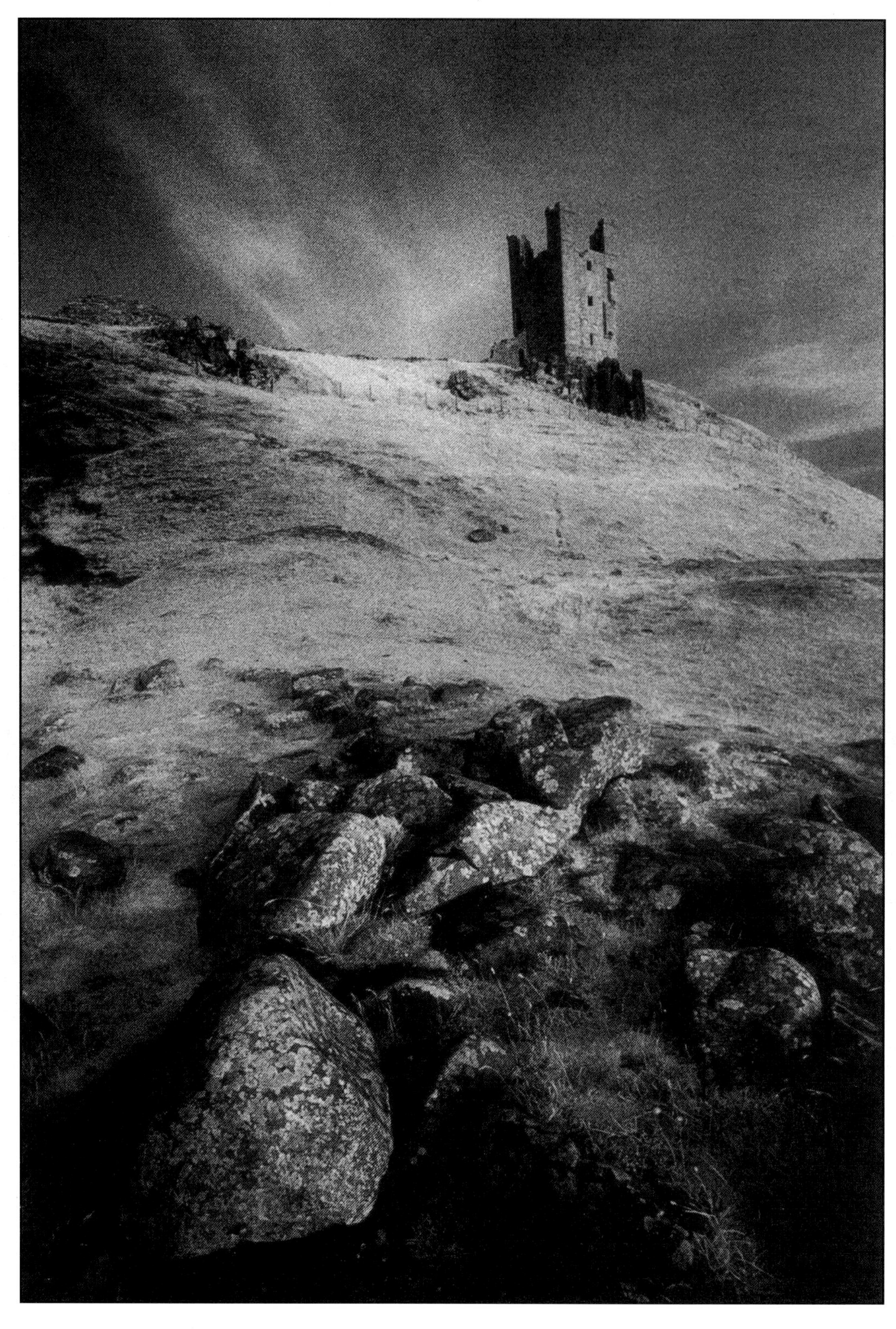

139
Dunstanburgh Castle
David Dixon

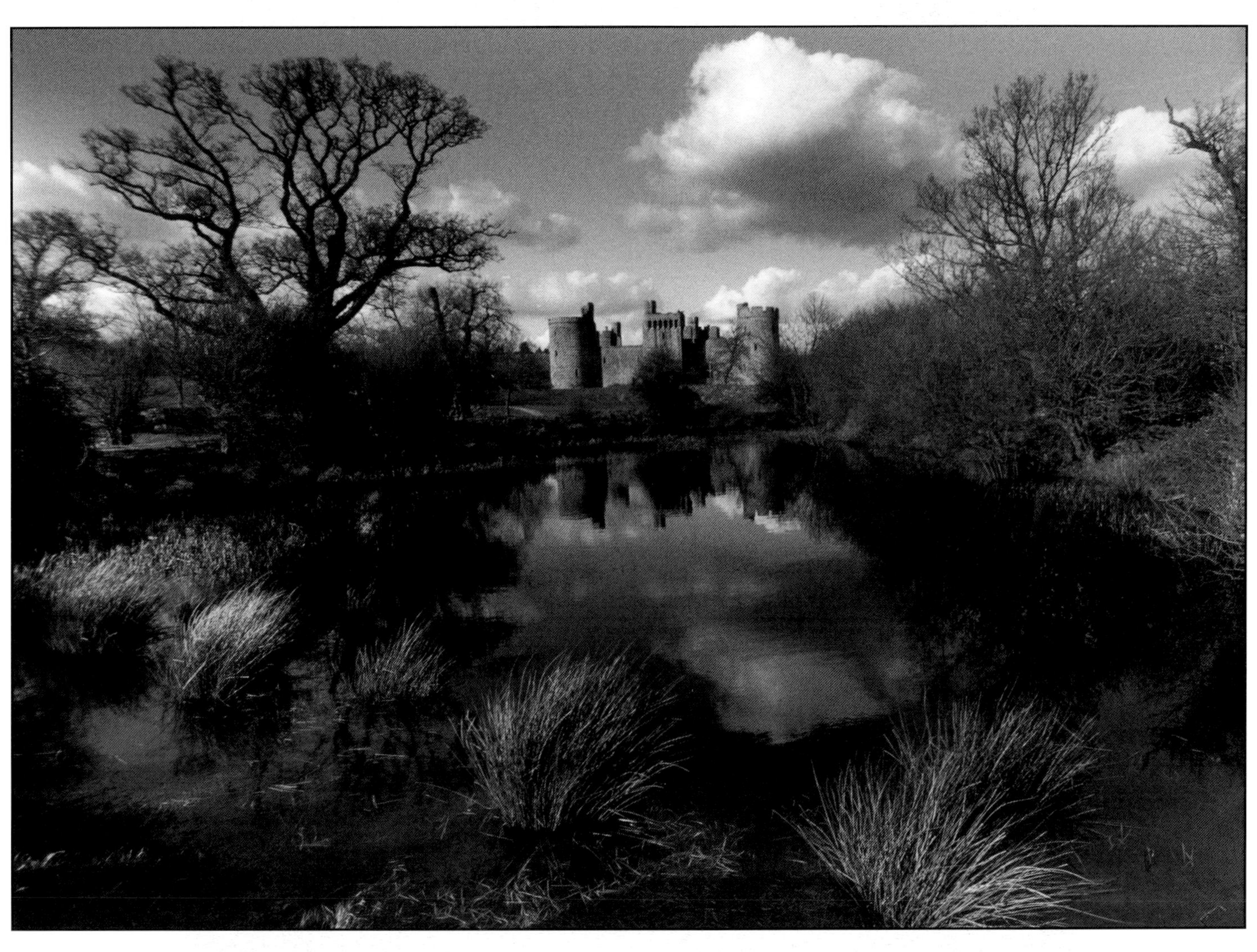

140
Bodiam in winter
Peter Moughton

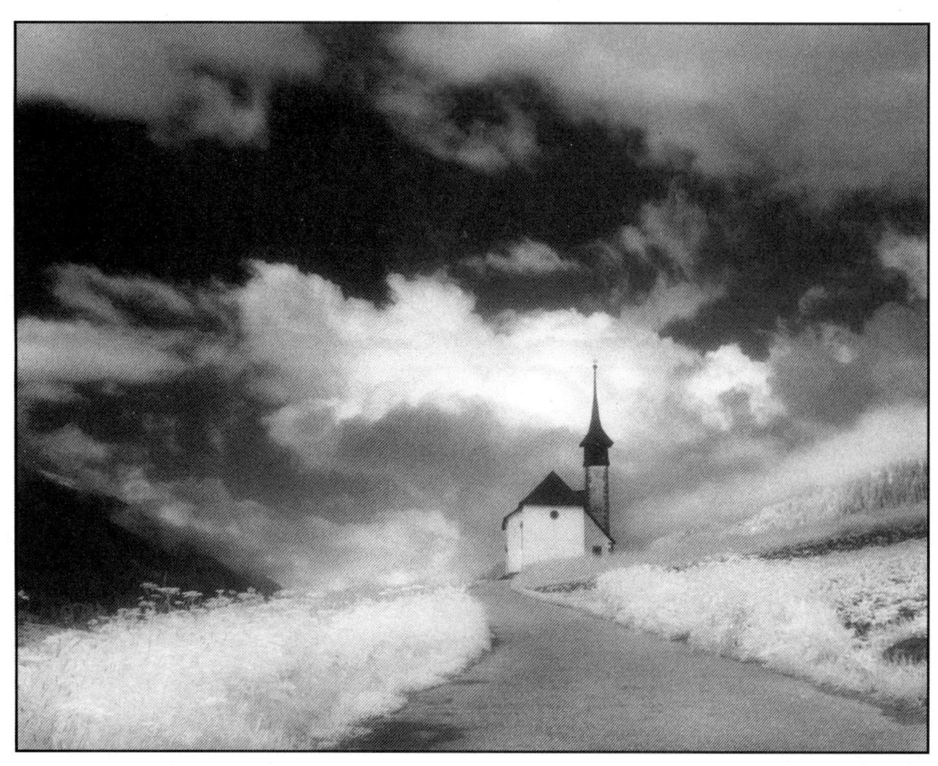

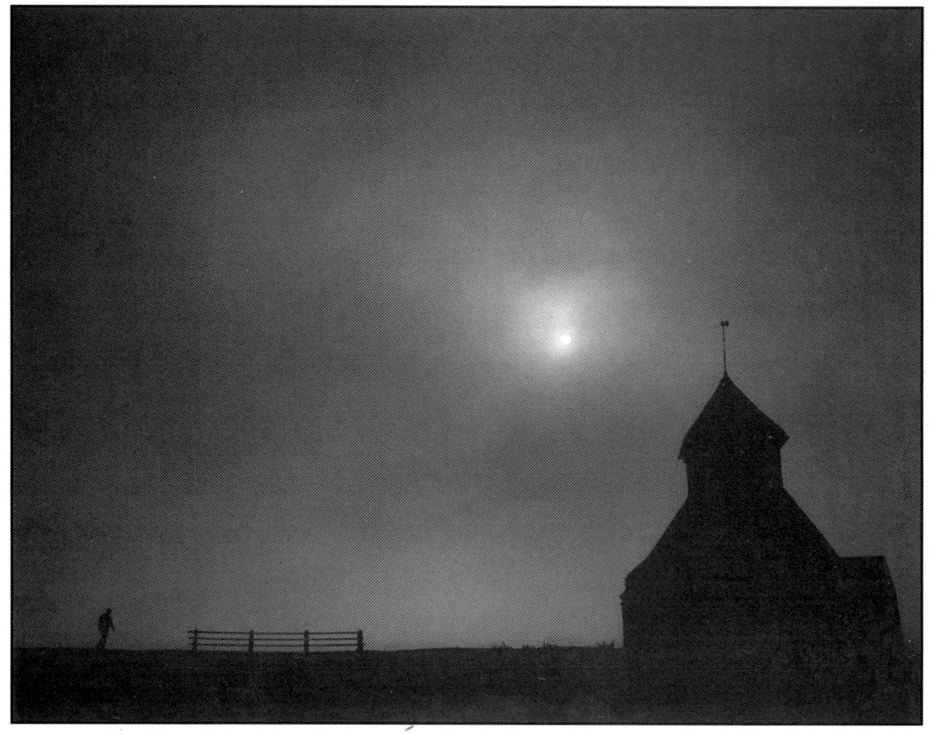

(top) 141, **Chapel in the valley, Switzerland**, *John Constable*

(below) 142, **Stranger at Fairfield**, *Chris Shore*

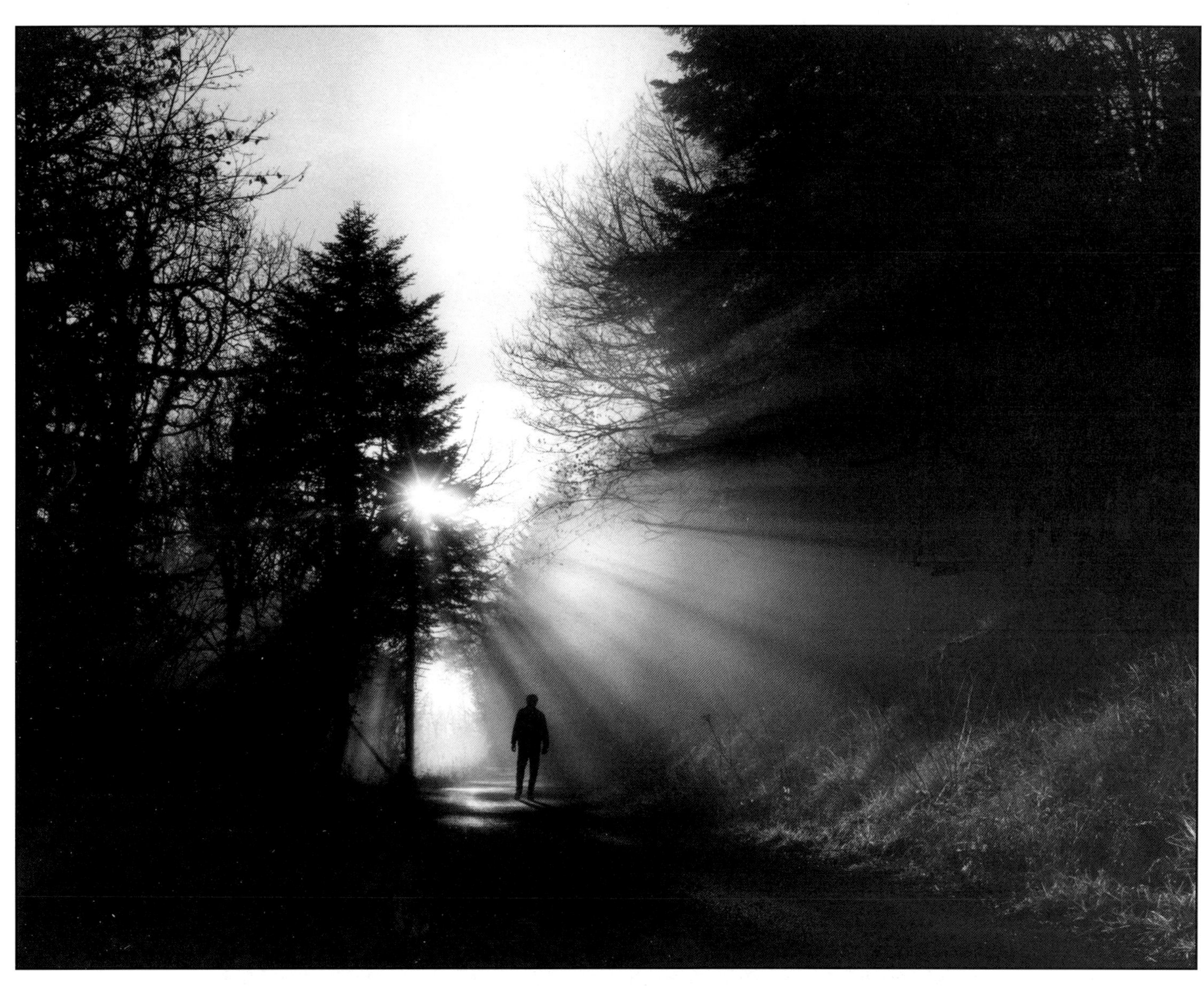

143
Lonely walker on the Jura
John Constable

Contributor profiles

All contributors were asked to provide a brief personal photographic profile. The available space dictates that they have had to be edited to the brief outlines presented below – with apologies for any vital information omitted or any inaccuracies introduced. The italicised numbers refer to the plate numbers (*not* the page numbers) of the photographer's images. There is a glossary of abbreviations used in the profiles on page 144.

Ron Abrahams *(Israel)*
A dental surgeon by profession, Ron has been active in photography for about 10 years. He works solely in monochrome and concentrates on landscape and outdoor figure work. *(79, 86)*

Rex Bamber *(Kent)*
Following his early interest in photography, Rex trained as a photographer in the RAF. After further training and working as an assistant, he worked as a freelance fashion and editorial photographer. An active member of Croydon CC, Rex is a Fellow of the RPS and member of its Applied panel. *(124)*

Jiri Bartos *(Czech Republic)*
Jiri took up photography in 1954 and since has had over 25 exhibitions in the Czech Republic and elsewhere in Europe, as well as participating in many international salons. Working mainly in monochrome, Jiri's main subjects are landscape, detail and structure, architecture, nature and creative photography. *(110)*

Ken Bates *(Manchester)*
Currently working for an arts organisation in Manchester, Ken has been involved in photography for about 15 years. He has taken part in many exhibitions and displays, where his fine art prints have achieved pleasing sales. *(15)*

Neil Bedwell *(Lancashire)*
Neil originally bought a camera in 1982 to use as a sketch pad for painting and drawing, but found that he preferred photography as a medium. Having learned how to develop and print at night classes, he enjoys the ability to produce his own work and control its appearance. His main subject interests are landscape and buildings. *(37, 40)*

Denis Bourg *(London)*
A chef by profession, photography has become a favoured creative outlet for Denis over the past 10 years. In the early 1990s, Denis encountered and stayed with monochrome, specifically infrared. He describes his aspiration as "to enlighten people's hearts and minds through showing the extraordinary within the ordinary; the beauty within the mundane." *(14)*

Kevin Bridgwood *(Staffordshire)*
Kevin gained a licentiateship of the RPS in the pictorial section and admits to having many colour slides placed with image libraries. He uses formats from 35mm to 5x4 and has produced work for *Staffordshire Life* magazine, including cover shots. *(27, 96)*

Alan Brown *(Tyne & Wear)*
Though known to turn his camera to most subjects, Alan's photographic preference is sport, which he feels is too often dismissed as offering little opportunity for creative work. He has been a member of South Shields PS since taking up photography in 1990. *(21)*

Peter Bryenton *(Worcestershire)*
Peter describes photography as his favourite means of self-expression. After over 30 years, he says that he is still enjoying learning about photography. *(2)*

Christine Chambers *(Surrey)*
Following her selection for *Best of Friends 2*, Christine continues to experiment with her graphic ideas. She also works along more traditional lines, including still life and landscape. A member of Selsdon CC, Christine has recently gained the Associateship of the RPS. *(11)*

Mike Chambers *(Surrey)*
Since early retirement, Mike devotes much of his time to photography, though often that of other people through his club and Federation work. An active slide worker, his first love continues to be monochrome, especially landscape. His prints have gained many exhibition acceptances, earning him the AFIAP distinction to go with his ARPS and DPAGB. *(54)*

Tom Chatterley *(Leicestershire)*
Tom's interest in photography dates back to the early 1960s, soon after he started work. An active mountaineer, landscape and mountain photography are his favourite subjects, although his membership of Earl Shilton CC has encouraged a very varied photographic diet. For monochrome work, Tom prefers to use medium format. *(133)*

Derek Christy *(Australia)*
Derek joined a camera club in 1988, returning to photography after many years. He now works mainly in monochrome and has had successes in club and national competitions, as well as several exhibitions in Queensland. *(80)*

Peter Clark *(Staffordshire)*
A member of Cannock PS for over 15 years, Peter is a well known judge and lecturer. He achieved his RPS Fellowship for his monochrome landscape work. With over 800 exhibition acceptances, including around 125 awards, Peter holds the EFIAP distinction and is a 3-star mono print exhibitor of the PSA. *(28)*

Mike Coles *(Avon)*
Mike has been working in monochrome for just two years and has been surprised by how it has held his interest: he feels there is a lifetime's work in trying new things out and looking for that really satisfying image. His favourite subjects are people, sports and landscapes. *(67)*

Mike Coles *(London)*
This Mike Coles (no relation) has been a keen photographer from the age of nine. A film cameraman by profession, Mike always takes a couple of stills cameras with him on assignments. He works mainly in black and white, and particularly likes photographing people and places. *(19, 109)*

John Constable *(Somerset)*
John is a member of Dorchester CC and Westland PC (Yeovil) and has been taking photographs for over 30 years. In terms of subject, his main love is nature, using his Nikon F3, and he now makes much use of infrared film in his medium format Mamiya. *(141, 143)*

David Conway *(Dorset)*
A retired scientist, David was recently invited to join the Arena group. He works almost wholly in monochrome and is experimenting with new aspects of toning. His ambitions are to publish a book and to convert his Associateship of the RPS to a Fellowship. *(25, 114)*

Rosemary Cooper *(Hertfordshire)*
Rosemary has studied photography as a part-time extra-mural student at the University of Hertfordshire for six years. In 1995, she gained her Associateship of the RPS. Her overriding passion in photography is for atmospheric black and white images. *(1, 12)*

George Coupe *(Lancashire)*
With a serious interest in photography for the past eight years, George pays tribute to the help and encouragement gained from joining local camera clubs. A Licentiate of the RPS, he has exhibited in local and national exhibitions. He works exclusively in monochrome and his main interest is in photographing people. *(29)*

Roger Crane *(Kent)*
Roger has been taking photographs for over 35 years and is particularly interested in landscape work and the use of early photographic processes. He is a longstanding member of a local club and a Friend of the London Salon. *(52)*

Trevor Crone *(London)*
Trevor became interested in photography over 20 years ago. He works mainly in monochrome and his work has been exhibited widely and published in magazines, books and cards. He is a member of Aperture club and currently has a Contemporary Portfolio book in preparation for Creative Monochrome. *(4, 101)*

Steven Cull *(Cornwall)*
Steven has a diploma in wildlife illustration, which involved some photography. He is an accomplished painter, working mainly in watercolours, and sells his work through a number of galleries. He is secretary of Wadebridge & District CC, whose members have proved a source of inspiration. *(120)*

Sue Davies *(Buckinghamshire)*
Sue became hooked on photography as a result of enrolling on a City and Guilds modular photography course. Encouraged to visit galleries and exhibitions, she was particularly impressed by John Blakemore's Inscape exhibition and freely admits the obvious influence on her own work. She is an Associate of the RPS. *(123)*

John Devenport *(London)*
John enjoys working in both monochrome and colour, and is a keen member of the Mirage Group, Beckenham PS and Ashford CC. Primarily a landscape worker, a keen sense of observation is the key to many of his images. He gained his ARPS in 1988. *(7, 8, 90)*

David Dixon *(Kent)*
A Fellow of the RPS, David enjoys club life at Tonbridge CC and submits work regularly to the international exhibition circuit, gaining the gold medal for best monochrome print at the British Open in 1995. Most of his work recently has been with infrared film, which he uses to create a sense of drama and austere mood. David's images won a gold and bronze medal in the 1996 BoF Awards. *(105, 139)*

Peter Dixon *(Tyne & Wear)*
Peter has been interested in photography for over 30 years, working mainly in monochrome. A member of Tyneside CC and Whickham CC, and holder of the ARPS and DPAGB distinctions, he lectures widely on photography. With five other local photographers, he formed the Imprint group, whose aim is to promote photography through exhibitions. *(60)*

Tom Dodd *(Gwynedd)*
Tom's photographic interest spans some 25 years and is inseparable from his involvement with the outdoor environment. A well known lecturer, exhibitor and judge, Tom gained his FRPS in 1979. He is a member of the London Salon and the licentiateship panel of the RPS. Tom is one of the very few to have work selected for each issue of *Best of Friends* to date. *(112)*

Peter Doughty *(Norfolk)*
Peter hasn't looked back, photographically speaking, since joining Hunstanton & District PS as a novice in 1991. He has now graduated to club chairman. Peter enjoys photographing people in their environment, but also likes creating images in the studio. *(13)*

Glyn Edmunds *(Hampshire)*
An active photographer for nine years, Glyn gained his Associateship of the RPS in 1991, and the AFIAP and DPAGB distinctions in 1996. As well as exhibition successes, Glyn has had images published in the UK and USA. His favourite subjects are "fuzzy/creative landscapes" and figure studies. *(75)*

Richard Egan *(North Yorkshire)*
A committee member and past-President of Ripon City PS, Richard has been involved in photography for the past 10 years, but has specialised in mono prints only in the last two years. He has used a very wide range of subject matter, but prefers portraiture and figure studies. *(82)*

Roy Elwood *(Tyne & Wear)*
Much of Roy's life centres around photography, especially monochrome – an enduring first love. Recently he has moved from individual images to sets of prints around themes, currently water, nudes and dancers. He gained his Fellowship of the RPS with a panel of 20 nudes, each featuring parts of the male and female body. *(78, 81)*

Trevor Ermel *(Tyne & Wear)*
Trevor takes many of his pictures around his native Tyneside, documenting the ever-changing local scene. After enjoying photography as a hobby for 30 years – much of this time as an active member of Whickham CC – he now runs his own black and white processing business in Newcastle. *(134)*

John Fairclough *(Lancashire)*
John became hooked on photography as a child, seeing the latent image appearing in the developer: a thrill that has never deserted him. An active member of Wigan PS, John finds monochrome work gives him more freedom of expression and satisfaction than colour. His main subjects are landscape and people. *(42)*

Mike Farrow *(Hampshire)*
Having been introduced to photography as a teenager, he "dabbled" for the next 35 years. Eight years ago, time and finances permitted a more serious interest, so he joined a local club and the RPS. He enjoys monochrome and particularly the challenge of printing. His current inspiration is Barry Thornton. *(59)*

Andrew Foley *(South Yorkshire)*
A journalist by profession, Andrew has been involved in photography for just six years, during which time he has gained his Associateship of the RPS. He is a member of Gamma photoforum, Mexborough PS and Doncaster CC and has had work included in major national and international exhibitions. *(122)*

Alan Fowler *(Tyne & Wear)*
Alan is a member of Gateshead CC and has gained the ARPS and DPAGB distinctions, both in monochrome prints. Whatever the particular subject matter, he describes his main interest in photography as capturing the light, mood and feeling within the print. *(34)*

Steve Francis *(Wiltshire)*
A sports injury 10 years ago gave Steve the time to follow his latent interest in photography, trying to capture images with atmosphere and emotion. He soon became interested in monochrome and darkroom work. An active member of Swindon and Highworth clubs, his main subject interest is the landscape. *(63)*

Gary Freeman *(North Yorkshire)*
Having been taking photographs for about 10 years, Gary describes photography as a passion, and a photograph as "life holding its breath". A fan of Sylvia Plachy, he says he can't better her comment: "everywhere I go I carry these weights, my cameras. Maybe I'd float without these anchors". *(66)*

Trevor Fry *(Essex)*
Trevor has enjoyed photography since the early 1950s and is currently a member of Cambridge & Saffron Walden club. He is a Fellow of the RPS and has had work exhibited in many exhibitions. Although he also works in colour, he retains a real love for black and white, particularly for his favourite subject, people. *(20, 22)*

Pavel Glebov *(Dorset)*
Pavel was born in Russia and has been making fine art photographs for the last 15 years. His early monochrome work in Leningrad, noted for its technical excellence and spiritual richness, concentrated on the city and its people. His more recent monochrome work focuses mainly on portraits and urban landscapes. *(65)*

Dave Gordon *(Devon)*
Dave gained his Associateship of the RPS in 1995 after several attempts. He has been making monochrome prints for about 12 years and has just started colour printing. His main photographic interests are landscape and looking for unusual patterns and shapes in rivers. *(62)*

Rob Gray *(Australia)*
Rob has been involved in photography for over 20 years. He recently opened his own gallery and, whilst not giving up his 'day job' yet, is working towards becoming a full-time landscape photographer. He specialises in "straight forward, high definition" monochrome landscapes using a 4x5 field camera. *(55, 56, 89)*

Kathleen Harcom *(Hampshire)*
Although enjoying many aspects of photography, Kathleen's main interest is landscape work. She has successfully completed a number of college courses in photography and gained her Associateship of the RPS with a panel of monochrome infrared images. *(116)*

Clive Haynes *(Worcestershire)*
An Associate of the RPS, Clive has been making photographs for some 30 years. He is a long-standing member of the Worcestershire CC, a founder member of Infinity Plus fine print group, and a member of UPP, Circle 11. In addition, he teaches photography and presents talks and workshops. *(95, 119)*

Dawn Heath *(Australia)*
Dawn emigrated in 1992 from England to Australia, where she is in her final year of an arts diploma in applied photography. She is fascinated by the trees and landscapes of her new home country and travels around recording these new wonders, mainly with infrared film. Dawn had worked only in colour until starting college in 1995. *(102)*

David Herrod *(Cumbria)*
David Herrod is a self-taught photographer who exhibits internationally, winning a large number of medals and prizes, and has had many solo exhibitions of his work. He holds the Artist distinction of FIAP. He has had two solo books of his photography published by Creative Monochrome, *Waters of Cumbria* and *Images by Design*. *(103, 127)*

Alfred Hoole *(Lancashire)*
Alfred has been interested in photography since he was 12, joining Accrington CC (where he is still a member) in 1955. He is a regular participant in club, federation and national exhibitions. Now into early retirement, he has much more time to indulge his passion for landscape and architectural photography. *(26)*

Arnold Hubbard *(Tyne and Wear)*
Arnold has been a member of Sunderland PA for about 25 years. His work has been seen in many national and international exhibitions. A Fellow of the RPS and holder of the EFIAP distinction, Arnold is a popular lecturer and regular judge on the club circuit. *(108)*

Ken Huscroft *(West Midlands)*
Having been taking monochrome landscape for many years, Ken is currently working on a 'trees in torment' series, most of which are accompanied by verse. He hopes to be able to have this body of work published as a book. *(58, 98)*

George Jenkinson *(Surrey)*
George started 'serious' photography about 35 years ago, on joining Sutton CC of which he is now Vice President. After 15 years producing Cibachromes, including his successful FRPS panel, he is now pushing himself to re-learn monochrome. A well known speaker and judge, George has gained the AFIAP and is a member of the Arena group. *(87)*

Dick Jones *(Surrey)*
Dick holds the APAGB, is a former Associate of the RPS, and is a past chairman of the Pictorial Group of the RPS. His work has featured in several anthologies alongside that of some of the country's leading professionals, artists and writers. *(31)*

Victor Kelly *(Northern Ireland)*
Victor took up photography five years ago and is a member of Banbridge CC. His main interest is in black and white landscapes and his favourite aspect of photography is the darkroom, where he loses all track of time. In 1996 he was the winner of the Northern Ireland PA monochrome section. *(104)*

Jerry Keogh *(Denmark)*
Jerry says he tries to use photography as a means of expressing thoughts, feelings and, perhaps, fears. Although time and practice improves technique, he finds the subject matter itself becomes more elusive – so the challenge remains. *(77)*

Ian King *(Perthshire)*
Ian became hooked at the age of 10 while watching a friend develop a print. At the start, it was just a way of spending spare time, but now he sees it as a means of expressing himself – "there's a part of me in every print". What he finds most interesting about photography is that everyone sees things differently, resulting in individual interpretations on paper. *(32)*

Keith Launchbury *(Lancashire)*
Keith has been a member of Preston PS since 1986 and its President for the past three years. He is also the President of a newly formed group, Lancashire Monochrome. His own photographic interest is currently the landscape and particularly Cumbria's Lake District, where it complements his love of fell-walking. *(47, 136)*

John Laurens *(Jersey)*
After graduating from college in photography, John spent six months travelling in the States where, but for work permit problems, he was set to work with a New York photographer. About four years ago, he found a position in his native Jersey with a new studio, where he still works, defining his style of black and white photography. He is preparing a book for publication by Creative Monochrome. *(83, 84)*

Andrew Machon *(Middlesex)*
Inspired by Nature, Andrew is both an artist and a scientist. His goal is to express Nature's 'soul', with both its beauty and spiritual qualities. He uses primarily infrared film and has a particular interest in alternative printing techniques, including photo-etching and gum printing. *(64, 71)*

David Mahony *(Australia)*
It would be impossible here to do full justice to David's three page photographic CV. His work has been exhibited around the world, gaining many awards, and published in many magazines and journals. He holds the Artist distinction of FIAP. *(5, 23, 115)*

Ian Mellor *(Buckinghamshire)*
Ian began taking photographs as reference material for painting and drawing, but since processing and printing his first monochrome film, he has not looked back. He gained the LRPS in 1986 and CPAGB in 1995. A member of New City PS (Milton Keynes), he has exhibited in both national and international salons. *(76)*

Dave Miller *(Tyne & Wear)*
Dave says that his reward from working in monochrome comes from the simplifying effect it has on the subject, freeing him to concentrate on the light, form and texture of the image. "Finally, with the resulting print, I have something to hold, display and enjoy." *(35)*

Roy Morgan *(Shropshire)*
Hooked at a very young age, Roy has been taking photographs "on and off" for 50 years. An Associate of the RPS, he has had two books of his colour photography published. He photographs anything that appeals to him, but as a retired architect, finds himself drawn to the built environment. "The joy is in the seeing and the worry is in the darkroom where it is easy to be dishonest." *(24)*

Peter Motton *(Australia)*
Peter became interested in large format photography while working in the graphic arts industry from 1960 to 1975. Since moving to Tasmania in 1975, when he bought his first 35mm camera, he has spent some years as a technician in print media at the University of Tasmania. He describes the work he now produces as a "reaction to the academic images of the age". *(38, 72, 128)*

Peter Moughton *(East Sussex)*
A photographer for more years than he cares to remember, he is currently the chairman of the Hastings and St Leonards CC. He has tackled most subjects, but has generally found most satisfaction in natural history and landscape photography. He holds the Licentiateship distinction of the RPS. *(140)*

David Pearce *(Hertfordshire)*
With a lifelong interest in photography, it is only recently that he has found renewed interest in working in monochrome. He is a member of the RPS Pictorial Group and an active club photographer. He occasionally participates in exhibitions, but is sometimes surprised at the work accepted for today's exhibitions. *(36)*

Moyra Peralta *(London)*
A self-taught independent photographer, Moyra spent her early years as a freelance. She now works extensively in the social documentary tradition in conjunction with part-time teaching of photography to adult students. She is an Associate member of the RPS and is currently undertaking an MA degree in the history and culture of photography. *(16, 17)*

Len Perkis *(Norway)*
Since taking early retirement seven years ago, Len has devoted most of his time to making photographs. His main subject interests are landscape, nature and travel. Len has had images published in many prestigious books and magazines and a major shipping line has used many of his landscapes to decorate its ships. *(61, 91)*

Frank Phillips *(Devon)*
A retired surveyor, Frank says he has been "a photographer of only average achievement for over 40 years". His primary interest is landscape and coastal images. An Associate of the RPS, this is Frank's second appearance in the *Best of Friends* series. *(97)*

Den Reader *(Norfolk)*
Den has a string of solo exhibitions to his name and his work has been seen in several publications. He currently has 15,000 original images lodged with a major picture library, bringing his work to a wide and varied audience. *(125, 130)*

John Reed *(North Yorkshire)*
John has been making monochrome images for about seven years and is an active member of the York PS. He holds the Licentiateship of the RPS. *(41, 53)*

Patrick Reilly *(Ireland)*
Patrick has been taking photographs since the 1970s, and enjoys a wide variety of aspects of the hobby, although still finding monochrome the most exciting medium. He writes, "While I think about my work, I don't feel the need to explain it in detail: if other people like it, I see that as a bonus". *(39)*

Ted Richards *(Berkshire)*
Ted came to Newbury about six years ago, after many years in Cheshire, where he had been an active member of the two Manchester societies. Newbury provided fresh subjects for his photography and also an excellent camera club. Ted gained the ARPS distinction in 1969. *(45)*

Margaret Rowntree *(Gwynedd)*
Margaret had been taking slides for around 25 years, until she decided about five years ago to try her hand at monochrome. "Under the expert tuition of my husband, I found that I really enjoyed printing, and haven't taken a slide since." Margaret has already had what she describes as a 'modicum' of success in competitions and magazine publications. *(92)*

Mike Salter *(Avon)*
Mike has been interested in photography for about 12 years, but over the last five years has become more involved in his own processing and printing. An active member of Bristol PS, he works only in monochrome, making mainly landscape and figure images. Mike recently converted his LRPS to Associate status. *(69, 70)*

Andrew Sanderson *(West Yorkshire)*
After a three year course at Dewsbury and Batley Art College, Andrew worked as a press photographer and black and white printer until going freelance in 1987. Posters of his work have been sold in virtually every country in the world and his work has been acquired almost as extensively for private collections. *(117, 132)*

Brian Scott *(Australia)*
It was as a sports teacher that Brian first became interested in photography and he has now broadened his image-making to encompass the challenge of recording the natural beauty of the local landscape. Monochrome

appeals to Brian because of the degree of control it offers through to the finished print. *(57)*

Laurie Scott *(Kent)*
An active member of Beckenham PS and Bromley CC, and a regular exhibitor in national and international exhibitions, Laurie has been interested in photography for over 25 years. He obtained his Associateship of the RPS in 1993 with a slide panel of outdoor portraiture images. His main interests are natural history, human interest and graphic subjects. *(111)*

Chris Shore *(Kent)*
For Chris, the joy of photography is to be in an isolated spot with good weather, finding an old derelict building and trying to turn it into a well composed image. He finds that his favourite haunts in the Romney Marsh offer these elements in abundance. *(43, 142)*

Ian Shorrock *(Lancashire)*
Ian switched from colour photography to monochrome about two years ago. He enjoys the way monochrome gives full control of the image-making process from pre-visualisation through to the finished print. His preferred subject matter is the landscape, especially the mountains and lakes of Cumbria. *(131)*

Derek Singleton *(Cumbria)*
Derek took up black and white photography in the mid-1950s, and like many at that time, was seduced by colour slides. He returned to monochrome in the early 1980s, specialising in landscape photography. More recently, he has developed a strong feeling for the West Highlands of Scotland, seeking to capture on film the atmosphere of this wild and remote part of the country. *(48, 50)*

Roger Skinner *(Australia)*
Although making photographs since 1963, Roger did not begin exhibiting his work until 1979. Coincidentally he met and worked with Frank Watters – a period which Roger describes as beginning his re-education in the arts in general and Australian photography in particular. This led to him successfully challenging the arts establishment prejudice against photography as a medium, winning several prestigious national arts prizes with photo-based images. *(85)*

Mark Snowdon *(North Yorkshire)*
Mark developed his interest in photography in 1986 whilst living in South Africa. He works almost entirely in monchrome, normally using medium format cameras, with a preferred combination of Agfa APX25 film and Rodinal developer. He became an Associate of the RPS in 1991 and is currently working towards the Fellowship. *(138)*

Ray Spence *(Warwickshire)*
Ray's passion for photography was kindled while taking a degree in microbiology and, after a 12 year stint as a biology teacher, he chose to lecture in photography and media studies. He is a Fellow of the Royal Photographic Society and has lectured and exhibited widely in the UK. In 1994, Creative Monochrome published a portfolio of his work, *Form and Fantasy*. *(73)*

Göran Stenberg *(Sweden)*
Although working as a professional photo-printer, mainly in colour, Göran's personal work is primarily monochrome, which he has been enjoying for the last 15 years. Most recently he has been exploring the use of infrared film and trying out the bromoil printing technique. *(30, 100, 106, 107)*

Ernesto Tarnoczy Jr *(Brazil)*
A civil engineer by profession, Ernesto joined a camera club in 1980, since which time he has been taking photographs of urban and rural landscapes as well as enjoying still life and abstract close-ups. He has gained acceptances in several national and international salons. *(68, 126)*

Priscilla Thomas *(East Sussex)*
Priscilla acquired her first slr in 1991 and discovered photography as a means of creative expression. She gained her LRPS in 1992, ARPS in 1993 and – on her fifth attempt "with blood, sweat and tears" – the Fellowship in 1995. She has enjoyed numerous successes in national and international exhibitions. *(118)*

Malcolm Thomson *(Tayside)*
Malcolm started working as a photographer when he was nearly 15, and describes it as "my life, my passion". Monochrome is the medium he grew up with and it still excites him 30 years on. *(129)*

Cliff Threadgold *(New Zealand)*
Cliff became seriously interested in photography after visiting New Zealand in 1988. On his return to the UK, he joined Potters Bar PS and the UPP, and more recently he completed five modules in the City & Guilds photography course, which generated his interest in monochrome. He gained his ARPS in 1995 with a panel of landscape photographs. He now resides in New Zealand. *(93, 94)*

Mike Tinsley *(Kent)*
Mike's interest in photography became more serious whilst living and working in the Solomon Islands, where his newly acquired joy in scuba diving prompted him to learn underwater colour photography. On returning to the UK in 1989, he took a conscious decision to use only monochrome. He now feels he is beginning to get to grips with this medium. He has just moved up from using 5x4 format to 10x8 plates. *(121)*

David Valdes *(Sussex)*
A semi-retired science and photography teacher, David has belonged to Brighton & Hove CC since 1952. He gained the Associateship of the RPS in 1959. David frequently gives illustrated talks to local camera clubs and other groups. *(113)*

Ton van der Laan *(Netherlands)*
Ton became interested in monochrome photography about 20 years ago and progressed through membership of a

local camera club. He started by concentrating on architecture, but has subsequently become more and more interested in nature photography. *(99)*

Clive Vincent *(Cornwall)*
Although starting with colour, Clive is now a confirmed monochrome worker with roughly 12 years' experience of the medium. He tends to specialise in landscapes, primarily of his native Cornwall and his other great love, Dartmoor. A member of Penwith Photo Group, Clive has exhibited his work widely. *(46, 135, 137)*

Robert Visick *(North Yorkshire)*
Rob describes his photographic career thus: "1946: given a 'Vest Pocket Kodak' camera and a roll of film by my French mistress. Developed the film in a dish in the little cupboard underneath the stairs at school. With the image appeared the addiction. Progress thereafter steady, if a little slow, to LRPS in 1992." *(3)*

Gerry Walden *(Hampshire)*
Specialising in monochrome photography, Gerry Walden is a member of Independent Photography in the South East and has exhibited widely. He works in the style of the famous French documentary photographers, such as Cartier-Bresson and Doisneau, believing that the image before the camera should not be orchestrated in any way. He follows this through by printing from the full, uncropped frame of the negative. *(9, 10)*

Per-Åke Wärn *(Sweden)*
Interested in photography since his early teens, Per-Åke works mainly in the contemporary/avant garde style. He has a particular interest in photographing rock music and his images in this field have been published in several magazines in Sweden and the UK. Per-Åke has had three solo exhibitions and has had work accepted for several international salons. *(88)*

Liz Williams *(Avon)*
Having purchased an slr, Liz joined the Bristol PS in 1992 to learn about photography. She quickly developed an interest in monochrome film and printing and in the past couple of years has used mainly infrared, both outside and in the studio, because she loves the surreal effect it creates. *(74)*

Peter Williams *(West Midlands)*
Peter became interested in photography over 20 years ago as a means of recording his fishing successes. He continues to enjoy both pursuits, enjoying the solitude of being engulfed in quiet surroundings. He was hooked (his word!) on monochrome with his first film – Kodak infrared – about eight years ago. *(33)*

John Winchcomb *(Bedfordshire)*
John has been interested in photography since 1960 and was an active member of Maidstone PS until a change of job and location in 1968 forced him to a more isolated pursuit of his hobby. He has recently returned to photography after some years involved with model engineering and horology. He is a member of the RPS and its Visual Arts group. *(44)*

Bill Wisden *(East Sussex)*
A well known club lecturer, Bill has spent much of his time encouraging others that "all is possible". He has recently retired from the Pictorial panel of the RPS after 33 years' service and has been awarded the Honorary Fellowship of the Society for his services to the RPS and pictorial photography. He is an Associate of PAGB and a member of the London Salon. *(6)*

Julie Woodhouse *(Derbyshire)*
Julie is primarily interested in landscape photography and particularly enjoys walking with her camera in Snowdonia, Scotland, and closer to home, the Dark Peak. She has achieved the LRPS distinction and is now looking towards the ARPS. *(51)*

Baron Woods *(Lancashire)*
After 20 years specialising in colour print photography, and achieving the Fellowship of the RPS, Baron has recently returned to monochrome. He hoped that the move away from reality, which is inherent in black and white prints, would generate more satisfying images. *(49)*

Steve Zalokoski *(Avon)*
Steve bought an slr camera in 1988 and hasn't looked back since. He has tried a wide range of techniques and styles in search of his 'niche', and became captivated by the magic of monochrome after making his first print. In 1994 he gained both the DPAGB and the ARPS distinctions: "I find that having something to aim for helps me produce 'the goods'." *(18)*

Glossary of abbreviations used in profiles

BPE British Photographic Exhibitor – 'crown' awards based on acceptances in recognised national salons

CC Camera Club

FIAP (translated as) International Federation of Photographic Art: awards distinctions including Artist, Excellence and Master, based mainly on acceptances and awards in recognised international salons

PAGB Photographic Alliance of Great Britain

PF Photographic Federation

PS Photographic Society

PSA Photographic Society of America

RPS The Royal Photographic Society (UK): awards distinctions at Licentiateship (LRPS), Associate (ARPS) and Fellowship (FRPS) levels, mainly by assessed submissions of work

slr Single lens reflex: camera which uses a prism and mirror to allow the photographer to view the subject through the camera lens

UPP United Photographic Postfolios